Praise for *The Playwri...*

"Stuart Spencer's meticulous handbook ... thought was almost impossible: it describes, clarifies, and analyzes the mysterious process of building a play. And moreover, he does so with the grace and respect of a first-rate teacher for the intelligence and potential of his students. There is no ideology, no formula for instant success here. Just the distilled experience of a real practitioner generous enough to share, and reliable enough to be trusted."

—Jon Robin Baitz, author of *Ten Unknowns* and
The Substance of Fire

"You learn playwriting from a combination of hard knocks and good advice. Stuart Spencer's book is full of the latter. Read it and save yourself some bruises."

—Terrence McNally

"A sensible, lucid, thorough, and tremendously helpful journey into the always mysterious realities of playwriting."

—Romulus Linney, author of *The Sorrow of Frederick*,
Holy Ghosts, and *Tennessee*

"At last! A straight-from-the-shoulder approach to playwriting that finally blows the dust off much of the mystique surrounding this craft. Stuart Spencer writes with wit, insight, clarity, brilliant first-hand knowledge, and yes, finally, offers genuine help! Refreshing and beautifully organized, this book is long overdue."

—Jack O'Brien, Artistic Director, The Globe Theatres, San Diego

Stuart Spencer

The Playwright's Guidebook

STUART SPENCER's play *Resident Alien* received numerous productions around the United States and is in development as a motion picture. His other plays include *The Rothko Room*, which was published in *The Ensemble Studio Theatre Marathon 2000* (Faber Inc., 2001); *In the Western Garden*, which was published in *The Ensemble Studio Theatre Marathon '99* (Faber Inc., 2000); *Blue Stars*, which was selected for *The Best American Short Plays 1993–1994*; *Sudden Devotion*; and *Go to Ground*. A three-part anthology, *Plays by Stuart Spencer*, was recently published by Broadway Play Publishing. His new play, *Alabaster City*, was commissioned by South Coast Repertory. Spencer teaches playwriting in private classes and at Sarah Lawrence College and can be reached regarding private instruction at StuartSSpencer@aol.com. He is a member of Ensemble Studio Theatre and the Dramatists Guild.

THE
PLAYWRIGHT'S
GUIDEBOOK

THE
PLAYWRIGHT'S
GUIDEBOOK

STUART SPENCER

FABER AND FABER

NEW YORK • LONDON

Faber and Faber, Inc.
An affiliate of Farrar, Straus and Giroux
19 Union Square West, New York 10003

Faber and Faber Ltd
3 Queen Square
London WC1N 3AU

Grateful acknowledgment is made for permission to reprint excerpts
from the following publications:

Counting the Ways and Listening. Copyright © 1978 by Edward
Albee. Reprinted by permission of William Morris Agency, Inc., on
behalf of the author.

"Conversation with Arthur Miller" by Otis L. Guernsey Jr., *The
Dramatists Guild Quarterly*, copyright © 1987. All rights reserved.

Act One. Copyright © 1959 by Catherine Carlisle Hart and Joseph
M. Hyman Trustees. Reprinted with permission of Random House,
Inc.

The Real Inspector Hound. Copyright © by Tom Stoppard.
Reprinted by permission of Faber and Faber Ltd (Worldwide
excluding the U.S.) and Grove/Atlantic (U.S.).

Library of Congress Cataloging-in-Publication Data
Spencer, Stuart, 1957–
       The playwright's guidebook / Stuart Spencer.
           p.   cm.
       ISBN 0-571-19991-7 (pbk. : alk. paper)
       1. Playwriting. 2. Drama—Technique.   I. Title.

PN1661 .S68 2002
808.2—dc21

                                             2001040694

Designed by Barbara Grzeslo

14   13   12

This book is dedicated to all the members—
past, present, and future—
of the Tuesday Night Workshop.

CONTENTS

YOU MIGHT have seen this recently: the word "playwright" spelled "playwrite." It may seem sensible to you, modern-looking and unpretentious. Let me suggest, though, that there's a good argument for staying old-fashioned.

In the dictionary, "*wright*" is defined as "constructive worker." In earlier times the term was applied to those people who wrote plays. This was because they not only wrote the script, but also directed, designed, acted, and produced. In short, they constructed the entire event.

But the metaphor holds even today, if for a different reason. A play is more wrought than written. A playwright constructs a play as a wheelwright once constructed a wheel: a general shape is laid out, and then hammered, bent, nailed, reshaped, hammered again and again, until finally a functional and artful product has emerged.

The writing of a play involves just such a rough, practical, lusty attack on the material. After all, a wheel is only a wheel once it's a wheel. Until then, it's something that resembles a wheel. "If it works," the playwright says, "then keep it. If not, go back to work."

This is the first lesson of creating a play and, as many a playwright before you has discovered, also the last. It's in the spirit of those words that this book is founded.

I have written plays for over ten years now and taught playwriting for nearly as many. In that time, I have seen many people (myself included) struggle with the forming of that wheel. In my early years of teaching, I hunted for books that would help me to make sense of this daunting task. Many of the books had some good ideas in them, of course, but they all had serious drawbacks as well. Foremost among these was the failure to be genuine how-to books. The authors philosophized well enough, but in the end they resorted to describing how other playwrights have managed to write their plays. (Worse, some of their examples were hopelessly out of date: obscure nineteenth-century melodramas, and so forth.) I knew from my own classes that this kind of information is not much help to the playwright struggling to write his own play.

A second problem was that the few guidelines these books did offer tended to express the idiosyncratic methods of that particular author. (Things like "Take a warm bath before writing," "Play your favorite music while you work," "Never work more than three hours a day," and so on.) It's not bad advice per se, but in my experience with actual students it simply wasn't very useful. Besides, the advice tended to be badly organized, wandering from one idea to the next without a sense of rational progression.

It seemed to me that a good playwriting text should deal first with the most fundamental building blocks of drama—its atomic structure, as it were. It should discuss them in a way that allows the would-be playwright to follow along as if the play were being written right now. And the reader should be told that there are actually specific things that she may do to understand and follow these ideas. The book should also talk objectively about the problems of playwriting, not with quirky suggestions that reflect the idiosyncracies of the author but with essential and universal principles. These principles should deal with everything from the "impulse" that lies behind every play's origin to the problems involved with rewriting when a first draft is finished.

And so, frustrated with my search for such a book, I sat myself down one day and started to sketch out ideas for a better way. It seemed to me that playwriting, like any other artistic discipline, must involve some ideas that could be learned and taught. We teach music and painting and dance using universally agreed upon precepts, after all. The music that results may be Liszt or Lennon, the paintings Rubens or Rothko, the dances Balanchine or Fosse—but the underlying techniques are the same, or at least share common ideas. In the past century we have even devised several coherent, systematic means of teaching an art as ephemeral as acting. Why should playwriting be any different?

I realized that I had indeed observed certain recurring patterns in the work of the very disparate writers I had studied, taught, and worked with. What's more, I found I could identify those same patterns in the plays of the greatest playwrights of world literature. I began to write down these patterns in note form and to work out how one related to the other. Further patterns emerged until I started to see that there are, indeed, certain knowable, learnable elements to the art of playwriting.

At first I intended to use my notes simply to help me in my classes. Knowing the patterns allowed me to speak from a framework (I resist the terms *system* or *method*) so that what I was saying was part of a coherent way of thinking about playwriting. The various parts were explainable and—just as important—harmonious with each other. This was deeply satisfying to me, and for the most part to my students as well. I could see that I was helping them more than I had been previously. By using my newly developed ideas I was better able to support them in the realization of their own vision. Most students seemed to like having a clear and comprehensive technique to which they could refer as they strove to create artistic order out of chaos.

Finally, a student of mine suggested that I put my notes into some sort of order so that I could pass them out to the class. Thus began the formal work of creating this book. That work has evolved over nearly ten years, and what you are about to read is the result of much trial and error. There is nothing in this book that I have not tried both in my classes and in my own work. I cannot guarantee it will work for you, but I can guarantee it has worked for others and, not incidentally, for myself.

We will begin by laying out the means by which your own play can be wrought. Part One will show you that there is an atomic structure to a play, and that there are tools you can use to build it. The tools, by themselves, are relatively simple. They are, for example, the idea of action—the thing that a character wants and which propels him forward through the play. Or the idea of conflict—that which gets in his way.

Part Two will show you that there are innate impulses in you, as there are in everyone. When these impulses are allowed out and onto the page, they become the basis for your play. And you will now have the tools of Part One (if you need them) to give it shape.

In Part Three, we'll see how once the play is written, you will almost certainly have work remaining: rewriting, cutting, and dealing with myriad other issues that may have come up in the first draft. I will show you that there are clear and specific ways to address these problems, while strengthening and supporting what's already good about your play.

Finally, in Part Four, I offer both general and practical advice that may come in handy for the working playwright.

In addition, one recurring theme of this book is that playwriting is a whole, a gestalt. To this end I've included in the text marks (>) or (<) directing the reader forward or backward to a page where the same idea was introduced or is developed further.

It's all quite simple, and quite difficult. Let's begin.

THE
PLAYWRIGHT'S
GUIDEBOOK

INTRODUCTION: HOW WE TELL STORIES

BEFORE WE discuss playwriting, let's talk a little about theater, what it is, and perhaps more to the point, what it does.

At this moment in history, we can divide storytelling into three basic forms: prose, theater, and film. (Let's agree to leave poetry out of this discussion, as most of it these days is not narrative.) By prose, we'll say that we mean novels, short stories, and even some of the new computer hypertexts. By theater, we'll agree to mean anything performed by live humans that incorporates language in front of a live audience. And by film, we'll mean not just movies but television, videos, and DVDs—all of which are mechanically or electronically reproduced.

To better visualize these three means of narrating a story, we can begin by laying them out on a spectrum.

← FILM   THEATER   PROSE →

Each of these forms serves a particular purpose and affects us in ways the others do not. Each is particularly well suited to a form of expression to which the others are less well suited.

Bear in mind that the following discussion does not imply, for example, that film is only suited to eliciting visceral responses or that prose is only suited to analysis. These are generalizations meant simply to suggest that certain media have an inclination toward certain means of expression and will provoke certain reactions in an audience more easily than might another medium.

With that caveat, let's start with film.

← FILM   THEATER   PROSE →

IMMEDIATE

VISCERAL

Touch a hot stove and the hand instantly recoils from the heat. One doesn't think about it, consider the options, and then decide to move the hand. In fact, the hand has moved before one even knows how or why. Our brains are structured in such a way that we have an immediate visceral response to information received through the senses.

If we hear the loud, piercing shriek of a siren, we clap our hands over our ears. If we smell delicious food, the mouth waters and the appetite swells. If we see someone to whom we are sexually attracted, certain physiological activities begin to stir in us, not because we have decided to stir them, but because we are human and this is how humans react. Indeed, we react this way whether we like it or not. That person to whom we are sexually attracted may be forbidden to us in some way, yet the attraction continues and may in fact increase, in spite of our attempts to repress it.

Which brings us to film.

Film operates on us in this same visceral fashion. When we sit in the darkened movie theater or in front of the television at home, we are receiving images in the same way we receive them in life: through the senses. But there is one crucial difference. Film images are even more intense than those in reality because they have been selected and deliberately distilled into a purer form in order to achieve greater impact.

In *Un Chien Andalou* (*An Andalusian Dog*), the classic (quintessential, even) surrealist film by Luis Buñuel and Salvador Dalí from the 1920s, there is a famous sequence in which a woman stands on a balcony, looking out at the moon. The scene at first suggests a conventionally romantic mood, which changes abruptly when a man appears on the balcony behind her, produces a long, straight razor, and pulls her head back by the hair. In extreme close-up, we watch as one of her eyes—wide open, though strangely emotionless—is sliced by the razor blade.

Certainly this is one of the most startling images in the annals of cinema. Its impact on audiences has not lessened in the seventy years since its creation. I have only seen the film once, in a college class many years ago, yet I can recall the image with absolute clarity. The memory of it retains the power to make me cringe.

Part of the potency of this image is its irrationality. We don't expect such a violent act in this romantic setting. The violence is not accompanied by any of the usual sexual overtones, nor is the act intended to take the life of the woman. We presume that she will go on living after this event, though certainly blind in one eye. We cannot predict the violence nor do we know what exactly to make of it after the fact. It simply *is*.

But while the image's force comes, at least in part, from its inexplicability, we also have to acknowledge that its impact is heightened by the medium through which it is presented. There is something in the camera's ability to select both this single image (the eyeball) and the moment of its violation that cannot be equaled on either the stage or the page.

For the sake of this discussion we are talking about pure film, without dialogue. We can allow music, because music operates on us just as directly, as viscerally, as images do. But dialogue in film diminishes the visceral effect. As we hear over and over again from media critics and Hollywood story editors, it is the image that makes films powerful. High-minded literary critics may not like this idea, and in fact they often criticize filmmakers for writing poor or inane dialogue and for relying solely on visuals to give their films impact. But this is like criticizing water for being wet. Take away the visuals, and the audience is left with nothing but talking heads. Even if those heads speak descriptive language in addition to dialogue, one often has the feeling that one may as well be reading a book.

Which brings us to prose.

← FILM	THEATER	PROSE →
IMMEDIATE		CONTEMPLATIVE
VISCERAL		ANALYTICAL

When we read a line of prose—the one you are reading at the moment, for example—the brain is required to go through certain analytical processes that are not required of it when watching a film. We are no longer conscious of these processes, at least not if we read well and often.

But if we think back to childhood when we first learned to read (or perhaps when we've tried to learn a second language), it becomes obvious that the act of reading in itself requires effort and analysis, regardless of the content. It requires that the reader go through a middle step, between the experience of the word on a page and the moment of understanding. This isn't necessary when we watch a film. It's true that we may want to reflect upon the meanings of the images in a film in order to absorb their full significance. But the act of watching or listening is a passive one, as compared to the active process of reading. It is this inherently active process that compromises the immediacy of the experience of reading prose.

What literature may lose in immediacy, however, it makes up for in its ability to plumb the depths of an experience. Prose can get to the inner workings of a person's mind. It can analyze a gesture, expound upon it, and reveal it from an endless number of points of view. The camera is unable to articulate its point of view beyond the presentation of the image itself.

A writer of prose, though, might take the same scene in *Un Chien Andalou* and turn it into a verbal study of the man's motives or of the woman's feelings of romance as they turn suddenly to horror and pain. A writer might even choose to describe in detail the surrounding scene—the balcony, the night air, the moon—which might, in turn, impart new meaning to the entire setting, as in this passage from *The Great Gatsby*:

The only completely stationary object in the room was an enormous couch on which two young women were buoyed up as though upon an anchored balloon. They were both in white, and their dresses were rippling and fluttering as if they had just been blown back in after a short flight around the house.

When F. Scott Fitzgerald describes the couch on which Daisy Buchanan sits, he manages, in so doing, to describe Daisy herself. In this way, we may well lose the immediacy of a Jean Renoir film, but we gain the insight of a great novelist. Is one better than the other? Only as a matter of taste. In reality, they are merely different forms of expression, both equally good. One is better than the other only insofar as the artist is able to exploit the medium of his choice.

Literature is full of examples of this peculiar power of prose. Marcel Proust is perhaps the quintessential model for a prose writer's ability to excavate the meaning of even the simplest gesture. Indeed, in prose it is often the throwaway look, the tiniest gesture, the passing phrase that is amplified into something of profound importance. Here, in a passage from *Remembrance of Things Past*, the narrator observes a man performing the perfectly ordinary act of winking as he escorts a lady companion from church one Sunday morning:

> He brushed past us, and did not interrupt what he
> was saying to her, but gave us, out of the corner of
> his blue eye, a little sign which began and ended, so
> to speak, inside his eyelids and which, as it did not
> involve the least movement of his facial muscles,

managed to pass quite unperceived by the lady; but striving to compensate for the somewhat restricted field in which they had to find expression, he made that blue chink which was set apart for us sparkle with all the zest of an affability that went beyond mere playfulness, almost touched the borderline of roguery; he subtilized the refinement of good-fellowship into a wink of connivance, a hint, a hidden meaning, a secret understanding, all the mysteries of complicity, and finally elevated his assurances of friendship to the level of protestations of affection, even of a declaration of love, lighting up for us alone, with a secret and languid flame invisible to the chatelaine, an enamored pupil in a countenance of ice.

Proust has taken this fleeting, seemingly simple gesture and interpreted it for us in a way that could never be done in film. We might get the wink in close-up, or in slow motion, or we might see it repeated several times. But we would never achieve the same depth of analysis, the same luxuriant ability to contemplate and analyze this momentary flick of the eyelid. Prose has the unparalleled potential to reveal alternative meanings. In prose, we can lift the veils off level after level of meaning. We can present different points of view, one after another, as William Faulkner showed us in *The Sound and the Fury*, or Virginia Woolf in *The Waves*.

Before we go on, remember that this is not a set of definitive rules, merely some observations that describe certain propensities. All other things being equal, a film will tend to elicit visceral responses, prose analytical ones.

So how does this bring us to theater? How does theater fit into this spectrum of visceral versus analytical? To which is theater best suited?

Both. And then some.

← FILM	THEATER	PROSE →
IMMEDIATE	— BOTH —	CONTEMPLATIVE
VISCERAL		ANALYTICAL

Obviously, there's a strong visual dimension to theater: we call it spectacle. Spectacle has always been considered suspect by serious theatergoers: a necessary evil by some, and a lovely but shallow diversion by others. The ancient Greeks deliberately kept sensationalistic spectacle offstage so that the audience would be forced to concentrate on what they considered the essential drama. Sophocles shows us not the moment when Oedipus blinds himself, but the moment when he realizes that he must blind himself in order to keep his oath and his honor. Euripides doesn't show us Medea as she murders her children, but the moment when that terrible deed becomes inevitable.

The Greeks understood that onstage sensationalism could never compete with the brutal and common viscera of life, and so they concentrated on something that is all too rare in the everyday world but to which the theater is well suited: moments of penetrating and profound understanding.

Still, the elements of stagecraft—sound, lighting, costume, not to mention the actors' bodies themselves—all contribute to an immediate, visceral effect on the audience, whether high-minded purists like it or not. Aristotle himself accepts the necessity of spectacle, so long as it is kept within certain limits and insofar as it is part of the organic whole. In other words: spectacle, yes; empty sensational thrills, no.

I think Aristotle gets the balance just right. When we watch Olivier as Othello (preserved in a film version) fall backward off a ten-foot platform, collapsing into an epileptic fit, this is spectacle extravagantly imagined but tightly integrated into the needs of the play. When we watch Mama Rose's dancers in *Gypsy* metamorphose from small children into adult teenagers before our eyes in the flickering of a strobe light, this too is spectacle, but again justified by the demands of the plot. When we watch the set of *Medea* collapse around Diana Rigg, the spectacle is warranted because it serves as a metaphor for Medea's shattered emotional state. It supports, and is supported by, the meaning of the text.

Yet even so, the theater cannot select and distill images as the camera can. A stage director can focus our attention in one area of the stage or another, but it will always be a clumsy effort compared to the work of a camera, whose focus is absolute. If Buñuel wants us to see only the act of mutilating an eye, he shows us that and only that. We're as close as he wants us to be. We look either at the image he provides, or we don't watch. There is no in-between. A stage director, composing the same scene onstage, would have a tough time getting us to focus with the same intensity on that eye. Especially from the balcony. And even if he could, would we have the same reaction to its violation by the razor? We're simply too far away, and there are too many other things to look at.

The theater is a medium based as much on words as on deeds. In this sense, it is more like prose. The story unfolds onstage through the use of words. Characters speak to one another, as they do in prose, though onstage the words that the characters speak are the *only* words. We have no narrator except in particular instances when the effect is either ironic, as in *Our Town*, or merely clumsy, as in many high-school pageants.

In the theater, we have no controlling narrative voice. What we do have is a variety of points of view. In fact, we have as many as there are characters onstage. This is a feature that prose only developed in the twentieth century with authors like Faulkner and Woolf, who were noted for being daring innovators.

But the shifting point of view is a central and eternal truth of the theater. Plays would not be plays if the point of view was not diffuse. What's more, the theatrical point of view does not shift clumsily around as it does in prose. We do not have to start a new chapter, or call attention to the new viewpoint by developing a new section. Instead, the shifting point of view in a play is a built-in reality. We accept it as readily as we accept that books are printed on paper or that films are shown on screens. When one character stops talking and the other starts, we've made the shift effortlessly, without even thinking about it.

But the question remains: What does theater do best?

The theater, at its most effective, is a mingling of the attributes of both film and prose. Or to be historically accurate, film and prose are splinters torn from the original tree of theater. Let's remember that theater preceded both those other forms. In Homer there are references to the singing and dancing of the Dionysian ritual, the predecessor of Greek drama. Even in Homer's time, those rituals were ancient, and they incorporated both spectacle and language. They were, for all intents and purposes, theater.

Since then, we've carved up that great tree of theater and distributed its potency to other forms for our own peculiar reasons—economic, technological, sociological, and so on. No one is complaining. Literature and cinema have their own important places in the culture.

The fact remains that it is theater as an art form that is the most vigorous way of telling a story. How could it be otherwise? It is the theater that combines all the best parts of those other media we also enjoy.

In Euripides' *Bacchae*, we are shocked not only by the spectacle of a mother, blinded by primal bacchic lusts, parading her murdered son's head on a pike; we are also horrified when, seeing what she has done by her own hand, she articulates, through language, her sense of horror.

We respond not only to Macbeth's tormented soliloquies on the nature of his crime but also to the moody, night-shrouded setting of the play.

It is not just Nora's words that stab us with their continued timeliness and painful truths, it's also the sound of that slamming door. It is Hedda Gabler's cries of defiance against a world that would confine her that engage our minds, but it is the sight of her burning Eilert's manuscript that fully reveals her character.

Chekhov's beautiful words artfully portray his characters in their struggle against stasis, yet what would *The Cherry Orchard* be without that distant, mysterious, ambiguous "sound of a breaking string" that he describes in the stage directions? And it's not just Tom's lovely words telling us of his anguish over his lost family in *The Glass Menagerie* but the sound of a violin in the wings that move us. Stage designers—sound, lights, set, costumes—are not adjuncts to our experience. When the play is worthy, and when these elements serve the text, they are fully equal partners.

The theater is demanding of its audience. We have to be willing to listen and watch carefully, to comprehend ideas and images emerging in complex, often multilayered patterns. And that comprehension must occur *now*. A book, which can be as demanding as a great play, at least allows the reader to put it down and come back later when she's ready to read the same passage again.

So in an age when we are inclined to seek instant and easy gratification—even if that gratification is superficial and transitory—good theater continues to demand more than many of us are willing to give. In turn, audiences today are flocking to other, less demanding art forms. If such forms are especially adept at offering satisfaction that is at best fleeting, then that is a price that many are willing to pay.

As a result, numerous playwrights are tempted to abandon the strengths that the stage alone can offer. But in the long run, this only makes the problem worse.

As playwrights, then, we must write the best plays we can, understanding what makes good theater, not good film or prose or some other art form. It is a balancing act, to be sure. We must write plays that contain compelling images that will collide with the audience and strike a spark in them. But we must also fan that spark into a flame with the ideas conveyed by our words and the ideas they express.

There are no strict formulas and no absolute rules, at

least none that cannot be broken. But there are ideas that can guide us and help us to write the best plays we can. Those ideas are what this book is about, and they are based on the critical work of Aristotle found in his essay on theater, *Poetics*. While this is only one theory of drama, it is the primary one, and the one that remains essential. All other theories have come after it and are, for the most part, a reaction to it.

The *Poetics* was written in the fourth century B.C., a century after the great playwrights Aeschylus, Sophocles, and Euripides had died. This chronology is important: Aristotle was not writing a how-to book from which the tragedians took their lessons. It was the other way around. Aristotle learned from the playwrights what he believed made a great tragedy.

As Francis Fergusson observes, the *Poetics* is less a rule-book than a cookbook. On certain fundamentals Aristotle is quite absolute; in other areas he allows some play for the idiosyncracies of a flowering artistic talent. The work is that of an opinionated theatergoer who is interested in exploring how he arrived at his opinions. Reading the *Poetics* is like reading the musings of a highly astute amateur trying to determine why some plays move and fascinate him, why some leave him utterly cold, and why others work in part but not as a whole.

Unlike many modern theorists, Aristotle does not appear to have any critical agenda except to discover the means by which the plays achieve their effects. He was an observer and a categorizer. His genius was to find order in what seemed like chaos. He did not ordain, and he did not prescribe. He took the world as he found it. Aristotle's observations on theater are similar to those of Newton's or Einstein's on nature: they did not make the laws of physics, they only revealed them.

While it's true that the laws of drama (like those of nature) may be mysterious and ultimately inexplicable, they are nevertheless present and quite powerful. You don't need to understand gravity in order to fall off a roof. Defy the dramatic rules if you will, plenty of great playwrights have. But first at least know what you are defying. Nothing is more disheartening than to hear a person rail against Aristotelian theory only to discover that the same person has never read, and has no real understanding of, what Aristotle actually wrote.

Because the *Poetics* is an ancient, philosophical tract and not a modern how-to book, it can seem forbidding. *The Playwright's Guidebook*, however, is a how-to book—though any book on artistic endeavor that purports to give you all the tools you'll need to create art is overreaching, to say the least. It can't. The effort and, for that matter, the art are up to you. But what this book can provide is a set of ideas, a toolbox of implements that will help you in your efforts.

Aristotle's ideas, timeless though they may be in some respects, must be rethought and reapplied with each new generation of theater. Aristotle was writing about a specific aesthetic form, of a particular time, for a unique culture. That form, that time, and that culture are foreign to us now. While we may reach into his ideas for their essence, we must not take him too literally, as the theorists and playwrights of the Renaissance did. And we must never hold his (or anyone else's) ideas higher than our personal measure of our own work. In the theater, practicality, like ripeness, is all.

In other words, if it works—keep it.

This book will try to show you ways of using Aristotelian ideas in a way that is current, flexible, and pragmatic.

In general, Aristotle's description of the dramatic rules was so persuasive, so complete, that for 2,300 years nobody challenged him. Many borrowed from him, and in the Renaissance they nearly worshiped him. But no one ever thought to question him.

Until the twentieth century.

Then, as Einstein with Newton and as Darwin with the Bible, all hell broke loose.

Bertolt Brecht was the first to rebel. Brecht's theories on theater, collectively called "epic drama," were a gauntlet thrown before the feet of the master. Brecht, himself a playwright, found that Aristotle's observations, though perhaps once valid, did not serve the needs of a modern audience.

Brecht set about to dismantle not just the more technical, dramaturgical Aristotelian ideas, but also the very function of theater itself. Instead of the arousal of fear and pity, he gave us the idea of alienation—that is, deliberately alienating the audience from the emotional experience of the drama so that it can attain a better grasp of its intellectual (or social, or political) meaning.

Other rebellions followed, each with its own theories and manifestoes. It's noteworthy that, in nearly every instance, the theorists were themselves playwrights. (Aristotle never did any work in an actual theater.) Among the more prominent genres are the absurdists, with their competing manifestoes, ranging from Artaud's early embrace of the irrational in his "theater of cruelty" to Ionesco's postwar Gallic shrug at life's futility; the naturalists, with Émile Zola proclaiming that all artifice in playwriting must be replaced by a raw, external representation of life; and the expressionists, who didn't entirely refute Aristotle, but in effect replaced his "imitation of an action" with an imitation of the internal life of the characters and of the universe in which they live.

There are many more. Indeed, today there are nearly as many nonlinear (read: non-Aristotelian) styles as there are writers who practice them. This is one of the great delights of contemporary theater. Robert Wilson, Meredith Monk, Anne Bogart, the Wooster Group, Richard Foreman, Mabou Mines, Théâtre de Complicité, and many others, create a theater that is entirely their own. They owe very little either to their predecessors or even to each other. Or they have synthesized so many various traditions as to have created their own. In nonlinear drama we are not dealing with an established group of conventions that happen to differ from another, already established set. We are dealing, instead, with an ever-burgeoning array of theatrical ideas that burst out in a seemingly endless, chaotic display.

But even for those writers who are interested in nonlinear theater, it's still useful to study what might be called the classic ideas of theater. In the worlds of painting and music, students take for granted that one must first study the classic forms before one can begin to develop one's own iconoclasm. This same principle is also true (or should be) in the theater.

Rebellion is an important process in the development of any art form. But rebelling in a bubble is not going to speak to anyone. First, you need to get some idea of what you're rebelling against.

I hope this book will tell you.

PART ONE

STRUCTURE

THE TOOLS we're about to discuss provide you with the means to begin writing your play. Even the expert use of these tools will not solve all your writing problems, but they can offer you a sense of craft. Then you can apply that craft to begin the infinitely more difficult job of actually saying what you're trying to say.

It's important to remember as you're reading and working on the exercises in Part One that these ideas really are tools, not rules. There may be the laws of drama I mentioned in the Introduction, but you're better off not thinking of them as that.

Many great plays do not use the tools I'm presenting here, or if so, they use them in such idiosyncratic fashion that they are almost impossible to identify. For example, one is hard pressed to find a clear action for Lear in *King Lear*. Even if one does find action and conflict in *Waiting for Godot*, an event for the play is very elusive. In fact, that's the point of Beckett's play—that there is no event. The contemporary work of playwrights such as Richard Foreman and Robert Wilson also lack any of my tools, yet many people—myself included—find their work fascinating and rewarding.

An audience goes to the theater to be entertained, informed, excited, provoked. People go because they are interested in your play, for whatever reason and on whatever level that may be. And your job is to keep them interested. If you have done that, then you have accomplished your task, no matter how little you may have used the tools I will tell you about.

Conversely, no matter how brilliantly you may have structured your play, if it can't capture an audience's interest, then you've failed.

Some students ask if they should think of these structural tools as a blueprint. My reply is an emphatic *no*. A blueprint suggests a preconceived plan, a rigid form into which you have to make your own ideas fit. It suggests also that the idea work has already been done and that all you need to do is follow instructions. Nothing could be further from the truth.

It bears repeating that the ideas described in Part One should be thought of as the tools that will come in handy while you are constructing your play. But it is your own play you are constructing, according to your own plan.

It's as though you have begun to build your dream house. It's conceivable (if highly unlikely) that you might even do the work without any tools at all. If you're like most people, you'll want a hammer, some nails, a saw, and so on. Soon you'll have them. And like building a house, the blueprint of your play may very likely change, grow, and evolve as you create it.

Other students approach me in the middle of learning some of the tools in Part One and say that they really don't want to use the tools they've been shown. They have a vague feeling of discomfort and suspect that there is something banal about them. They're afraid the tools will drain their work of creativity and that if they employ them, it will be embarrassingly obvious to the audience, who will see the play's scaffolding.

This apprehension about craft is peculiar to our modern age in which we value creativity over artifice, not realizing they are two sides of the same coin. Still, it's an understandable concern. Certainly none of us wants our audiences to see the scaffolding. But that's no reason not to have it. It's only a good reason to make sure that it isn't visible. Good scaffolding is by definition invisible—it's intrinsic to the play you are writing. You'll see, in the course of using this book, that structure is not something that must be artificially imposed onto your play. It is part of your play, the foundation of it. You know you've struck gold when what you are trying to say and the way you are trying to say it, are one.

ONE: WHAT IS STRUCTURE?

DO WE REALLY NEED STRUCTURE?

IF YOU'RE like most people who pick up this book, you're a little nervous about the thought of writing a play.

Very possibly you have never written a play (or anything else). But the prospect of transforming those bits of characterization, the fragments of dialogue that have already formed in your head, the intense emotional climaxes that you can feel even if you can't quite fully conceive of how to bring them off—the prospect of fashioning an actual play from all that amorphous material swirling around in your brain is too tantalizing to resist.

Or perhaps you've taken a crack at writing a play and things didn't work out well. You got frustrated and never finished. Or you might have finished a draft, but what you've written was nothing like that beautiful vision in your head.

You may be in a class, or you may be on your own with this book as your guide.

Whatever the case, there are two things we can be pretty sure of: you're excited about the prospect of writing a play—otherwise you wouldn't be throwing yourself into the task; and you're a little anxious about the journey that lies before you.

If you're excited, that's terrific. If you're nervous, it means you're sensible. Writing a play is daunting. As a playwright, I know from personal experience. I also teach playwriting, and I go to see a fair amount of theater. This book is based on my own experiences as writer, teacher, and theatergoer. And my experience as all three tells me that it's difficult to mold a statue from a formless lump of clay. If it were easy, everybody would do it.

And yet, writing a play is, paradoxically, simpler than many people imagine. Fortunately for you, people have been writing plays for several thousand years now, and you can learn from their experience. Playwrights have learned over the centuries that there are a handful of rules to guide you in your work if you need them. They are a means toward an end: devices that can often help you in designing the overall shape of your play, tightening down the bolts, drilling some new holes if needed, buffing it to a fine finish.

In general, you'll find that the structure of playwriting is liberating. If you use it properly, it will free you to write the play you must write. If you view it as a means to an end, and not an end in itself, it will always be at your side, ready to help you solve problems.

You must never judge your work by going down a check-list of all the various fundamentals of playwriting that you have followed or broken. You must never set out to write your play so that it adheres to the structure first and to your own vision second.

These tools aren't necessary, either. They are there to help you when you're trying to understand your own play and make it better—make it closer to that vision in your head. If they help you realize that vision, terrific. If they are only getting in the way, let them go—for now, anyway. Go ahead and write what you must write, the way you must write it. The material that you write without thinking about the rules may, at the very least, be a terrific beginning. Rough, perhaps, and not totally formed, but a beginning that the rules may help you to shape and polish.

We'll talk much more on this in Part Two (> Chapter 9), but for now think of it this way: sometimes, you just want to go out and tend your garden by hand, down in the dirt. Just you and the earth and the plants.

But at some point you may also think to yourself, why not pick up that trowel?

THE UR-PLAY

In anthropology, an ur-myth is a story whose source is typically lost in the distant, unknowable reaches of prehistory, yet deeply embedded in the subconscious of the culture—present but mysterious. The ur-myth often has contemporary manifestations, later versions of the same essential tale. Wagner's *Tristan and Isolde* is a good example of this: an ancient Germanic myth that became a nineteenth-century opera.

Within you there is what I call the ur-play. In fact, there

are many ur-plays inside you—one for each play you intend to write. What ends up on the page is, one hopes, a close approximation of this ur-play. But the actual ur-play itself is ultimately unknowable, buried deep in your own subconscious. Your job as a playwright is to summon it forth and set it down in the form of words and directions—"certain ciphers on paper," as Peter Brook called them.

But, as Brook implied, those words and directions only represent the ur-story. They can never be the ur-story. As playwrights, we write words that come as close to that as we can, words that evoke a world that is as similar to our ur-play as possible.

When we've done this, we've written the play that we need to write. Sometimes, when we get into trouble, it's because somewhere along the way we've allowed the ur-play to be lost. In its place, our conscious minds have created an artificial story, one that bears little or no relation to the play inside us. This has less to do with following (or not following) the rules of dramaturgy than it does with staying in touch with the original impulse of your play (> Chapter 9).

A private student of mine, Linda,* had read the first several chapters of this book while it was still in manuscript form and had completed the exercises on which you'll soon be working. She'd done them quite well, in fact. The scenes she had written were excellent not only in the sense that they showed a good grasp of structure, but they were elegant in language and understanding of character. They were good scenes, not just mechanically proficient exercises.

Then she started work on her own play, and it all fell

---

*Names of people and titles of plays have often been changed.

apart. Even when she stopped forcing herself to use the tools, as I suggested, and just tried to write what she was feeling regardless of whether or not it was dramatic, she still hated everything she did; in all honesty, I wasn't much more enthusiastic. The tools had not, apparently, been hindering her. There was simply nothing in this play that she (or I) liked well enough that these instruments might have honed.

What had been so seemingly effortless for her in the isolated exercises was now torture. "I know exactly the play I want to write," she said. "I know exactly what I want it to be, but I just can't seem to get it out onto the page. The tools are only getting more in the way, making it harder. I'm at the point where I don't even want to turn on the computer. It's just too frustrating."

In talking to her, I noticed that she kept referring to the play she wanted to write, as if to suggest there were another play that she didn't want to write. I asked her about this, and she immediately agreed. "Sure," she said, "there's this whole other way of writing that keeps trying to come out. But that version has different characters, a slightly different setting, but most of all—it's not what I want to say."

It was not what she wanted to say, I agreed, but perhaps this was, in a sense, at the heart of the problem. She had lost track of her ur-play. I suggested she needed to think less about the play she wanted to write and start to give some room to the play she needed to write. There's a difference. Sometimes it's a big difference, sometimes not so big. But there's always a difference.

In Part Two, when we discuss the impulse, we'll talk more about this idea. We'll see how it's possible to hang on to the ur-play. When Linda learned more about this, she was able to return to her play and, though it changed considerably, she found she was able to release what was needing to come out. Until we get to more on this subject, just remember that you, like Linda, must always pay attention to the play you need to write. It's the only one that's really there.

THE INVISIBLE THREE ACTS

Carl Jung, the early-twentieth-century psychologist, observed that our dreams are constructed in the form of three-act plays. He meant partly that, like three-act plays, our dreams have beginnings, middles, and ends. But his comment also implies that in our dreams we express our needs, find that there are certain obstacles that prevent us from fulfilling those needs, and either fulfill those needs or don't.

Those ideas—"beginning, middle, end," and "needs, obstacles, fulfillment"—are intimately related, and they are virtually all of what you need to know about basic dramatic structure. The point is this: three-act plays are not constructed as such because someone, somewhere made an arbitrary intellectual decision that they ought to be that way. Rather, plays are constructed in this fashion because it's a reflection of who we are, of how we think. We tell ourselves stories at night, in the form of dreams, which have beginnings, middles, and ends.*

---

*For a fascinating, in-depth discussion of the three-act concept, see David Mamet's *Three Uses of the Knife*.

And why do we dream like this? Because our lives are themselves a constant process of need, obstacle, and fulfillment (or fulfillment's dark twin, failure). We perceive the world this way. Even this very effort on which you are now embarked—the writing of a play—can be thought of in these terms: you need to write a play; you have encountered an obstacle in the sense that you don't yet know how you're going to do it; and someday you will be fulfilled when your play is finished.

At this point in my college course, there is usually a well-read student who pipes up and says, "But not all plays are three-act plays. The Greek tragedies aren't. Shakespeare's aren't. Most of the plays being written today aren't either."

In a literal sense the student is right, of course. All the Greek tragedies occur in one act of about ninety minutes. And today, it's become common to see plays like *Talley's Folly*, *'night Mother*, *Master Harold and the Boys*, and *Six Degrees of Separation*—none of which have an act break.

Even some two- or three-act plays have continuous action. Arthur Miller's *The Price* is technically a two-act play and Tennessee Williams's *Cat on a Hot Tin Roof* is technically three, but both plays occur in one place and in one time frame. When the lights come up on each succeeding act, the characters are in the same place and time that we left them at the end of the previous one. These plays could easily have been written as one-acts except that, for various reasons, the authors chose otherwise.

And further, there are many four- or five-act plays which, when they're produced, have only a single intermission. Sometimes—particularly with Shakespeare, whose act divisions were later editorial interpolations—the break is taken in the middle of an act. If you hadn't read these plays, and if there were no playbill telling you so, you'd never know whether you were seeing act breaks or only scene transitions.

So this well-read student is literally correct, but we aren't speaking here of how a playwright decides to write "End of Act One. Lights up on Act Two." There are many considerations that go into that decision which have nothing to do with what we're dealing with here. We're looking at the underlying dramaturgy of a play, which is invisible to the untrained eye. In this sense, the arrangement of almost any play is (like a dream) in three acts.

The essential, invisible play is arranged as follows: the need is introduced in Act One, in Act Two the need confronts the obstacle, and by the end of Act Three the need has either been fulfilled or denied. (The latter, by the way, being a good working definition of comedy versus tragedy.)

The length of these invisible acts varies widely. Sometimes the obstacle is established immediately after the need, making the invisible first act very short, even concurrent with the second. Sometimes the obstacle isn't introduced until much later. That makes for a longer invisible Act One. The other invisible acts will also vary according to the same principles. This is a natural thing, and a good thing. It's part of what makes each play a unique work of art. Plays, while they have a mechanical aspect, are not simply widgets that can be turned out according to rigid specifications.

SIMPLICITY ITSELF

So basic dramatic structure is that simple.

Of course, simple does not necessarily mean easy. In fact, it's usually most difficult to be simple. But it does mean that, while their execution can prove to be challenging, the basic concepts we're dealing with here are not that hard to grasp. It means also that the structure of your play can be simple. I'll even go out on a limb and say that, as a rule, the simpler the better.

Jeff, a student from one of my workshops, listened to me discuss the merits of simple dramaturgical structure. We were talking about his play, and my point was precisely focused on how he might think about improving it. He was the first to agree that his play was not all he wanted it to be, but nevertheless a worried look crept over his features when I got to the subject of simplicity. I wasn't surprised when he approached me at the end of the workshop and asked if we could talk.

Jeff is quite bright, and there was a wealth of ideas running through the play he was working on. It was thematically dense (that's not pejorative) and he clearly had a lot to say as a writer. He was also a good student, eager to learn whatever he could from the workshop. But this idea that structure should be as simple as possible obviously disturbed him. It seemed to challenge every instinct of what he considered his work to be.

When the others had gone, Jeff said, "But my play is complicated. It's not just that I want it to be—it *is*. The play inside that wants to come out is full of ideas and contradictions and nuances. And that's the way I like it. I know it's not perfect and I have a lot of work to do, but I like it complicated. Why do I have to make it simple?"

First, I agreed with him: the play he was writing was indeed complicated—and was all the better for being so. On one level. But that wasn't the level I was talking about.

So I reassured him that he was right about one other thing, that the play he was writing was indeed the play he needed, not just wanted, to write. That's not always true in cases like this. Some writers discover that when they allow the play, which they need to write, to emerge, it's much simpler than the one they wanted so badly to be complicated.

But this wasn't Jeff's problem.

In the workshop, I had been telling him that this structure should be simple. He heard something else. He thought I was asking him to make his thematic ideas simple—or simplistic, as he complained. I pointed out the distinction: the psychology of the characters, the layering of imagery, the subtlety of theme, the delicate nuances of language—all these factors can be as finely wrought, as complex as you like. And the more so, we would generally agree, the better.

But I encouraged him to let his structure stay simple. His structure is simply a foundation, a framework within which he could then do the work that interested him. The stronger and simpler the foundation, I said, the more freedom he would have to fill in those all-important details.

Good stories are simple. Good stories can be told, briefly, in a few sentences. Bad stories go on and on, never get anywhere, and no matter how interesting and subtle your ideas may be, the audience won't hear them. Why? Because they're asleep.

So no—I'm not suggesting that the ideas in your play be simple, much less simplistic. There's a world of difference between the ideas that your play conveys and its structure, which is the means by which they're conveyed.

That's why structure is liberating. If you build it strong, build it clean, and build it simple, it will be a firm, reliable pillar on which you can always lean. And then you're free to write the complex, intricate play that's within you.

TWO: ACTION

WHAT IS ACTION?

I ONCE went to the workshop* production of a new play
in which there was a great deal of physical activity onstage.
The actors leapt about athletically, at times almost gymnasti-
cally. There were two fight scenes and a dance sequence. At
one point an actor bounded around as though he were an
enormous dog, barking and drooling; in another scene two of
the actors prepared (and then ate!) a complete meal. Much of
the activity was funny, some of it breathtaking in its physical-
ity, all of it well choreographed and well performed.

---

*A workshop production is generally one that has a set, lights, costumes—all
the things that one normally expects at a play. But it's inexpensively and
quickly produced; the run is short, and the rehearsal period may have been
short as well (> p. 311, Readings and Workshops).

Yet, for all this activity, I thought the play was dull. And the rest of the audience, from what I could tell, felt the same. I counted at least four heads buried in programs, several more resting wearily in cupped hands, and any number of torsos slumped in seats. The applause at the end was polite—and over before the actors left the stage. Why should this be, you might well ask, with all that excitement onstage?

I'm going to venture that the reason for our disappointment—and this may surprise you—is that there was no action. You've probably heard this said about a play, and maybe you've even said it yourself: "There wasn't enough action . . . Nothing happened . . . I wanted less talk, more action." Yet how could I say this about a play that was manifestly bursting with it?

Sophocles advised that "knowledge comes through action," and the Bhagavad Gita returns, "On action alone be thy interest, not on its fruits." Hamlet bemoans that he may "lose the name of action," while Henry V exhorts his troops to "imitate the action of a tiger." James Russell Lowell opined that "all the beautiful sentiments in the world weigh less than a single lovely action."

Are all these writers talking about the same idea? Or does the concept of action take on new meanings in new circumstances?

Aristotle proposes that drama is, at its core, "the imitation of an action," and it's Aristotle's definition with which we, as playwrights, are concerned. (It's what we could call dramatic action, but for our purposes we will refer to it simply as action.)

Before we find out what Aristotle actually meant by his

word (*praxis*, in the ancient Greek), it's a good idea to understand his approach to philosophy in general.

Aristotle loved categories. In order to study his subject, Aristotle typically divided it into categories, then subcategories, and sometimes sub-subcategories. In studying the arts, he divided them much as we would today: painting, sculpture, music, writing, etc. He further divided writing into epic and lyric poetry, and comic and tragic drama.

All art, according to Aristotle, is an imitation of something. The thing that an art form imitates is its object. In other words, the object of Da Vinci's *Mona Lisa* is a rather pretty woman with a mysterious smile: she is the person that the painting imitates. The object of Beethoven's Symphony no. 6 (the *Pastoral*) is a bucolic setting. Each movement portrays a different aspect of that environment. "A gathering of villagers," "a thunderstorm," etc., are those things being imitated by the symphony. The object of Michelangelo's *David* is the biblical hero of the same name: the man, David, is imitated in the form of a sculpture.

What do all these objects have in common? For one thing, they're all found in the physical world. They are all concrete, observable phenomena. That's why Aristotle's observation about what drama imitates is so startling. When he says that drama is the imitation of an action, he doesn't mean a physical action. He means an internal, psychological need. The Aristotelian scholar S. H. Butcher called it "psychic energy moving outwards." Dante called it a "movement of spirit." Playwrights, prone to more practical phrasing, call it "what a character wants."

But however we phrase it, the crucial distinction is that

drama is different from all other art forms in at least one aspect: it imitates not the external world, but an inner one—an invisible world, a world we would never see if we did not have drama to reveal it.

This idea I find to be astonishing. More important, I find it true. Deeply true.

Dramatic action is not doing something. It is not physical activity. It is not characters moving around the stage, gesturing and performing business. It is not fight scenes, or dances, or behaving like large dogs, or preparing and then eating a meal. Characters onstage may do all these things with great exertion and extraordinary polish, but it will bring them no closer to dramatic action unless the fact of their wanting something drives them to do so.

Action is what a character wants.

To further illustrate, let's look at another problematic play, this one at a small off-Broadway theater with a good reputation. It concerns three brothers who have gathered for their father's funeral. One brother is grief stricken, another is secretly glad that his father is dead, the third seems above it all, as though he looks down arrogantly on the other two for caring so much one way or the other. The brothers' emotions soon become apparent, and for the length of the play they laugh, cry, fight, rage, sob in each others' arms. Finally, having released all their feelings about each other and their father, they go off to the funeral and the play is over.

The play wasn't melodramatic. It was truthful, well observed, subtly written, well acted. It was clear that the emotions had sprung from the playwright's own personal, painful experience.

But again, as much as I wanted to like such a deeply felt, truthful work, I couldn't deny that I was bored. And again, I wasn't alone. Nearly a quarter of the audience didn't come back for the second act.

The reason? Once again I can only postulate, but I say: no action. Those brothers wanted nothing from each other. They felt deeply, truly, and honestly. But emotions are not action. They're important, and we certainly wouldn't ever want to see a play without them. But they don't take the place of action. Characters may feel profound sadness, or joy, or anger, or love. They may speak at great length about these feelings, shout about them, sing about them. But these remain feelings, not actions.

This is what action isn't. Let's find out more about what it is.

Let's say that we have a character named Joe. Joe wants a glass of water. Wanting that glass of water is his action. Different people will use other words. They may say it's his objective, or his goal, or his need. I use action, but what matters is the concept not the word. (I once had a student who for some reason absolutely hated using the word action. It just really bugged him, made him freeze up and feel uncreative. So he and I only talked about his characters' goals, and that was fine with both of us.)

Joe may do something about the want—the desire—that he is experiencing, or he may not. He may ask for a glass of water, he may demand it, he may beg for it. He may stick out his tongue and pant, and hope that someone gets the message. He may simply stand up, walk to the sink, and pour himself a glass. He may do a lot of things that indicate he wants a glass of water.

Or he may do nothing. He may just sit there.

In terms of whether he possesses an action, it doesn't matter whether he acts on it. In either case, he still has an action. He has an action because he wants something: the glass of water.

Action is what the character wants.

Whether a character chooses to do something about attaining his action is a second, distinguishable step. A crucial step in the development of a drama, to be sure. Without it, there's no play—but it's the second step, not the first.

A man who buys a lottery ticket, and then goes home wanting to win, is not pursuing a dramatic action. The character must want something that we can watch him pursue.

When Joe speaks up and says "I want a glass of water," his action becomes clear. It also becomes clear if someone passes by him with a tray of drinks and he desperately grabs one of the glasses, drinking it down in a gulp. We learn that a character has an action by his behavior—either through what he says or what he does. Language or spectacle.

And, typically, the character should want something of another character. If Joe says he wants a glass of water, but he speaks those words into the void, it will not be nearly so effective as if he says them to a character who stands before him holding a glass of water.

In some plays, there is hardly any physical activity at all. This is true of playwrights as disparate as Sophocles and Beckett. Oedipus has hardly any physical movement in Sophocles' play; Winnie remains buried in her mound throughout the entire length of Beckett's *Happy Days*. Some would say that these plays have no action. They couldn't be more wrong. There is overwhelming need in both of these plays—and in many others like them. And that need is expressed almost entirely through the most wonderfully precise, nuanced, revelatory means known to humanity: it's called language.

The important thing to remember is that neither physical activity nor language alone is action. By themselves they're either mere activity or mere talk. Words and movement are there for a larger purpose: to serve the action, to reveal it, to convey it to the audience.

Action is what a character wants. It is the wanting itself.

HOW TO THINK ABOUT ACTION

In practical terms, you'll probably end up talking about action a lot—both while you're writing (and rewriting) your play and while you're in rehearsal. In the former case, you'll be talking with teachers or fellow writers about how to work on and improve the play. In the latter, you'll be talking to your director, your dramaturg, and perhaps your actors and designers. There are a few good ways to keep things clear and simple.

The first is to settle on a vocabulary. Make sure that, even if you use different words, you at least mean the same thing.

Also, try to avoid another common problem—one that happened to me early in my career. In preparation for rehearsal of a one-act play, I asked my director what she thought the action of the play was. In some ways that's a perfectly good question, probably the most important question a playwright and director can discuss. It's the one you want to get hammered out before making all the other decisions that will flow from it (> p. 317, Collaboration Issues).

Unfortunately, though, phrasing the question in that way—the action of the play—led to a lot of confusion and, ultimately, an unnecessary fight. And frankly, a large part of it was my own fault.

My director responded to my thoughts by offering all kinds of perfectly good but rather abstract ideas about theme and images and symbols. Never did she mention what the characters wanted. I got angry and said she didn't know what action was.

Many harsh words later, I realized of course that I hadn't asked her that. I asked her about the action of the play. But plays, strictly speaking, do not have actions. Characters do. Of course, many plays have a main character who in turn has a main action. This is what I meant when I asked her the question. Since it was quite clear in my mind who the main character was, the real meaning of my question was apparent to me. But not to her.

When we got this worked out, she and I agreed who the main character was—and we also agreed about the nature of his action. So the discussion proceeded easily from there.

The problem is not always so easy to solve. Sometimes you and your director will disagree on who the main character is or what his action is. (It happens.) In that case, you've got a longer discussion to look forward to. But at least you'll be using the same vocabulary.

So whether you're just thinking about how to work on your play or speaking to a director about how to mount it, always be sure to take a moment and make sure you're talking about something real. Trying to talk about the action of a play is not real. Talking about a character's action is.

WHO SHOULD HAVE AN ACTION?

Every character in a play should have an action, which means that a play will have as many actions as it has characters. Many of them may be small, momentary, unremarkable in comparison to that of the main character. But they will be a necessary part of the general movement of the play. Indeed, one of the hallmarks of the greatest playwrights is that even the character who is onstage only for a few moments wants something.

Take Sophocles' *Antigone*. Antigone's sister, Ismene, is a minor character. She makes one appearance at the beginning of the play, then is in another brief scene later on. Yet in both scenes she is very active. In the first, she desperately tries to convince Antigone not to violate Creon's edict against the burial of their brother; in the second scene, she begs to share in the blame that will otherwise be Antigone's alone to bear. Powerful needs, both.

Or take the paperboy scene from Tennessee Williams's *A Streetcar Named Desire*.* The Young Man, a paperboy, has entered with a simple but clear action—he's "collecting for *The Evening Star*." The deep, emotional need of the scene is clearly Blanche's. She longs romantically and sexually for the boy. But he is not simply passive. If he were, he wouldn't be there, and

---

*There will many references to this play, and to a handful of others, throughout the book. You can find a list of these plays in Appendix A, p. 323. They are all well known. But if you are not already familiar with them, I recommend that you read them now before you go on with the book. Or at the very least read them as you make your way through this text.

he wouldn't stay even for the short time that he does. He is there simply because he wants to collect his money.

Or is there some faint, frightened hint of longing on his part as well . . . ?

THE FIRST STEP

Finally, the way in which you think about the action may not be as important as the fact that you make sense of it for yourself and that you use the concept of action to support yourself in your work.

Like any tool, dramatic structure should help and not hinder you in your job. There may be an awkward period when you are still learning to use that tool. During this time, it may seem that the tool is more trouble than it's worth. But once you've mastered the technical aspect of dramatic writing, you'll find that your technique makes your work simpler and your problems easier to solve.

The exercise at the end of this chapter is meant to help focus your understanding of action. Treat it as just that, an exercise. It's like a laboratory experiment that isolates one singular process and allows you to concentrate on that process only. You shouldn't expect to write a terrific scene when you do the exercise. Do the best you can, of course. (And who knows? You may end up loving the results.)

But writing a scene that's excellent in all aspects isn't your objective if you're doing the exercise well. Your objective is to get a firm grasp of what action is and isn't. Use the exercise to explore that idea, and that idea alone. All other aspects of the scene—the mood, the characterizations, how interesting it may be—these are all secondary. If you come away with a better, surer sense of what action is (and isn't), then you've done the job.

As I've suggested in Chapter One, I don't recommend that you put the tools first when you're working on your play. So why am I telling you to sit down and do an exercise like this, which demands you think about the tools ahead of time? Because you're not writing your play now. You're writing an exercise that will help you discover how those tools work, how you will end up using them. So for the moment, you are going to put them first and foremost. Later when you've got a better grasp of them, they'll become second nature and you'll start to deploy them as needed, without even thinking much about them.

When you've finished the exercise, set it aside for a few days. The Roman poet Horace wrote that if he wanted to know if a poem of his was any good, he waited eight years. If he still liked it after that much time, only then was he sure that it was a keeper. You may not want to wait so long, but a few days or a week seems reasonable for a short exercise. It's enough time to get a little perspective, to step back from the writing and try to see it as others do.

When you look at your exercise, try to evaluate it as you would someone else's writing. Assess it critically and coolly, but fairly. Don't let yourself get away with anything, but resist the urge to make blanket condemnations like, "I hate everything about it." That won't get you anywhere. This is an exercise, so try to identify where you've succeeded and where you haven't.

If you're in a class, your teacher is an obvious person to go to for more feedback. But so are other students or friends.

It's important to ask them specific questions about the scene. You want to know whether the action is clear, so ask them precisely that. Ask, "Do you know what Character X wants in the scene?"

Like you yourself, they may want to respond to all sorts of other elements of the scene—theme, characterization, mood, dialogue, humor, etc. Let them. But remember also that you have just conducted a laboratory experiment, and you want to know the results of that experiment. So while it may be interesting to hear about those other elements, be sure to get a clear answer about your specific area of concern. If everyone you ask identifies the action in the way you intended it, you know you've done your job. If not, you've got more work to do.

Be sure not to ask leading questions, such as: "Was it clear that Character X wants a book from Character Y?" If you suggest the answer, chances are much more likely that you'll get the answer you're looking for. But, just as in a scientific experiment or a court of law, it won't mean very much. Leave the reader open to give his own answer free of suggestion.

One other thing: if you're working on your own play, don't try to incorporate these exercises into it. Keep them separate. Your play is too important to be submitting it to the rigors of a laboratory experiment. There's plenty of time to get to your play later, once you've begun to grasp the basics of structure.

EXERCISE 1: THE ACTION SCENE

Write a short five- to ten-page scene (> p. 297, Standard Manuscript Format) in which there are only two characters and the first character wants a book from the second character. All the details of the scene (who these people are, where they are, what their relationship is, what the book is, why the first character wants it, why the second has it, etc.) are up to you. In other words, you have been given the action for the scene, but nothing else.

WHAT IS MOTIVATION?

IN REHEARSALS for my own plays, I often hear the actors using the terms *action* and *motivation* interchangeably. At one moment, an actor might say, "The action I'm playing is to flatter her." And in the next moment, the same actor says, "My motivation is to flatter her."

While that may be fine for actors, to my mind it's useful to draw a distinction between these terms. And not for some abstract intellectual reason, but because separating them allows me to delineate the difference between what characters want and why they want it. They are flip sides of the same coin—deeply intertwined but distinct.

If action is what characters want, then motivation is their reason for wanting it.

• • •

Let's suppose, for the sake of argument, that we go back to the time when *Six Degrees of Separation* was still being written. In this imaginary scenario, John Guare knows that Paul's specific, immediate action is to ingratiate himself into Ouisa and Flan's home. But he hasn't yet decided on Paul's motivation for doing so.

Guare contemplates the possibility that Paul is really a conventional con man who intends to strip their apartment of all its valuable artwork. Then he floats the notion that Paul has seen Ouisa on the street, is attracted to her, and hopes to have a sexual encounter with her. Other ideas occur to him too: that Paul is a psychotic murderer out on a spree of random violence, that he's homeless and wants a place to live, that he's an artist hoping to show Flan his work.

But Guare doesn't choose any of these options. They're perfectly good from a strictly mechanical point of view, but it's obvious to him that they're not the play he wants to write. (Thank God.) He settles instead on the subtle, highly nuanced motivation that can best be summed up in Paul's own words when Ouisa asks him, at the end of the play, what he wanted the night he first stumbled into their lives: "Everlasting friendship."

In some ways, your character's motivation will influence, more than any other single factor, the kind of play you write.

To illustrate, let's go back to the paradigmatic Joe and his glass of water.

If Joe wants his glass of water, it may be because he is thirsty. It is the most common reason, after all. But he may have other motivations. He may want the glass of water so that he can throw it in Mike's face. He may want it to mix color dye into it and make Easter eggs so that Mike can hunt for them in the morning. He may not have any use for the water at all, but only wants it because Mike wants it too, and he doesn't want Mike to get hold of it. Same action, different motivations.

WHAT IS SUBTEXT?

I once had a reading of a play of mine, a work in progress. The reading went well. I had good actors and a small audience of friends, all of whom were very politely interested. And nothing more.

I was confused. I thought I had a good play on my hands. One thing I knew for certain: the action was clear. Or was it? Suddenly I wasn't so sure.

After the reading I asked some friends what they thought. I got the usual polite comments: "Really interesting," "You've got some good moments there," and other damning words of faint praise.

So I asked one particular friend if I could buy him a drink. We went out to a bar and before the first beer was finished, he laid it on the line. "The action is clear, yes. God knows, the action is clear! In fact, it's so clear you don't have a play."

He went on to explain that he knew everything about the main character's action (and everyone else's for that matter) right up front. There was nothing left for him to discover. All he did after the first fifteen minutes was watch the character reveal over and over again the same action, about which he already knew everything there was to know (> p. 217, Suspense).

There was no subtext.

How many plays have you seen that on the surface are perfectly well-constructed works which nevertheless leave you with absolutely no sense of surprise, suspense, or delight? Probably too many.

The reason may be that there's no subtext. The idea of subtext is related to that of motivation. They're different ways of thinking about the same subject.

When a character seems to have one motivation, but in fact has another (or for that matter, when he seems to have one action, but really has another) we call it the subtext. It lies under the text—hidden, just as motivation often is. It is either waiting to be discovered or serving to add other levels of meaning to what's happening on the surface.

I saw the 1999 revival of Arthur Miller's *Death of a Salesman*. Though I had seen the play and read it many times, I found it once again to be full of mystery and suspense. What happened in that hotel room years ago? Are Willy's memories reliable, or are they the visions of a deteriorating mind? Most of all, what is wrong between Willy and Biff? Why can't they get along? Where does this undercurrent of rage and resentment come from?

Much of this sense of mystery can be traced to Miller's use of subtext. I found myself wondering, all over again, what is Willy's deepest need? By the end of play, I learn that he wants to earn Biff's love and respect. But for much of the play that information is subtext, deliberately withheld by the author, buried under other actions that relate to it but don't reveal it directly. It's always present, but never explicitly stated.

Indeed, in earlier scenes Willy wants the following: Biff to ask Bill Oliver for a job; Biff to get the hell out of his house and go back out West; Biff to think more highly of himself; Biff to apologize. All very different specific needs on the surface, and all of them operating on various levels that disguise Willy's truest desire. But in the end, they all make perfect psychological sense because they all erupt out of the same core need—Willy's deepest subtext.

Subtext creates a sense in the audience that they are detectives and must get to the bottom of the matter. Audiences enjoy doing this—it keeps them interested. Certainly your play need not be a literal detective story. But you may wish to withhold some aspects of a character's action until the last possible moment.

Joe and Mike provide us with another illustration.

Joe may lead us to believe he wants the glass of water because he's thirsty, but, in fact, it's because he wants to mix poison into it and murder Mike.

Or Joe says he wants a glass of water (his text) but really he just wants to get a closer look at the lovely waitress who is serving it (his subtext).

Or Joe says he wants the glass of water, and in fact he does, but he leads his friend Mike to believe it's because he's thirsty—his text. When he gets the glass, he throws it contemptuously in Mike's face. Clearly Joe had some subtext.

ACTORS AND SUBTEXT

Good actors often have the ability to create a sense of subtext when it's evoked in the script—and even when it isn't. Their sense of inner life is so strong and convincing that we perceive a vast pool of information (emotions, secrets, desires, contradictions, etc.) somewhere below the surface of their performances.

Watching Judi Dench in David Hare's play *Amy's View*, I had precisely this experience. I admired the play as well, but her performance added that subtextual something that another actress might well have missed. Apparently Hare also thought so, to the degree that he confesses he sometimes had the sensation while watching his own play that he had not written the very lines she was speaking.

If you have an actor like this in your play, congratulations. You got lucky. But don't count on it. If you rely on good actors to make your play interesting, you're asking for trouble. Make your own good fortune (> Chapter 13).

HOW TO THINK ABOUT SUBTEXT

Here is another paradigm, a schematic way of thinking of motivation and subtext. It may help you to think of the problem clearly and simply.

Conceive of the action as existing on several levels simultaneously:

Level One: On this topmost level we have the most apparent action. For example, Joe's desire to get that glass of water.

Level Two: On this level, a deeper, hidden meaning: what Joe really wants is to throw the water in Mike's face.

Level Three: Let's say that Joe accomplishes that by the

end of the first act. Only then do we discover yet a deeper action: Joe wants to humiliate Mike in public.

Level Four: At the same time, we may discover that Joe wants to humiliate Mike so that Mike will leave town. Why?

Level Five: Joe wants to have an affair with Mike's wife.

Each level of the action is (to borrow a term from capitalism) vertically integrated. Each is connected to and dependant on both the one above it and the one below. Indeed, one could even say that all these actions are really an expression of the action that we discover only at the end: Joe's desire to have an affair with Mike's wife. Just as, in a far more subtle way, Willy's need for Biff to think highly of himself is a cover for Willy's more penetrating need for Biff's love and respect.

HOW TO CREATE MOTIVATION AND SUBTEXT

A very eager student once responded to all this by saying, essentially, "Great! So how do I do it?"

My answer is that if all goes well, you don't do it. It does you.

I hope it was obvious that my imaginary scenario of John Guare and his writing of *Six Degrees of Separation* was pure fantasy. Not only did I make it up, but it's a fair guess that Guare never went down a checklist of options for Paul's motivation.

It's far more likely that he relied on his instincts, his sense of who Paul is, guided by the same ineffable compass that pointed him toward writing about this subject in the first place.

In other words, it's most likely that you, like Guare,

won't have to create motivation/subtext so much as you have to allow it to rise up out of the situation. Your best way to create motivation/subtext is to let it happen on its own (> Chapter 9).

On the other hand, you do want to be aware of it—if not now while you're writing the play, then at least as you consider the rewrites that will make it clearer. At some point, you should be able to answer the question: Why is this character behaving in such-and-such a way?

Still, there will be those moments when you simply can't answer the question: Why? These are times when it doesn't "do you." You have to "do it." In those cases, you can do one of two things.

You can keep writing and hope that the character eventually reveals himself to you. This may be the longer route and will require a leap of faith on your part. On the other hand, it could end up providing you with the truer, more organic answer.

Or you can sit down and create a list such as the one I suggested in my mock-writing of *Six Degrees*. This will be faster and give you a surer sense of where the character stands, but you do run a greater risk of creating a false motivation/subtext that runs against the grain of your character's true nature.

I have also found that this second method runs a greater risk of creating more sensational motivations like murder, thievery, sexual exploits, and so on. While these have an obvious superficial appeal, they are not necessarily the most interesting in the long run. Often the most interesting motivation is the simplest, the quietest: "Everlasting friendship."

Nevertheless, I have used both methods in my own writing. Both have worked on different occasions. Both have failed me on others. There is no sure answer, only the one you feel most comfortable with at the time.

Up until now, we've been discussing the first basic tool of structure: action. Want, need, objective, motivation, and sub-text are all aspects of that basic tool, a subcategory of it.

Let's move on now to the second basic tool: conflict, obstacle, problem.

WHAT IS CONFLICT?

IN MY college course I once had a student, Ken, who wrote a scene that he insisted wasn't very good.

The scene was set in the 1920s. The characters Aila (eight) and her sister Marie (sixteen) speak rather quietly throughout. Aila wants Marie to come outside and play hopscotch. Marie allows that she'd like to, but it's more important that Aila stay inside and do her homework. We already know from earlier scenes that Aila has a debilitating and incurable lung disease. Marie's action to keep Aila inside doing her homework is really an effort to protect her health, indeed her life.

The rest of the class loved the scene. So did I. It was a simple and moving rendering of these girls' lives. The action was clear, as was the deeper motivation, which came out elegantly and subtly.

Ken agreed that the scene used all these tools, and allowed that he liked how they were employed.

I asked Ken why, then, didn't he like what he had written?

"No conflict," he said.

"But there is," I said. "The scene is full of it."

"No it isn't. They're just sitting there being nice to each other all the time."

"They are being nice to each other," I returned, "which only makes the conflict that much more poignant."

Ken continued to protest. "But I want it to be more exciting. Conflict should be about fighting and confrontation and, you know, people going at each other!"

That, of course, is the layman's definition of conflict—fighting, confronting, yelling. And while it's certainly one way conflict can work, and a good one, it's not the essence of what conflict actually is.

Conflict is that thing (or person) which prevents a character from getting what he or she wants. (We could call this "dramatic conflict" but here we'll simplify it to just "conflict.")

Conflict is a structural device, like action. It is (or should be) operating all the time, whether the audience is aware of it or not. Sometimes it's apparent to them: characters get louder and angrier. Sometimes it's not so apparent but is nevertheless a crucial factor in drawing us into the scene. Ken's lovely scene about Aila and Marie was like this.

Too often conflict is used to mean a vague state of tension, anxiety, anger, or some other heightened emotion in the characters. This is partly because those are the times when the layman perceives conflict. It's also because, as in the case of action, emotions can look like conflict. But they're not.

Conflict is not emotion anymore than action is emotion.

Conflict is that which prevents a character from getting what he or she wants.

Early in my writing career, I was working on a short one-act play called *Ticket* that I couldn't seem to get right. I thought I had all the components I needed for a good play. The two characters, a brother and sister named Jack and Marla, had very strong feelings about each other. The resentment they felt went back fifteen years to a time when they were both teenagers and Jack had persuaded his parents to send him off to a fancy private school so he could study music. Marla was forced to remain at home and was never able to pursue her ambition to go to law school.

In the play, Jack has come to visit Marla in their old hometown where she still lives. He wants to take her back to New York with him where he can show her the city. She, in turn, has always longed to go to New York. His offer could be the fulfillment of that dream, even though she remains deeply bitter toward him.

The dramatic problem of the play, as I saw it, was the tremendous resentment on the part of Marla—this, and the shock and anger Jack experiences when he discovers for the first time how bitter she really is.

In the first, incomplete draft I had written, once these feelings were revealed, the two siblings let each other have it with both barrels. Anger! Resentment! Recrimination! Volcanic emotional eruptions!

All this, and no play.

I simply couldn't find a way to get past these emotions. The characters sat there being volcanic page after page. It seemed that I could write them this way with no end in sight, and frankly it was getting mighty dull.

How could all that conflict seem so boring to me?

Because it wasn't conflict at all. Not dramatic conflict.

It was name-calling, for sure. It was also an argument of sorts, because they certainly disagreed over what had happened fifteen years ago in their youth.

But it was not conflict. Why? Because they could both have what they wanted, which was to go to New York. He wanted her to go to New York, and she wanted to go to New York.

She was angry about it, to be sure. Angry that he hadn't asked her before. Angry that he was living in New York at all, while she had become a suburban housewife. Angry that she knew she couldn't stay once she got there. But underneath this anger, she wanted the same thing he wanted: to go to New York. When both characters want the same thing, there is no conflict.

Conflict is that which prevents a character from getting what he or she wants.

EXTERNAL CONFLICT

An inanimate object can, in theory, provide conflict. If Joe is tied in a chair with a rope (a favorite scenario of the action/ adventure movie), then it is the rope that is Joe's conflict. While the playwright should be aware of this and use inanimate objects when it's appropriate, there's generally not much opportunity here for the playwright to do her work.

Far more fertile ground is found in other characters. In fact, when one character wants one thing and another character wants something incompatible with this, we have a more interesting kind of conflict than that between a man and a rope. We have what we call "external conflict."

In other words, Joe's action can be, to Mike, a conflict; and Mike's action can be a conflict for Joe. External conflict can be thought of as two actions of two different characters—when the two actions face off and prevent one character from getting what he wants.

In Act One, Scene One of David Mamet's *Glengarry Glen Ross*, Levene, a formerly great but now down-on-his-luck real estate salesman, pleads with Williamson, his boss, to give him the good leads. A lead is a name, but not just any name. It's the name of someone whom the company has reason to believe is a hot prospect—somebody who has indicated they may want to buy real estate. Therefore, a lead is valuable. It can mean the difference between success and failure. And Levene very much wants to be successful again.

He begs Williamson for those leads. He insists other people waste them; he explains away his recent failures; he pleads seniority. His action is quite clear.

Williamson refuses. He has an answer to each of Levene's reasons. He will not give Levene the good leads. Period.

Williamson presents Levene with a conflict. He prevents Levene from getting what he wants. Specifically, he presents an external conflict—which is a conflict that occurs between people.

"I want this; you won't let me have it." That's an external conflict.

Let's go back to the Joe and Mike paradigm for another example.

Suppose that our parched friend Joe still wants his glass of water. And let's suppose that he sits alone in a room, tied to a chair that is bolted into the floor. A glass of water sits on the table in front of him, but he can't reach it because the rope restrains him. His action remains the same as before: wanting the water. His conflict is the rope. The rope is what prevents him from attaining what he wants.

Let's face it. This isn't as intriguing as Mamet's scene. The potential for interesting dialogue between a man and a rope is limited. But it does illustrate in simple, concrete terms the idea of external conflict. Keep that image in your head. Because now, as good students of Aristotle, we're going to break down external conflict further, into two types.

Direct External Conflict

I call it direct external conflict because the conflict occurs directly between two characters who want to possess or control the same object.

Let's imagine Joe in the same room, with the same action, and the same glass of water on the table before him. Mike is present, and he's also thirsty, so he also wants the glass of water. Joe wants the water; Mike wants the water. There's only one object (the glass of water) and they both want it. Here, Mike is Joe's conflict; Joe is Mike's.

The first scene of *Glengarry* is also a good example of direct external conflict. Levene wants the leads; Williamson also wants them. The scenario varies from the paradigm only so far as Williamson already has possession of the leads and therefore doesn't need to attain them. He only needs to retain possession of them by denying them to Levene.

Indirect External Conflict

Indirect external conflict also occurs between two characters. While the action of the first character is directed toward the second, the action of the second is directed elsewhere. This kind of conflict can be illustrated by again using Joe and Mike.

Joe still wants the glass of water, but Mike has no interest in it. What Mike wants is to kill Joe, and he's very busy trying to do so. This keeps Joe sufficiently occupied in defending himself that he is unable even to get to the glass of water in order to drink it.

Again, we have conflict. Joe cannot get what he wants; Mike cannot get what he wants either. Mike is Joe's conflict: he is the one preventing Joe from getting his glass of water. And Joe is Mike's conflict, but for a different reason: Mike wants to kill Joe, while Joe is doing his best to prevent that.

Hence, indirect conflict.

It's this type of conflict which often involves positive feelings rather than negative. We have just seen a negative example of indirect conflict; here is a positive example.

Joe still wants to drink the glass of water. Now, though, Mike wants to kiss Joe. He's in love with Joe. Joe is attracted to Mike, but he already has a lover and wants to be faithful, and so no kissing. Besides, he's still thirsty and wants that elusive glass of water.

Again, we have conflict. Joe can't get his water: he's too busy fending off Mike's advances. Mike can't get a kiss: Joe is insisting on doing what he thinks is right.

One might even say that, far from lacking conflict, this is the most interesting conflict scenario between Joe and Mike so far, though there's not a negative feeling in sight.

There would seem to be a third example of conflict, such as the one in *Romeo and Juliet* in which there appears to be no conflict at all between the two star-crossed lovers. The audience sometimes has the impression that the rival families battle it out while the two lovers merely bill and coo, speaking pretty words to each other.

How dull a play it would be if this were so.

To the contrary, though, Shakespeare has constructed each scene with the lovers so that the conflict between their families comes to bear on Romeo and on Juliet in such a way that the conflict between them grows very strong indeed. Their type of conflict falls into one of the categories we've already discussed.

Take, for example, the morning scene. Romeo wants to leave, to escape and save his life; Juliet wants him to stay and must persuade him that it is not yet morning. It's a terrific example of indirect conflict.

Or you could think of it as direct conflict, if you prefer. Romeo's own person, his physical body, becomes the object over which they both seek control. He wants to take his physical self out of the bedroom; she wants it to remain.

What matters, as always, is not the fact that the tools are being applied or even that we agree on which tools, but that something is happening here that works beautifully.

And in either case, Shakespeare then provides a delicious twist and reverses the flow of action and conflict. In the second half of the scene, Romeo now decides he can afford to stay awhile after all, while Juliet urges him to escape with his life.

There is more external conflict (whether you think of it as direct or indirect) in that scene than in many shouting matches of lesser plays.

INTERNAL CONFLICT

Internal conflict occurs often in novels, where the conflict may be entirely within a character. Virginia Woolf's *To the Lighthouse* is one of the supreme examples of this. Indeed, in *To the Lighthouse*, the action itself is mostly internal. The characters think about what they want, contemplate it, mull it over, but almost never state it out loud to another character. In turn, any conflict they may encounter comes not from the other characters, who after all are silent, but from themselves, with whom they are carrying on an internal monologue.

As a novel, *To the Lighthouse* has the advantage I discussed in the Introduction: the ability of prose to plumb the inner workings of the mind. Action and conflict rage throughout Woolf's book, though they remain silent and invisible to the external world.

Plays, of course, exist only in the external world, and therein lies the crucial distinction. If a playwright were to adapt *To the Lighthouse* to the stage, he would be faced with the central problem of how to bring the conflict out into the open and speak it aloud so that it could be seen and heard.

He could choose to break the fourth wall and allow the characters to speak their internal thoughts in the form of direct address to the audience (> p. 258, I'm Talking to You). Many great playwrights have chosen this avenue (Shakespeare springs to mind), but when they have done so, it was with great selectivity and restraint. The proportion of soliloquy to dialogue even in such a contemplative play as *Hamlet* is tiny. Playwrights who insist on writing vast sections of their plays in the form of a monologue to the audience often find the audience wondering why they didn't visit the bookstore instead of the box office.

The playwright may also choose to reveal internal conflict by incorporating it into the character's words and behavior and interactions with the other characters. This is the method I prefer because it is the method most suited to the theater. The theater is a place of words and deeds, of language and spectacle, a place where, in the words of Peter Brook, the "invisible is made visible."

In his autobiography, Elia Kazan describes the experience of his wife, Molly, as she wrote plays. Molly was apparently a brilliant woman, full of passion, and quite knowledgeable about the craft of theater. She wrote plays that were emotional, intelligent, and well-structured, but strangely unmoving. Kazan wondered why.

Molly, he knew, was a forceful, strong-willed person and her plays reflected this: her main characters were relentless in the pursuit of their action. Nothing got in their way. Far from being a fault, Kazan mused, this ought to be a strength in her writing—a quality that we admire in all the great plays.

Still, Molly's plays never seemed to work, which led Kazan to realize a deeper, more complex truth about drama. The most fascinating character often is not the one who is able merely to pursue his action relentlessly. The most interesting characters are often ambivalent. The character does have an action, yes. And he does pursue it. But there is something else: something in him complicates that pursuit. This complication makes the character more interesting because it gives fuller dimension to his dramatic journey.

The complication that causes the ambivalence is a second action that the character himself pursues, one that is in opposition to the first. In a basic scene, when a first character has an action and a second character has an action that opposes it, we call it conflict. When the same character has both these actions, we call it internal conflict.

Internal conflict is two actions within one's self that give rise to a conflict.

If a character has an internal conflict, along with the external ones we've already talked about, we in the audience are in even greater doubt as to the outcome of the play. Things are more complex. We perceive a struggle that is both greater and deeper than when we only see a conflict between two separate characters. Greater because there is, simply, more conflict in the scene. Deeper because a struggle that is within one's own conscience (or soul or mind or what have you) is perhaps the most profound struggle that we humans know of.

It's not necessary for every character, or for every play, of course. There are plenty of great characters who don't seem to have much if any internal conflict. But if you, like Molly Kazan, find that there's an ineffable something missing from your work, take a look at your main character to see if an internal conflict might not fan the flames.

Let's use *Oedipus the King* as an example once more. Aristotle admired the purity (what he called the unity) of Oedipus's action. Everything in *Oedipus* relates very clearly to the title character's pursuit of the central action: I want to stop the plague. Or it could be phrased in its more concrete form: I want to find out who killed King Laius. (Although these might sound like two different actions, remember our discussion of vertically integrated actions in Part One. That's what these are. Integrated actions are intimately dependent on each other and do not lead to internal conflict.)

Everything Oedipus does is a pursuit of that objective— whether we call it "stop the plague" or "find the murderer." Correct?

Well, yes. And no. Here is where the intricacy, the subtlety of internal conflict comes in.

Oedipus has an ever-growing fear that this pursuit may lead to disaster. That fear (an emotion) also rises out of his generally noble, responsible character. And his fear leads to a second action, which contradicts the first. This action might be phrased "to avoid the truth." Hide it, bury it, ignore it, deny it. Which is precisely what he does through much of the play—alongside his more overt action. It's like a shadow action, parallel to the first, popping up occasionally only to be quashed by his first, more driving action.

He keeps saying how badly he wants the unvarnished truth—but the facts are staring him in the face all the while, growing more and more insistent. When he quite deliberately puts them aside as though they meant nothing, this is his second action. Together with the first action, it creates an internal conflict: I want to know the truth, yet at the same time I don't.

It's part of what makes the play so fascinating. If Oedipus had no fear (and a consequent action to deny the reality which arises from that fear), he would have no courage—the former being essential to the latter. And if he were not a courageously noble man, we would not feel nearly the same about him. It is his fear that gives us a chance to sympathize with him. We are involved in the fear, we understand it. It gives him dimension. It helps to make him what we used to call in high school a "well-rounded character." If he had no fear, had nothing at stake (> Chapter 5), then his role could easily be reduced to that of an automaton, plodding through the play like a robot mouthing the words.

Think of other great plays and interesting characters: Blanche DuBois, for instance. Her action is often described as "wanting a safe haven," or as "wanting magic, not reality," or "wanting to be pure again." I would agree with any of these, and they all more or less fit together. They're expressions of the same basic need in her.

But she also wants to sleep with Stanley. She's clearly aroused by him and feels the need, the compulsion, even, to have sex with him. This could lead to disaster, and it does when he finally rapes her. It's the last action in the world she ought to be pursuing if she really, unambivalently wanted her safe haven. But she doesn't want it unambivalently. There's something else in opposition to that first need. And it's one of the things that makes the play great.

This might sound like an impossible contradiction, a conundrum: to want two things simultaneously. I can hear you saying, "How the heck am I supposed to do that?"

Good question. I won't say it's easy. There's not a lot about playwriting that's easy. But it's quite doable.

First we need to put the concept of ambivalence into dramatic terms. That's why it's better to call it internal conflict—because onstage, that's what we really want. Not ambivalence, strictly speaking, but two separate and distinct actions that come into conflict with each other, both actions being within one person.

As any actor will tell you, he can play only one action at a time. Therefore, don't try to show a character literally struggling with his two conflicting actions simultaneously. We may do this in real life, it's true. And when we do we're usually frozen in place, unable to make a move in any direction. We usually call it depression. Your character will have the same problem, but the audience will probably perceive it as passivity or stasis. And they will almost certainly not be interested in it.

Instead, create the illusion of real-life internal conflict by allowing the character to pursue one action for a beat, then another in the next beat (> Chapter 7, if you don't already know what a beat is). The audience will be given the impression of simultaneity, but you will actually be writing only one clear action at a time for your actor to play.

For an illustration of how this might work, let's go back to Joe and Mike. Let's suppose that Joe wants his glass of water for a simple, obvious reason: he's thirsty. But Mike is also thirsty and has complete, unquestioned control over the glass.

But let's also suppose that Joe is angry at Mike—not because of the water issue, but for some other reason. Something that precedes this scene. Because of Joe's anger (an emotion), he also has another action: to make Mike cry. This is a second action, completely unconnected to his thirst.

Not only are Joe's two actions distinct from each other, they also conflict. For if Joe pursues the glass of water, he'll try to be nice to Mike, and surely this will not lead to Mike's crying. And if he tries to make Mike cry, surely Mike will not relinquish the glass of water. Joe can't have it both ways, but he still wants to. That's an internal conflict. I could spin out the rest of the scene for you, but I don't think it's necessary. You know what happens when you have external action and conflict. The same thing happens when you add internal conflict to the mix—only more so.

THIS IS NOT AN ARGUMENT

One final word on conflict. It is not an argument. An argument is a discussion between two people who disagree on a subject. Joe thinks the glass of water is half full, Mike thinks it's half empty. That's an argument.

In my unsuccessful play from my early years, the brother and sister disagree about what transpired in the past. That alone was an argument, not a conflict. It was a disputation of the facts. Characters may have differing opinions, and they can argue about them all day, but it will never be conflict.

A play may contain arguments along with conflict. Many good plays do have arguments in them. Antigone and Creon have an ongoing argument about whether loyalty should be to the state or to the gods. This is, thematically speaking, what the play is about. It is a profound question, and it has much to do with what makes *Antigone* a great play. But in addition to—and as part of—that argument, Antigone wants to bury her brother and Creon won't let her. Those opposing needs create the conflict, and without it there would be no drama.

⁂

EXERCISE 2:   THE CONFLICT SCENE

Write another two-character scene. In this scene, the first character wants a tangible object (like the book, but choose your own object this time) from the second character. The second character wants something intangible (love, forgiveness, adulation) from the first. Be sure that neither character can get what they want, at least not easily. Again, all the other details of the scene are up to you.

FIVE: HIGH STAKES AND HIGH HOPES

LET'S SUMMARIZE what we know so far.

We know there are two major tools of structure: action and conflict. A character wants something and she is unable to get it. Everything else we've discussed up to this point is just a way to further understand those two ideas. When these two tools are being used, we have what is called the dramatic situation.

There is a third basic tool in structure, but before we get to it, let's take a moment to elaborate on conflict. There tend to be two problems with conflict: there's either too much of it or not enough.

WHAT ARE HIGH STAKES?

A typical scenario from a play by one of my "beginning" writers is what I call the "strangers on the park bench" scenario:

two strangers meet on a park bench (or on a train, or in a coffee shop, etc.). They get involved in a conversation, and before long they are sharing intimacies. Perhaps, with a little luck, they're also pursuing actions and running up against obstacles. In the end, they walk away a bit happier, perhaps a bit wiser, or sadder, or knowing a little something they didn't know before.

The scene is sometimes amusing, sometimes serious. It is often diverting in one way or another. But when it is over I am usually left feeling unmoved.

It may be my own bias, but I often find it hard to get very involved with scenes like this, and I believe it's because there is very little at stake in them.

What does it mean to have something at stake? Why are high stakes good and low stakes bad?

For that matter, what are stakes?

First, let's dispel the mystery and obfuscation. High stakes are not high emotions. High stakes are not created by injecting false drama into a situation by, for example, making the character's life more miserable than Job's. Conversely, stakes are not low merely because the character speaks quietly and sits still.

Stakes are what the character has to gain or to lose.

Thinking about stakes is a way of thinking about conflict. In a high-stakes situation, the character thinks, "If I don't overcome this obstacle, I'll die. If I do overcome it, I live, and I marry the woman I love, and I'll have pots of money besides."

In low stakes, he thinks, "If I don't overcome this obstacle, life goes on, and I'm only out fifty cents. If by chance I do overcome it, what I get is a peck on the cheek from a woman I never liked much in the first place."

You could also think of stakes as a function of action. "If I don't pursue this action, I'll die," etc. If that works better for you, fine. Putting it in terms of conflict works best for me.

In either case, remember this: high stakes equal much to gain or lose; low stakes equal little to gain or lose.

"Much to gain or lose." It's sounds so . . . relative. How much is much? How is a writer supposed to know how much is enough? Or too much? Besides, one person's gain might be another's loss. How do you know you're making the right choice?

As with any other aspect of your play, it's not a question of a right choice or a wrong one. There are good choices to be sure, and better ones. Certainly worse ones. But no right and wrong.

Hamlet has much to gain: the knowledge that his father's soul will rest in peace.* That knowledge might not matter to everyone, but it matters to Hamlet. And Shakespeare was obviously convinced of it. He believed that Hamlet believed.

And guess what? The audience believes it too.

That's how it works. Not because it's right or wrong. But because you believe that your character believes.

So what's wrong with the "strangers on a park bench" scenario? My answer is that the characters typically have little to

---

*Also the throne, but interestingly that's scarcely referred to in the play. Shakespeare has chosen to make the stakes personal; it's not a tragedy of ambition like *Macbeth* or *Julius Caesar.*

gain or lose. They meet, they talk, perhaps a dramatic moment (i.e., one of high emotion) occurs. But had these characters never had this scene, would their lives be very different? Had they met other people and played out other scenes, would it not have been much the same?

Did they need to meet this person and enact this moment? When the answer is no, we have a case of low stakes.

But why are the stakes low? And how do we make them high?

There are many aspects to the problem, and many solutions. But let me suggest the most common reason for the problem—and the most obvious.

Aristotle, in his discussion of fear and pity, and how best to evoke them, reminds us that "when the tragic incident occurs between those who are near and dear to one another, if, for example a brother kills, or intends to kill, a brother, a son his father, a mother her son, a son his mother . . . these are the situations to be looked for by the poet."

Why? Because when the characters care deeply about what happens to themselves and those around them, the audience also tends to care deeply. Aristotle is saying, in effect, that when you have close ties ("emotional bonds" we might say today), high stakes are much more likely to follow.

Indeed, familial situations are just the ones we find over and over again in the great drama of the ancient Greeks: *The Oresteia, Oedipus the King, Antigone, Medea,* the *Bacchae.* All of them are what today we would call family plays.

If a literal family doesn't suit your designs, try to find other connections between the characters. Are they old friends? (Think *That Championship Season.*) Lovers? (Think *Romeo and Juliet.*) Old, long lost friends? (Think *The Iceman*

Cometh.) Enemies who were once friends—or lovers? (Think *Private Lives.*) Are they people who ostensibly have a rather distant relationship, but who, underneath, actually harbor strong feelings for each other? (Think *Talley's Folly.*) I'll bet for every play you really love, you can find a connection in it, a strong feeling produced by relationships like these.

For it is the *strong feeling* that matters most. We're not necessarily looking for positive feelings—love and affection. We're also interested in strong negative feelings—resentment, bitterness, and so on.

What we don't want is indifference. We want the characters to matter to one another.

Witness the example of one of the great pairings of dramatic literature: Blanche and Stanley. Strangers when they meet at the beginning of the play, they have nevertheless heard of each other. They're also in-laws. They know something of what to expect from each other, and already they don't like what they think is coming.

Then, upon meeting, they form an immediate bond of both attraction and repulsion. (Late in the play, Stanley will acknowledge this connection just before he rapes her: "We've had this date with each other from the beginning.") Stanley and Blanche resent each other—but are also drawn inexorably together. They fight bitterly over Stella, over their cramped living quarters, over lost fortunes and old lies. They also try to seduce each other. It's a complicated relationship, full of seeming contradictions, but the one thing we could never say about Blanche and Stanley is that they don't care about each other. They care deeply. Neither can walk out of that apartment until the other is destroyed.

That's what we're looking for.

Another famous pair from dramatic literature is Peter and Jerry of *The Zoo Story*. This is literally a "strangers on a park bench" play. But most would agree it's a powerful drama. How does Edward Albee do it?

First, his essential point is that this is a play about strangers. It could not be anything else. He cannot fudge the issue by making Peter and Jerry friends or even acquaintances. That would destroy the idea that Jerry has sought out a man completely unknown to him; if not entirely at random, then at least without any knowledge of who Peter is.

The play is about the need to communicate, to touch another person across the unbridgeable gap that separates us as humans. If Jerry and Peter know each other, this effect would be impossible to portray—at least the way it's portrayed in this play. So the fact that they are strangers is essential.

What happens over the course of *The Zoo Story* is that Jerry works aggressively, sometimes seductively, often ferociously to engage Peter. And Peter finds himself quickly drawn into Jerry's emotional orbit. They slowly become "friends" so that by the end of the play they arrive at the ultimate act of communication and intimacy—the murder/suicide of Jerry.

Albee's solution, dramaturgically speaking, is to acknowledge that Jerry and Peter are strangers, and to write a play which is primarily about the forging of a bond between them. He makes them grow to care about each other very much. He gives them something to gain (friendship, intimacy, a connection) and much to lose (friendship, intimacy, a connection, and life itself).

Unless you have an overriding reason not to do so, as Albee clearly does in *The Zoo Story*, it's wise to choose characters who already know and care about what happens to each other. Because characters who care will have high stakes.

A story from a college class of mine shows how a play can develop from a low-stakes situation to one of high stakes.

A student, Veronica, brought in a "strangers on a park bench" scene which, like *The Zoo Story*, happened to literally take place at a park bench.

In the first version, a young man named Cosmo tries to romance a woman named Angelina. They are strangers.

I said that, although the scene was well written in many ways, Cosmo's stakes seem rather low. "Why is Angelina so important to Cosmo? I understand he likes her, is attracted to her, but there's nothing I can see that suggests this is anything more than a mild flirtation that he might conduct every day of the week. For all I know he does this every day with a new woman. For her part, it seems to me that Angelina could take him or leave him without so much as a second thought."

Veronica agreed that, while the scene was pleasant enough, it wasn't terribly interesting. It didn't have the fire and ice that she had imagined it would.

She agreed to work on it some more.

The next week, in a new version, Cosmo tells Angelina that he has had his heart badly broken by his girlfriend, Jackie, who just dumped him. He had come here to the park to lick his wounds and finds himself very attracted to Angelina. In other words, Veronica's solution was to give Cosmo an offstage event that makes Angelina more important to him than before (> p. 272, In Medias Res).

The scene was better, no doubt about it. Cosmo now had a specific and credible reason why connecting with Angelina should matter to him. There was, at least, some fire. But I had to point out that, though Cosmo certainly now had more to gain (the mending of his broken heart), it was hard to understand why Angelina was the answer. Wouldn't any woman have done as well? Wasn't Jackie the real object of his desire? Wasn't that why his heart was really broken?

Veronica had already acknowledged that the scene only felt partway there to her. Now she also agreed Cosmo was really still in love with Jackie, that Angelina was only a rebound.

"In that case," I said, "the stakes remain low between Cosmo and Angelina. If he doesn't get her, life goes on. Another woman will serve just as well as a rebound."

Veronica returned again with a third draft. In this version, Cosmo had broken up with Angelina a year before after a long and passionate affair. In the intervening year, he had gone out with Jackie, and that affair also ended with tears and bitterness. He runs into Angelina, by accident, near the same spot in the park that they used to frequent as lovers. In seeing her again, he realizes his mistake and pleads with her to take him back.

The scene worked beautifully. Why? Because (I believe) it was now Angelina who mattered most. Cosmo had much to gain or lose from the other character onstage, the person with whom he was playing the scene.

Fire and ice.

When a character has much to gain or lose, he will care deeply. If there is little to gain or lose, then he will tend to be indifferent to the outcome. And that indifference will almost surely be matched by that of the audience.

Make them care.

WHAT ARE HIGH HOPES?

Can there ever be such a thing as too much conflict? Absolutely.

Remember what conflict is: that which prevents a character from getting what she wants. If there is too much of this thing—if, in other words, the obstacle is so great, so impenetrable, so unmovable that the audience senses there is no possibility that she will ever attain her objective—then we have a problem.

If, for example, you make it impossible for Joe to obtain his glass of water, and if Joe knows that, the audience will soon enough figure that out and lose interest in Joe's struggle.

It must remain plausible that Joe may get his water. There must be some ray of hope, and he must believe there to be one, no matter how dim.

Consider a play I once heard at a public reading, I'll call it *Father and Son*, in which a young man, Sam, has come home to care for his dying father. Sam's deepest action, beneath the upper layers of trying to keep his father alive or at least out of pain, is to obtain forgiveness for having deserted the family many years ago. A good action and a playable one.

However, in this particular draft, there wasn't a snowball's chance in hell that the father was ever going to grant forgiveness. He refused to be decent to Sam, would barely even speak a word to him.

Fortunately, there were several other characters, so there was a chance for dialogue between them. But at the center of this play was a hopelessness. Sam was out of luck, up the creek without a paddle. Worse, he as a character knew that he was up that creek. There was never even the slightest opening, not the slimmest opportunity for him to get a foot in the door of his father's bitterness. And sure enough, by the end of the play, the father died without uttering a syllable of forgiveness.

It was frustrating to watch as this play, so promising in other ways, floundered on its core issue.

In the feedback session afterward, several voices raised this issue. The playwright defended his choice saying it was "true to life." He may have been right about that. Certainly there are unforgiving parents out there. But the playwright forgot that people don't go to the theater merely to see things that are true. They also go to see that which is interesting.

As far as I know, the playwright never rewrote this play, and as far as I know it has never been produced. When there is no hope, there's usually little interest.

But, you say, what about the great tragedies—*Oedipus the King, Hamlet, Death of a Salesman, Waiting for Godot*? Oedipus, Hamlet, Willy Loman, Vladimir and Estragon all find themselves in hopeless situations, don't they?

In some sense, yes. If you know these plays, you know that all these characters come to a tragic end in one way or another. And that there was an inevitability to their tragedy. But that's what we know now—after the fact of the play. The actual experience of all these plays, and, I would argue, of any good play, is one of great hope.

Let's take *Godot* as an example. Vladimir and Estragon have become synonyms for despair in our colloquial references. And yet, if we examine the text, we find that both characters are endlessly hopeful. They have to be, given how dismal their circumstances are. Even in the final moments of the play, they are willing to believe that tomorrow Godot will come. We in the audience have perhaps lost hope; Vladimir and Estragon have not.

The same with the other examples. Oedipus truly believes he can save the city without peril to himself. That's why he keeps getting deeper and deeper into the quagmire until at the end of the play he realizes the truth. Hamlet believes there must be a way to exact revenge successfully and morally, yet stay alive at the same time. He continues to believe this until he is mortally wounded in the play's final moments. Willy's belief in his own salesmanship and in Biff's essential greatness remains undiminished until the very end. He rages at Biff, to be sure, but he also defends him, clutches him to his breast, loves him.

It's important that the character remain hopeful, and that you give him the way by which to do so. This might mean the character is deluded (as we could say of Willy or Oedipus), or it might be that he cannot see the entire picture clearly (as with Hamlet or Vladimir and Estragon). But whatever the case, if the character has hope, chances are good that we will too.

IN MY college course a student, Kate, was trying to finish a one-act play based on Jack Kerouac and Allen Ginsberg. The play was a fictionalized account of an encounter between the two men in the early 1960s, when Ginsberg's star was continuing to rise but Kerouac's had fallen sharply. At this moment, Allen has come to visit Jack in the Long Island home of Jack's mother, where Jack has been living and drinking himself into oblivion.

So far, it was a very affecting piece, with Allen playing a very strong action to get Jack out of this house, away from his mother, and back to some semblance of the life they once led. Jack was in the reactive role, resisting Allen at every turn.

Kate was ready to bring the play to a conclusion and expressed concern over just how she was going to do that.

"I don't really know what happens at the end," she said. "I haven't figured that out yet."

What happens at the end. It's a colloquial way of saying it, but it's as good a way as any to describe what we mean by the event of a play (> p. 271, The Passover Question).

WHAT IS AN EVENT?

The final basic tool at your disposal, after action and conflict, is event. It is related to action and conflict in the sense that it provides their culmination or climax—the moment to which the action and conflict have been leading.

The event is sometimes thought of as the moment of change in the play. When, for example, Oedipus moves from ignorance of King Laius' murderer to knowing his identity. Or when Hamlet moves from seeking revenge for his father's murder to exacting that revenge. Or when Blanche moves from a woman seeking refuge to a woman who's last possible refuge has been taken from her.

In all these instances, we have the main action of the character (Oedipus wants to find the murderer of the king) and a conflict (everyone he talks to either doesn't know or isn't saying), which lead at last to the event (he discovers who the murderer is).

The event is when a character either gets what he wants or definitively does not get it.

Oedipus gets what he wants. So does Hamlet. They both pay a heavy price, to be sure. Oedipus destroys his life and Hamlet is killed. But dramaturgically speaking, they get what they want.

Blanche, on the other hand, does not. Her main action is to seek refuge, to find a place where she can, at last, be safe.

(This is open to interpretation, but let's assume it for the sake of argument.) Her conflict is, primarily, Stanley. He doesn't want her in his house; he isn't sympathetic to her desire for a place to rest. While Mitch and Stella both offer some hope at first, in the end they also side with Stanley. Blanche grows more desperate until Stanley lashes out and brutally rapes her, robbing her of any chance that she will find the refuge she seeks. This is her event. It is the moment when she changes from seeking refuge to knowing there is none.

Further illustration from Joe and Mike, our dehydrated, long-suffering protagonists.

Same room, same original situation: Joe wants the glass of water; Mike does too. That's our action and conflict.

But now let's suppose that Joe is more clever than Mike, or stronger, or perhaps just more intimidating. In any case, Joe succeeds in getting the glass of water and drinking it down in one gulp. The moment that Joe seizes the glass and drinks the water is the event. Joe has gotten what he wants.

Or, conversely, Mike succeeds in getting the glass of water and drinking it down. This too is an event, even for Joe. Why? Because he has definitely not gotten what he wants. The glass of water is gone, down Mike's hatch. That is the event.

Or perhaps Joe and Mike struggle over the glass of water and they spill it. Now the water is on the floor, undrinkable. That is the event: neither man gets what he wants—and fails to do so definitively.

The event changes the dramatic situation (meaning the action and conflict) in some significant way. Once Joe has gotten what he wants or once he has definitely failed, the situation changes. He either wants nothing at all, or he wants something new.

The event is when a character either gets what she wants or definitively does not get it. But it can also be useful to think of the event not only as what happens but as a change, the moment when things are different.

Let's go back to my student, Kate, and her play about Jack Kerouac and Allen Ginsberg. Recall the basic structure of the play: Allen's action is to get Jack out of his mother's house and back to the life they once led. Jack is depressed and drinking too much. He's fighting Allen. He doesn't want to go.

In discussing the problem of the ending with Kate, I pointed out that structurally speaking she had a fairly simple choice: either Allen succeeds in getting Jack out of the house, or he doesn't.

She said she didn't feel in her gut that Jack would ever leave.

"Then that's what happens in this play," I said. "Allen leaves empty-handed. He realizes he can never get what he wants, and he goes."

She did go on to finish the play as such, and it was a lovely, sad, elegiac, and, most important, truthful piece.

The deeper, subtler lesson of this episode is not the finding of the event. It is the nature of the event.

Remember that when we examined action, we noted that it is internal. Dramatic action occurs within a character's mind. It is the wanting of something, the desire to attain something. We know about it through external means—what characters say and how they behave. But the action itself remains invisible.

The same is true of the event. Strictly speaking, it's usually smart to think of the event of a play as occurring within a character's head.

Oedipus realizes who his parents are—and only then cries out that all has come to light. Hamlet decides at this moment to plunge the poisoned sword into Claudius—and then does so. Blanche sees that disaster has finally arrived in the form of one Stanley Kowalski—and faints into a swoon. Or, in another interpretation, we could say that the event is Stanley's, his decision to commit the rape. That works equally well if you suppose that he has had the main action.

The event is a thing of the mind. This is why Aristotle called it the "recognition." He meant that it is a recognition of the truth, that the character has traveled from ignorance to knowledge.

This particular type of event (recognition of truth) does not apply to every play, not even to all the ancient Greek tragedies. But the general idea of what Aristotle was getting at, that the event is mental not physical, applies just as well today as it ever did.

The event of *Oedipus the King* is not the mutilation of his own eyes. That happens offstage for one thing; it's a consequence of the event. The event of *Hamlet* is not the sword fight. That happens both before and after the event. The way the sword fight concludes is a result of the event. The event of *Streetcar* is not the rape; it's the recognition that the rape will occur (or the decision to commit the rape, depending on your interpretation).

In the Joe and Mike scene, we might describe the event as Joe's decision to give the glass of water to Mike. The event itself is invisible, yet we know it has happened because Joe lifts the glass and hands it to Mike.

In Kate's play about Kerouac and Ginsberg, the event is Allen's realization that he will never reach Jack, will never get him out of this house, literally or metaphorically. We know about that event because Allen says words to that effect, then leaves.

We must be able to perceive the event by activities (speech and behavior) that occur in the actual, concrete world. Often these activities occur after the event—we know the event has happened because of the shock waves that ripple away from it.

But the event itself, in nearly all cases, is inside the character's head.

GOD FROM A MACHINE

Imagine you're sitting in the Theatre Dionysus in Athens, circa 410 B.C. You're watching the new Euripides tragedy called *Orestes*, the story of Orestes and Electra after he has murdered their mother, Clytemnestra. It's the same subject that Aeschylus had already treated in *The Libation Bearers* many years before. This version is very different from Aeschylus'. The purported hero of the piece, Orestes, hardly acts like one. He is selfish, brutal, devious.

By the end of the play, Orestes finds himself trapped on the roof of the palace with his friend Pylades. They're holding Orestes' cousin Hermione captive in the hope that they will be allowed to escape the city. His uncle, Menelaus, stands below demanding they release her. Finally, in desperation, Orestes orders the palace to be set on fire. It's a very suspenseful moment. Will Hermione be saved? Will Orestes and Pylades escape? Will the palace go up in flames and kill them all?

And what happens?

Apollo appears out of the heavens and descends onto the stage. All the characters stop what they're doing. The fire is extinguished—presumably by divine decree. Everyone listens while Apollo decides who will marry whom, who will be banished, and in general how this play will end.

Disappointed? So was Aristotle.

The event of Apollo's arrival certainly is something that happens, and it certainly changes things. Yet it isn't very satisfying.

The Greeks had a term for an event like this. They called it the *deus ex machina*, meaning literally "god from a machine," a phrase that loses none of its piquancy in translation. It refers to the Greek stagecraft practice of flying in the character of a god using a machine—probably some sort of contraption like a crane with ropes.

This is a perfectly legitimate device of stagecraft, of course, and we still use it today, in a more sophisticated form, when we mount a production of *Peter Pan*. But it's a lot less interesting as a dramaturgical device.*

Why?

---

*In fairness to Euripides, his use of the *deus ex machina* in this instance might very well have been intended ironically, as a cynical comment on this practice.

Because the *deus ex machina*, while it's certainly an event, doesn't grow out of the action and conflict. It is a consequence of nothing at all. It stands apart. It would have happened regardless of what the characters had been doing onstage.

You probably won't be tempted to write a literal *deus ex machina* into your play. But you may be tempted to write a modern equivalent, which would be any event that stands outside the action and conflict.

The event, to be truly dramatic, must be the result of the action and conflict.

To illustrate the difference between a real dramatic event and a *deus ex machina*, let's put Joe and Mike back in that room again, desiccated though they must be by now.

They struggle to gain control of the glass of water for some time. Then, while they aren't looking, a third character, Henry, walks in, drinks the glass of water, and then leaves.

Is Henry's drinking the water an event?

Not a dramatic one.

It's an event in the sense that Joe and Mike have definitively not gotten what they wanted. And it's an event in the sense that something has changed.

But Henry's entrance had absolutely nothing to do with the action or the conflict of the scene. He was going to enter and drink that water one way or the other, regardless of whether Joe and Mike ever struggled over it. His drinking the water is arbitrary, structurally speaking. It might be funny, to be sure. It might a good way to end a skit. But you're writing a play, and that's one good way to distinguish between the two.

Henry's entrance was introduced by the playwright as an

awkward device to end the play. It's not organic, as Aristotle would have said. And so, for us, it is not an event.

The dramatic event of the scene, whatever it is, must result from the action and conflict.

THE THIRD WAY

You may be feeling that this is too limiting, too reductive. After all, the end of a play does not have to be a simple choice between option A and option B.

You're right. There's another way, another choice, a third type of event at your disposal. It's a good choice, maybe even an essential one.

This third type of event is also the result of the action and conflict, but it's not simply a matter of whether the character gets what he wants or doesn't. Not that we're leaving this idea behind. The character will still experience the getting/not getting event—but in addition, another event may happen that overshadows the simple zero-sum kind.

Oedipus the King, one of earliest dramas in Western literature, remains one of the best examples of this third type of event.

Oedipus wants to discover the murderer of King Laius. He confronts many obstacles along the way, until at last he discovers the murderer: himself. In making this discovery, he has in some sense merely gotten what he wanted.

But this is hardly the whole truth, and certainly not the kind of truth that the audience experiences. We don't say to ourselves, "Oh, he caught the murderer. Very nice. Now let's all go home."

Our experience is far deeper than that. We feel that Oedipus's life is ruined, his sense of self destroyed, his entire world shattered, broken into pieces that can never be repaired. We cannot simply say, "He got what he wanted. That's that." Indeed, the power of this event is such that we forget for the moment that in a strict, structural sense, all that has happened is: he's gotten what he wanted. We forget because another change has occurred that is bigger, more important, more significant.

This third type of event is also the result of the action and conflict. Oedipus would never have made the discovery of his parentage had it not been for his own action. Had he not been pursuing that objective so relentlessly, the secret of his own birth would never have come out. But he did pursue it, and it did come out.

That's why it's a bonafide dramatic event—but also why it's not simply a matter of his getting/not getting what he wants.

From the sublime, once more to the earthbound.

Joe and Mike still want that water; they're still in that room. But let's add a bit of history. Suppose they're enemies. They've nurtured a loathing for each other over the years, reaching back farther than even they can remember.

Now they're locked in this room, struggling to get that glass of water. But they're evenly matched, and the struggle— perhaps both verbal and physical—goes on for some time. In that time, they begin to know each other in a way they never have before. They slowly come to see each other differently. Indeed, they come to love and admire each other. Finally, they offer the glass of water to each other, and they share it, half and half.

In some sense the event is simply that they both get what

they want—the glass of water. But there is another event as well, a third type of event that is neither the getting of the water nor the not getting of the water. That third type of event is the change of heart from hatred to love.

In this scenario, the event is experienced by both Joe and Mike, but that isn't necessary in order for it to be an event. In another scenario, for example, only Joe changes, or only Mike. If Joe changes, it's only an event for him. If Mike changes, then it's only an event for him.

Notice again the use of the word *change*. An event is a change. If Joe gets the glass of water, it changes him, his action, and the scene he is in. It may change him in some deep and profound way, or it may change him only in the sense that he is no longer thirsty. But it is change nevertheless.

If he does not get the water, it changes him in some sense. He may still want a glass of water, it's true. But it will have to be another glass of water. The first one is gone, and there is no hope of its returning.

This third type of event is a way of thinking of that idea of change. It's also a way of thinking of high stakes, high consequences. If it really matters that your character gets what he wants, then the event will resonate beyond the simple, literal meaning.

Hamlet gets what he wants, but he's killed in the process. Willy Loman gets what he wants (the knowledge that Biff loves him) but then can no longer bear to live. Blanche doesn't get what she wants, and it destroys whatever sanity she had to begin with.

You now know about the basics of dramatic structure. They aren't complicated. They're actually quite simple, and that's why they're so difficult. In writing your plays, you will almost always find that the answer to your problems lies in finding the simplicity that underlies the complexity you've created because you thought it was necessary.

There is more to know, of course. But in knowing these three basic ideas—action, conflict, event—you will be ready to tackle all other problems.

***

EXERCISE 3:   THE EVENT SCENE

Write a two-character scene in which the third type of event occurs. In other words, one character either gets what she wants as a result of the action and conflict or does not get it. Regardless, however, she also gets a third thing—something unexpected, something more than was bargained for. Remember, this third type of event is also a result of the action and conflict. As always, all specific details of the scene are up to you.

SEVEN: BEATS, SCENES, ACTS

YOU GO to see a play that you love. You're swept away by the words, the feelings, the ideas, the images. It all seems a great and beautiful mass, a formless, seamless tapestry that somehow, magically, all leads to a single climactic moment, and then is over.

One thing's for sure, it's not magic. You know that. And it's not seamless, either. It might look seamless, but I guarantee you, it's not. Even plays without any break at all, like *'night, Mother* or *Talley's Folly* or *Endgame*, are composed of small discrete units.

How does the playwright organize her drama into a coherent form? How does she apply the basic ideas of action, conflict, and event in a way that makes sense, that allows a natural progression from one moment to the next, that tells the story?

That's what this chapter is about. It's about arranging the action, conflict, and event into what appears to be a seamless tapestry.

WHAT ARE BEATS?

If action, conflict, and event are the subatomic particles—the neutrons, electrons, and protons—of dramatic writing, then a beat is the atom of the dramaturgical world. And although a beat,* like an atom, is composed of these smaller particles, the beat itself is the smallest possible functional dramatic unit.

A beat is the smallest unit of dramatic structure that contains action, conflict, and an event. It is the basic building block of any scene and, therefore, of any play. In a well-structured play, beats are not only present but readily identifiable.

Beats are not an abstraction. They are practical tools that are also used by directors and actors to break a scene into manageable, playable units.

You will often find that you've written beats naturally, without thinking about it. Great. But you should also know how to do it when it doesn't come naturally.

Here, for example, is a beat from Edward Albee's *Counting the Ways*. It happens to be the first beat of the play:

(HE is alone onstage. SHE enters.)

---

*Don't confuse beats in this sense with another use of the word. Sometimes playwrights will write "beat" into their stage directions in order to indicate a pause.

SHE

Do you *love* me?

HE

Hm? Pardon?

SHE

Do you *love* me?

HE

Why do you ask?

SHE

Well . . . because I want to know.

HE

Right *now*?

SHE

Well . . . yes. Or . . . no, no, not really. (pause) *Yes.*

HE

Of course.

SHE

Well . . . good.

(SHE exits.)

She has an action: She wants to know if He loves her. We may even deduce that She wants him to love her. But that would be interpretation.

The beat also has conflict: He doesn't want to tell her. Or perhaps He doesn't mind telling her, but doesn't understand what She means. Or He has to think about it for a few seconds before answering. In any case, He provides a conflict: She cannot get what She wants.

Finally, the beat has an event. He tells her what She wants to know: yes, He loves her. He might also have told her, "No, I don't." If He did so in a definitive way, a way that convinced her that this was the final answer, that too would be an event. Or if He convinced her that He could not possibly give her an answer at this particular time, this could also be an event.

You might have supposed from the last chapter that a play has only one event, and that it happens at the end of the play. That's understandable, given the way we were talking about events in that chapter. But the reality is that plays are full of events.

Every beat of a play has some kind of event, no matter how small. They are tiny changes that allow the narrative to go forward, to give us the sense that the story is constantly evolving, growing, transforming.

Not all beats are as short as the one from *Counting the Ways*. Just as some atoms are quite large in comparison to others, some beats are long, others are short. But typically they are no longer than a few minutes of stage time, and frequently they are quite short.

Regardless of their length, the definition remains the same: they are the smallest dramatic units that contain action, conflict, and an event. When the action and conflict have led to an event—no matter how small—the beat ends and a new one begins.

Let's return for a moment to Joe and Mike, our hydrophilic friends, for another illustration.

They are locked in their room with their glass of water. Here's a breakdown of a series of possible beats for that situation.

First Beat: Joe plays "mister nice guy" and tries to sweet-talk Mike into letting him have the water. He gives up when Mike says that he knows Joe is faking it.

Second Beat: Joe, angry at his failure and humiliated at being found out in his ploy, now tries to browbeat Mike into letting him have the water. This method also fails when Mike says he isn't afraid of Joe.

Third Beat: Now Mike initiates an action. He tries diplomacy. He suggests that they divide the water evenly. This fails too, though. Joe refuses to share.

Fourth Beat: Mike tries again, suggesting that he is willing to fight Joe. He says he is confident that he can beat Joe in a physical confrontation. But Joe calls his bluff, and Mike is forced to back down.

Fifth Beat: Now Joe is active again. He attempts a trade. If Mike will let him have the water, Joe will give him money once they get out of the room. But Mike doesn't trust him and refuses the offer.

This could go on indefinitely, as long as the playwright provides the characters with new ways of pursuing their actions. And there we have another good way of thinking about what a beat is. It's a new way for the character to get what he wants.

In this example, Joe and Mike use tactics. They scheme and plot. This is one good way to construct a scene, and you would do well to keep it in mind. As one idea, it's useful.

But don't think that this is the only way for a scene to un-
fold. Characters are not always scheming and plotting. Often
they behave unconsciously, without guile. Even when they are
acting consciously, they are not always scheming, at least not
as overtly as here.

Remember that the demarcation of beats is open to interpretation. There is not always an absolute right or wrong way.
The director or actors may come up with different places
where they begin or end beats.*

WHAT ARE SCENES?

The next largest dramatic unit is the scene.† A scene is a con-
catenation of beats. If the beat is an atom, the scene is a mole-
cule. Though you can break the scene into its disparate beats,
when you consider them together they form a whole that is
greater than the sum of their parts. They become a different
entity, a new thing. They become a scene.

The classical French dramatists had a convention that
whenever a character entered or exited, one scene ended and a
new one began. (It is the source of our term "French scene,"
still in use today.) They presumed that if a character were en-

---

*This is a matter for artistic debate and discussion with your director and ac-
tors; often the meaning of your play changes depending on where the beats
are marked. Remember, if the beats are well delineated in the script to begin
with, the disagreement rarely arises (> p. 317, Collaboration Issues).
†Not to be confused with the labels (Scene One, Two, Three, etc.) found in
manuscripts and published plays. These "scenes" are conveniences for the
purposes of reading or staging a play, and may or may not have anything to
do with dramatic structure.

tering a scene, he was doing so because he had an action that forced him to enter it. He was compelled to come on and pursue his action. And if that character were exiting it was because an event had occurred that ended his action or at least changed it substantially. Among other virtues, this method made it easy to know when a scene began and when it ended.

Today, however, characters in plays often enter and exit with no particular, identifiable action. We would never be able to label a scene from Chekhov or Lanford Wilson as we do Molière's. In some ways, this is a good thing. It allows us greater flexibility in terms of the shape and texture of our plays. Indeed, to be able to bring characters on and off incidentally could be considered an essential component of the modern naturalistic style. But too often playwrights take advantage of this laxity and allow characters to wander on and off the stage for the duration of an entire play, never once bothering to give them an action.

Joe and Mike, as we know, each have an action. Above, I described five possible beats for Joe and Mike to pursue that action. Together, these five beats form a sequence, but they are not a scene. Why not? Because they have not led to a major event, a significant turning point. Neither Joe nor Mike has gotten the water; neither has failed definitively. Certainly no third type of event has happened. It's true that smaller events have occurred, but these events only served to end the beat. The larger actions remain. (While this is a matter of opinion, let's accept it for argument's sake.)

Therefore, we'll continue to develop the beats until we have created a scene. We'll pick up where we left off.

Sixth Beat: Joe remains active. In fact, he now walks over to the glass of water and tries to drink it. Mike has to physically prevent him from doing so, wresting the glass from him in the process.

Seventh Beat: Mike is angry now. He has gotten the glass of water away from Joe, and he threatens to pour it onto the floor. Joe agrees to drink only half if Mike will do the same. It's a deal, and they each drink half.

This is a scene. Perhaps not one to enter the literary hall of fame, but a scene nevertheless. Each beat has led inevitably to this final beat, and the final beat has an event that changes the nature of the action. In this case, it happens to end the action.

At this point, a number of things might happen, and any of them will be the beginning of a new scene. There may be a blackout, and when the lights come up again, we may be in a new time and place.

Or there may be no blackout. Instead, another character may enter, perhaps Joe's wife who wants to talk to him alone.

Or Joe and Mike may remain alone, but now, having solved the water question, they will have a new action and conflict. Perhaps, for example, Joe wants Mike to leave so he can be alone, but Mike insists on staying so he can build a kite. New actions, new conflicts, and potentially a new event.

WHAT ARE ACTS?

The largest dramatic unit, next to a complete play, is the act. Frankly, in terms of dramatic structure, it's relatively unimportant. The ancient Greeks did not even use acts. Their plays are divided into sections (strophe and antistrophe, ode and episode, etc.), but the action is generally continuous, and there is certainly no intermission in which to pop out to the agora for a quick libation.

Acts are primarily convenient ways to divide long plays so that the audience can stretch its legs and the theater management can make a little extra money on concessions. Dramatically speaking, they serve little or no purpose. The division of acts in Shakespeare or Pierre Corneille or Kleist is highly arbitrary from a dramatic standpoint. In Shakespeare's case, the divisions were made by later editors, and we've kept them only because they make things convenient. Shakespeare himself simply wrote a string of unnumbered scenes to be performed without intermission and called it a play.

Modern producers typically ignore the act divisions of classical plays altogether. Instead, the plays are bifurcated according to the modern audience's expectation that they will have at least one opportunity to visit the bar or the rest room.

The standard form for plays at the end of the twentieth century is two acts. We'll avoid the discussion of how theatrical convention has ranged from no acts to five acts to three acts, with the occasional one-act thrown in for good measure. Instead, we'll simply discuss how the two-act form works.

But only reluctantly. Some students ask how a play should be structured, by which they mean, "Which scenes should I write, and where should I put them?" But that isn't really asking for a lesson on structure so much as it's asking someone to write your play for you. You already know all you really need to know of structure. Far more important than act structure is the basic structure of action, conflict, and event, and how they combine to form beats and scenes.

Still, it can be useful to examine what we might call the Platonic idea (if there is such a thing) of a modern two-act drama. But one must always keep in mind that this is only the idea of a play. No real play would ever look like what we'll be describing. Real plays have flaws and rough edges. That's part of what makes them great. They're made by humans and they're about humans, not neat and tidy abstractions.

So keeping this in mind, let's draw a picture of the perfect play. Because we're talking now about ideas, not people, the best tool to use is a graph, not words.

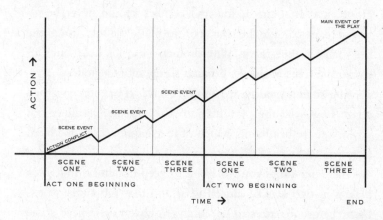

As you can see, in theory it's very simple. In Act One, Scene One, the action and conflict rise to the moment of an event, then fall slightly, though not back to the beginning point. Scene Two takes up again using some of the information, tension, etc., that was introduced in the first scene. The action and conflict again rise to the point of another event, then fall slightly, and then begin again with Scene Three. The end of Scene Three is also the end of Act One. It is the highest point of action and conflict in the Act.

Act Two, Scene One begins slightly lower again—a sort of regrouping of forces, but it quickly exceeds the height of action and conflict in the first act. And so on through the play until the ultimate event, after which the action and conflict may take a few moments to end completely.

Do plays really look like this? Of course not. They are full of tangents, scenes that are much longer or shorter than the ones portrayed, action and conflict that cannot possibly be described by a line on a graph.

But if there is one general lesson to be learned from the graph, it is that the action and conflict should never be allowed to lessen over the course of the play. The fortunes of the hero may decline (Lear, Willy Loman), but his need only increases, and his problems become all the more legion.

In writing your play, you don't have to be too concerned about how well the play fits into this scheme, certainly not when you are beginning. Much of the shaping can come later, after you've finished the first draft.

The one thing you will want to keep in mind is that your play is in two acts (if indeed it is) and that the audience expects, before it retires to the lobby, to have experienced some sort of significant dramatic event. Therefore, shape your play accordingly. Save the major event of the play until the end, certainly, but it's a good idea to give them some significant event at the end of Act One that will persuade them it is worthwhile to come back into the theater.

EXERCISE 4:   THE BEAT SCENE

Write a scene that has action, conflict, and an event, and which can be divided into at least five distinct beats, more if you like. Mark the beats, indicating precisely where you believe one beat ends and the next begins. Be prepared to explain why you've made your marks where you have.

PART TWO

THE CREATIVE PROCESS

PROLOGUE: DRAMATIC ELEMENTS

THE NOTION that a play can be broken up into what I call the elements of playwriting—theme, or character, or dialogue, or plot—is a dangerous one. The elements in Part Two are different in nature from the tools of Part One. They help to give form to a play, to be sure; they can be used to organize aspects of the play in one's mind and on the page. But in my opinion they are not, strictly speaking, structure. The tools of playwriting are all you need to know of structure.

Obviously, I believe it's useful to separate and examine the tools of playwriting structure—meaning action, conflict, and event. We've now spent a hundred pages doing just that. Dividing up those three ideas may help you clarify your thinking, make sense of otherwise amorphous material, and allow you to give a structure to your play.

But the second part of this book is generally not divided in a conventional way according to the dramatic elements.

You will indeed find the elements of theme, plot, dialogue, etc., discussed in the following pages. But I believe that there is a larger, more important organizing principle to those ideas. This dimension embraces all those elements; it is the creative process itself. This is a subtler but truer way to understand playwriting. It's one which, I believe, will lead you to writing more easily, faster, and, most important, better. So I've arranged Part Two along those lines and allowed the conventional categories to enter into the discussion as they will.

In other words, all these elements that we're about to examine in detail have a gestalt. The gestalt is your play. It is a whole, greater than the sum of its parts. It is organic, complete, indivisible. Character is indeed action. One character's action is another's conflict. An event is connected inextricably to them both—it's the consequence of them. As you'll see in what follows, exposition is everywhere, not just where you happen to see it. Your plot proceeds from your story, which in turn is related to your theme, which is another way of stating the action, which is a way of describing character.

As we embark on this next section, we will sometimes break the elements down into smaller pieces, otherwise there would be virtually no way to discuss them. But we compartmentalize, as Aristotle did, only to better understand. Our objective remains simple: to put them all together again.

With the fundamentals of dramatic structure behind you, you now have some understanding of the essential tools you'll need to work on your play. We've worked from the most basic tool (action) up to the consequence of that action (the event). You've also considered the various levels of composing those structural tools into larger units—beats, scenes, and acts.

At this point, we will begin to talk about the play itself.

As I've just suggested, we will talk about it, as much as possible, as a whole, organic entity—while breaking it down into smaller elements when that's essential.

But, more important, this section is concerned with the difficult job of saying what you're trying to say. The ideas involved with expressing yourself are more complicated, more subtle, and more ambiguous than the tools of structure. Part Two is a collection of problems and questions concerning the creative process that I've run into as a playwright, or that I've encountered with my students.

This is a discussion of the creative process, not a compendium. No book could be that. There are some problems that are *sui generis*. Plays are infinitely complex. Each play, while it will always have some things in common with others, is unique. For a book to honestly claim that it could address every dramaturgical issue, it would need to have as many chapters as there are plays in world literature.

As I did in Part One, I provide exercises throughout. But not every section has an exercise because not every section has an element that should be practiced. Sometimes, it's just something to think about.

The elements I deal with in this section are the most common. And the creative processes I describe and discuss are the ones I've observed in most people, including myself. I believe that many problems that may seem unique and impenetrable are really generic and solvable. And that many (if perhaps not all) of the answers that you seek can be found in what you're about to read.

THIS MAY seem like a strange chapter title with which to start a discussion of the creative process. It may suggest to you that we're going to talk about college teaching departments. We're not, of course.

We begin with a discussion of the difference between the concepts of theater and drama because down the line, as you get into the creative process itself, you'll want to be clear as to how distinct and fundamental these ideas really are. As you'll see, the creative process for developing a theater piece has a broad set of guidelines, or conventions. The drama, on the other hand, has narrower, more specific guidelines.

VERY THEATRICAL

The first sentence of Peter Brook's seminal work, *The Empty Space*, is: "I can take any empty space and call it a bare stage." Brook means that the idea of theater, the act of theater, does not require a particular building, or particular lights or sets or props, or any of the trappings we generally associate with the word theater. Theater can occur anywhere, anytime, under nearly any conditions.

Brook continues: "A man walks across this empty space whilst someone else is watching him, and this is all that is needed for an act of theatre to be engaged." In other words, the only conditions required for theater to happen are two human beings: one to perform, the other to watch and listen.

The idea of theater is just this broad. Its arms embrace a wide spectrum of experience.

Theater has always existed. It was never invented. It has been around as long as human beings—even before. The mating dances of animals can be thought of as a form of ritual, of showing and telling, and therefore of theater.

The idea of theater arises spontaneously in all of us. In the dawn of humanity, men and women began to perform for others around the fire, at the mouth of the cave, in the shadow of the tree. These performances may have taken the form of singing, or dancing, or storytelling. They might have served as a religious ritual, or as a celebration of the hunt, or were perhaps merely a means of telling a story for enjoyment. Whatever form and purpose they assumed, they arose unconsciously as part of the collective spirit of this new species.

As infants, we understand the nature of theater when we delight in watching our parents perform for us by making faces and nonsense noises as we lie in the crib. As young children we instinctively feel the urge to perform for our parents and our siblings and our friends: putting on shows for them, dressing up, or imitating our elders in a thousand different ways. Aristotle tells us that

> the instinct of imitation is planted in man from childhood, one difference between him and other animals being that he is the most imitative of creatures, and through imitation learns his earliest lessons; and no less universal is the pleasure felt in things imitated.

As adults, we continue both to perform and to be an audience every day of our lives, sometimes knowingly and sometimes not. A man stretches his broad shoulders to get the attention of a woman on the other side of the café. The movement catches her attention, and she admires his build. An act of theater has transpired.

A young boy shouts "Mommy, Mommy!" and, having gotten his mother's attention, does a cartwheel across the grass.

A businesswoman enters a restaurant where she is having a business lunch. As she sits down across from her lunch partner, she flicks her hair back with a confident twitch and meets his gaze evenly, showing no fear or apprehension—though she's feeling plenty of both.

All of this is theater. All of it is spontaneous, unplanned, without guile, without name, and without form. Any form it may possess is as idiosyncratic as the person performing it.

There are other, more deliberate acts of theater also performed every day. The President strides down the grand hallway into the East Room of the White House where reporters wait to ask him questions. A priest celebrates Mass. A man puts on women's clothes and goes to a club to dance all night, attracting the attention of curious onlookers. A teacher lectures to her class about the physics of elasticity, using a rubber band as a prop.

All of this is theater too. Even when the primary purpose of the act is not theatrical, events like these, and a thousand others in our everyday lives, contain the essential idea of theater.

We also have the more obvious instances of theater, those events we're more accustomed to identifying as such: circuses, carnival acts, the mime in the park, civic parades, and so forth.

And, finally, there is that theater that occurs in a particular building with its specialized lighting, its peculiar arrangement of chairs, its box office in front, and a marquee that announces the current show.

All these, and everything in between, are theater. If you're going to create something which is, simply, theater, you have virtually no guidelines to help or hinder you. It can be as fundamental as walking across a bare stage while someone watches you—and as difficult to make interesting.

MAKE IT DRAMATIC

Drama, on the other hand, is a narrower idea. It is one small subcategory of the all-embracing theater. It has specific definitions. It is the sonnet to theater's free verse. The problem is how to work within the prescribed limitations of the art form. The creative process is just as essential here as it is in any other art form, but the exigencies of form are among the most demanding. So it's important to know just what those demands are.

Drama had to be invented. In the Western world, the ancient Greeks are credited with the job. In particular, individuals like Thespis (from whom we get the word *thespian*), Aeschylus, and Sophocles gave a particular shape to what had been until then a religious ritual of dance and song and declamation. The ritual already had a specific shape; these men drew from that shape and caused a new one to evolve from it.

This shape they called tragedy, roughly analogous to what we would call drama. Drama has certain conventions that are peculiar to it. Unlike its larger, freewheeling parent called theater, drama is restricted by certain laws, which, as a philosopher, Aristotle made it his business to observe.

As you know from Part One, Aristotle did not prescribe. His intention, like any philosopher, was only to describe; that is, to make note of the way in which good dramas seemed to follow—over and over, and in the hands of many different playwrights—certain rules. The more successfully the playwrights followed these rules, the better received their work seemed to be by audiences, and the longer they seemed to last in the public's affection.

Aristotle, writing about a hundred years after Sophocles, observed that Sophocles' work had remained vivid and important, while the work of Aristotle's contemporaries was forgotten almost as soon as it was written. Aristotle surmised that his own contemporaries were failing, at their own peril, to follow the rules.

In *Poetics*, Aristotle made his own assessment of what he considered to be the rules. Others who have studied or practiced the art of playwriting have arrived at their own rules, though for the most part they are only expanding upon those ideas of structure that Aristotle was first to note. I myself have written Part One of this book with a particularly heavy debt to Aristotelian rules. I prefer to call those ideas tools because I'm a playwright, not a critic like Aristotle. As a writer, I don't care much for rules, but I'm always glad to have a tool to help me if I want it. For the moment, though, I'll call them rules.

Playwrights who ignore these rules do so at some risk. As I'm sure you expected, I don't say a playwright may not, under any circumstances, ignore the rules. The history of dramatic literature is full of moments—indeed entire plays—when the playwright seems to be ignoring every rule in the book, and yet his play still grabs the attention of the audience.

The great absurdist playwrights spring immediately to mind: Ionesco, Beckett, Anouilh. But there are others, including, at times, Shakespeare, Molière, Euripides, and Chekhov. You don't get a much better pedigree of rule breakers. But it seems obvious, at least to me, that these writers knew the rules very well, but made a conscious choice to ignore them.

Only a person who deeply understands the theory of, say, the dramatic event could write a play like *Waiting for Godot*. *Godot* plays upon our expectation of that particular tool, keeps us in suspense waiting for it, then deliberately, agonizingly, withholds it. And not just once, at the end of Act One—where we might accept it as part of traditional playwriting—but again at the end of the play. *Godot* has been described as a play in which nothing happens, twice.

Whether you like *Godot* or not, it's hard to deny that

what Beckett has done requires a knowledge of dramatic structure so profound that he was able to play with it, turn it on its head, confound our expectations, and make us laugh and cry in the process. That's a very different tune than the sorry song of ignorance that many playwrights find themselves playing.

Today, it would seem, we live in an age when artists are rebelling against the idea that art has rules. Many contemporary artists prefer free expression, unhindered by form and the rigors of convention.

But true free expression is very rare, and even, I would argue, nonexistent. The successful play, which seems to follow no rules and to be utterly free of conventions, does in fact have conventions. The difference is that its conventions are peculiar to itself. The conventions are that of the particular playwright and may apply only to this particular work. For his next play, he may invent others. Nevertheless, they exist.

This is exciting when it is done well. It means that the audience experiences not only new ideas but also a new means of expressing those ideas. One could say that Beckett's convention in *Godot* is: "There shall be no main event in this play." But at the same time, Beckett does not ignore the expectation that there might be an event; he does not dismiss the fact that events exist in plays and that audiences instinctively anticipate them. He acknowledges traditional convention, but gives us his own unique version of it.

When idiosyncratic conventions are badly done, the audience feels confused and let down, as though they're aware the playwright had something to say but lacked the means to say it. The playwright has neither followed the established conventions of his day nor has he created new, comprehensible conventions to take their place.

A play—a drama—is a particular form of theater but there are many others. Some of the others have well-established, recognizable conventions. About the opera, for example one could say: everyone sings all the time.

Even the spontaneous forms of the theater of life have conventions. There are conventions in my scenario above, what we might call "getting Mommy's attention and doing a cartwheel." That little *pièce de théâtre* has conventions that are repeated nowhere else, and in this case, the conventions are pretty much embodied in the title of the piece. It's a brief form of theater, though it can be repeated over and over, as any parent will tell you. Still, it satisfies its audience and its performer just as much as any other form because the conventions are known and followed. In this instance, it may satisfy Mommy long before it satisfies Little Boy. But what would Mommy think if Little Boy yelled relentlessly for her attention, then simply stood there looking dreamily at a butterfly once she was watching? She'd be confused because he hadn't delivered on the convention of his piece.

The modern urge to dispense with convention goes hand in hand with our modern sense that we should satisfy ourselves first and let others find their own way. It's a solipsistic and lazy approach to art, and probably goes a long way to explaining why audiences turn away from serious theater to the pablum offered up to them by television and film. It's not that audiences are afraid of being challenged. Quite the contrary: audiences love a good workout in the theater. What they don't like is spending their time and money on a play that, for all intents and purposes, is a private conversation between the author and himself. Theater is about communication. It is about the expression of an idea, not about hiding it in the privacy of one's own personal vocabulary.

Theresa Rebeck, whose work has appeared on both the stage and television, writes in *American Theatre* that one of her great frustrations as a playwright is that she is always expected to push the envelope, to avoid the conventions of narrative and realism at all costs. She observes that much of the theater that does push the envelope is simply "incomprehensible and boring" and audiences "don't understand it . . . We may be pushing the envelope, but if no one gets it, what's the point?"

Her message, with which I agree, is that the artist has two duties: one to herself, the other to her audience. She must be true to herself, digging within herself to arrive at the truth as she sees it. But she must also communicate that truth to the audience. To communicate an idea that does not express the artist's truth is pap, hack work. But to have an idea and not bother to actually communicate it is simply masturbatory.

The conventions in theater, whether they're generally accepted or only invented for a particular occasion, are the means by which ideas find expression. What we call drama has certain conventions. We don't all have to agree on every last iota of which they're constituted, but, as a playwright, it's best to acknowledge two and a half millennia of a tradition that offers some basic ground rules. If you're not following them, you're not writing drama. You're in another form, which, I emphasize again, is fine. Other forms of the theater are equally valid and equally interesting—assuming they're well done. But they are not drama.

Let's agree, in other words, that everything that is on a stage is theater, but everything that is theater is not necessarily a play. This is not a judgment. It is not a claim that plays are better than other theatrical forms, only different. A chair, after all, is not a table. And a table is not a chair. We don't criticize one for not being the other; they're both perfectly good. But we don't sit on the table and eat our food off the chair. By making that distinction, we keep things clear in our heads.

Arthur Miller, in an interview in the *Dramatists Guild Quarterly*, offers an analogy from engineering:

> If you build a bridge to go across a river it obviously has to go from one point to another point. If it doesn't do that, it's not a bridge, it's something else, perhaps an art work of some kind. [Or, I would add, maybe an unfinished bridge. With a little work, it might still get to the other side.] . . . If you want to build an automobile, probably it has to have wheels, and if you hate wheels you should build something else, maybe a table.*

In other words, do what you like. But have the honesty and integrity to call what you have made by its proper name. People will respect you for it, and, more important, they will probably understand you better as well.

---

*Vol. 24, no. 2.

You will also serve yourself. If you are going to write a play by creating your own conventions as you go, you won't want to be impeded by a lot of trappings of conventions that have preceded you. Many plays are written that are struggling to be unique, using their own exclusive, idiosyncratic structures and rules, only to be dragged down by an unintentional faithfulness to the forms of conventional drama.

Such plays, underneath, might be conventional melodramas or drawing-room comedies or classical tragedy. There's nothing wrong with any of those forms, but when the writing is not true to the conventions associated with them, and when it has not found its own idiosyncratic forms to replace those conventions but only dolls up the proceedings with zany dialogue or gratuitous acts of obscenity or endless flashy little blackout scenes, then the material becomes a mishmash that is true to no one, not even the author.

Robert Wilson is, for me, a good example of a writer (and director) who knows exactly what he is doing, and what he is doing has nothing to do with playwriting. Watching a Wilson piece is like watching architecture in motion—very slow motion indeed. But I admire and respect Wilson's work because I find that he has thoroughly dispensed with the trappings of conventional drama and replaced them with his own highly idiosyncratic dreamlike visions. There is no action in his theater, no conflict, no event. Often the language itself is nonsensical—clippings from newspapers, random syllables. But I find his images very compelling, and the slow, almost mechanical movements of the actors to be mesmerizing. I appreciate these works on a subliminal level that confounds the conscious mind, but which provides enormous satisfaction to something deeper in me.

Wilson has the integrity to be exactly what he is. And he also has the integrity and the strength of vision and the rigorous self-discipline of the true artist to create his own conventions, replacing those he has so deliberately tossed out the window.

We must all strive to have that same integrity, that same fidelity to our visions, regardless of how traditionally conventional (or not) our work happens to be. That fidelity is the basis, the very bedrock for the creative process. We must be true to our vision, our impulse, ourselves. Then, as we'll see in Part Three, we must try to see our work from afar and judge whether we are actually communicating what we wish, or whether we are merely indulging in our own private fantasy.

⁂

EXERCISE 5

1. Write five incidents from your own life which you consider examples of theater.

2. Read a play you admire. Identify the tools that the playwright has used in order to make it a drama.

NINE: THE IMPULSE

NOW THAT we've talked a bit about the foundations of the theatrical and dramatic experience, it's time to discuss the actual creative process itself. We'll talk about how it works in general, and also about the very specific steps you will be able to take to begin to understand your own creative process better.

Finding your impulse can be the answer to many problems in your writing. It can help you get closer to finding your own ur-play; it can clarify the structure of your play; it can provide you with a strong sense of character. The list of benefits from finding your impulse is very long.

Among the many other benefits, it can help you overcome writer's block. Regardless of your level of experience, you probably have some idea of what writer's block is, so let's start there.

FINDING THE IMPULSE

Like so many other aspects of the writer's craft, the idea of writer's block has attained an air of mystery. It has become the unsolvable, baffling bugaboo of the writer's life. "I'm blocked" is the most common complaint you'll ever hear from a writer—so common that it's a cliché, the one aspect of a writer's life that everyone else seems to have heard about. It's that time when the writer says, "I can't work. I can't write. Nothing is coming out of me."

Students say it to me often enough, fellow playwrights confide it to me in dark, despairing tones. And, God knows, I've said it to myself often enough.

In my experience, writer's block is one of two circumstances. It's either that vague but nagging feeling that we have something to say but don't know quite what it is or how to say it. Or it's that we have already written something, perhaps written many drafts of it, but it's all wrong, and we can't seem to get any closer to making it right.

In either case, there is a creative process wanting to happen and it's somehow, mysteriously, being stifled. We can call it writer's block or just plain frustration, but in either case the answer does not have to be to sit back and hope something good happens.

Instead, we can do something about it. That something is getting in touch with the impulse. The impulse is that which is making us want to write this play in the first place. We can get in touch with it, understand it better, and derive creative energy from knowing what it's really about.

It's interesting that we never speak of painter's block. Or composer's block. Or choreographer's block. Only writer's block. Perhaps this is because artists in other disciplines don't have to face the same process of translation from impulse into art as we writers do. We have to translate the impulse into language, an intellectual medium that conveys thoughts, ideas, concepts (< Introduction). Other creative arts do not have this same concern. They are more direct in this sense; the impulse to create them is never channeled through the medium of words, where it has more than ample opportunity to get lost in the shuffle of intellectualizing. (That's not to say that the other arts are easy and writing alone is hard. All artistic pursuit has its challenges. After all, we writers don't have to play an instrument, or know brush techniques, or be able to dance.)

But I personally don't believe there is any such thing as writer's block. At least not in the sense that it is some indecipherable dilemma in which one simply has to be patient and hope that it passes. Instead, I think that what we call writer's block is a particular state in which we sometimes find ourselves: the state of being out of touch with the impulse.

The first, and perhaps hardest, step in getting back in touch with your impulse is understanding that most of the elements of your play which you consider to be essential are not.

Your story, for example, is expendable. There are a million stories, you can always get another. Your characters may evolve as you work on them. You'll mold them according to your needs, and if you find you don't need some of them, they'll get changed or cut. The dialogue, too, will be in a constant state of change. Setting? Nothing is easier to change. It's a question of rewriting the stage directions. Title? Lots of good titles out there.

There is nothing about your play that is utterly unique or irreplaceable, except one thing: the impulse that makes you want to write it.

You must learn to believe that the impulse is crucial and you must learn to protect it. What follows is about that impulse: what it is, how to find it, and how to protect it.

FOLLOW YOUR GUT

The impulse is somewhere within your subconscious. It is the amorphous, unshaped, difficult-to-define combination of thought and feeling that is making you want to write a play.

The impulse usually comes from an experience one has had. It is, typically, a fleeting occurrence, a fragmented shard of life, of which it is difficult to grasp the meaning. We may overhear a conversation that interests us. We may witness a relationship, or be involved in one ourselves, that fascinates us and makes us want to write about it. We may know an interesting character and want to portray him or her. We may have a story or an anecdote told to us. We may simply have a sensory experience that fills us with a general feeling of wishing to express it.

We all know such moments. What distinguishes the playwright from other artists is that he feels compelled to translate them into drama.

Our definition of what an impulse is will broaden as we discuss it. But for now, think of it in this way: an experience that causes you to want to write.

YOU'RE SO IMPULSIVE

First, what not to do.

The tools you learned in Part One won't do you any good in finding the impulse. They are used by your conscious mind to help shape your play once it is written or as you are in the process of writing it. Finding the impulse is a process of delving into your subconscious and discovering what's there. One of the most common sources of writer's block comes from the attempt to give form and structure to an idea that is not yet ready to be given form, so put the tools away for the moment.

Also, you'll need to forget about all the other intellectual constructs of playwriting. You are not going to perform any of the traditional business of preparing to write a play. For example, you aren't going to think about how to begin telling the story at the proper moment. You aren't going to have the various incidents planned out ahead of time. You won't contemplate how the play ends. You won't worry about what your theme is. You won't have a biography for all your characters. You will not have an outline to follow. You will not develop characters. All these concepts are ways to give your play form, and by using them you run the risk of losing the impulse itself.

It's true that more experienced playwrights are sometimes able to begin by doing this sort of work. They have learned through years of practice to jealously guard the impulse from the harsh requirements of structure. But for many neophyte playwrights (and even for many experienced ones) all that traditional work is a dead end. We're going to put them aside for now.

You must also unburden yourself of all the other little private rules that you may have. I know you have them; we all do. You may not realize you have them. They may be unconscious choices that you've assumed to be essential to writing a play. But they are choices nevertheless. They are things like, "This play has to be written without scene breaks." Or, "This play must have only three characters." Or, "It must all take place in the attic," or "Every scene has to be in a new location," or "The title has to be spoken by one of the characters in each scene." Let go of any private rules like these that you've developed for yourself.

You're going to forget them because they, or something like them, are almost surely what is blocking you. At least for the moment, let them go. Know nothing. Be ignorant. It's bliss.

Here's what you can and should do.

The impulse won't necessarily come on its own. You will probably have to go out (or should I say "in") and discover it. Here's an example of an impulse, and how you might go about investigating it.

Let's say that you are walking in the park one autumn day and you see two people, a man and a woman, sharing a blanket on the grass. He is lying down, she sits beside him, cross-legged. Something in her posture and the way she talks earnestly, gesticulating with her hands, fascinates you. In addition, you're taken by the moody late-afternoon lighting, the faint odor of earth and decaying leaves, the slight chill in the air.

You can't help slowing down to watch these two people on the blanket. You try to overhear their conversation but only get bits and pieces, nothing you can really make sense of.

You walk past them, craning your neck around to get another glimpse of them. But you don't want to get caught eavesdropping, so you walk on.

Later that evening you are still thinking about this couple. The image of them, and of their atmospheric setting, continues to strike an emotional chord in you. You don't know why.

What was it about these two people that fascinated you while a hundred other people passed them by without bothering to notice? Even if every one of those hundred people were themselves playwrights, you may still have been the only one to have been so taken by the tiny drama on the blanket. Indeed, you may have been the only one to have considered it a drama at all. And we may even suppose that if a hundred other playwrights were assigned to write a play based upon the same scenario you observed in the park, each would write her or his own unique play. Why is this?

No one knows.

The nexus between the experience and the scene that unfolds from it onto the playwright's paper is utterly mysterious.

But something of that experience collided with your subconscious and a spark flew. Perhaps the couple reminded your subconscious of an experience you once had yourself, one that is lost to your conscious memory. Or perhaps the connection is very clear and you recognize in them the image reminiscent of your own life.

It doesn't matter. What matters is that your feelings are very strong and you want to write a play about these two people, even though you don't know anything about them beyond what you witnessed in a few brief moments in the park.

This is not the only way an impulse can happen, but it is

a typical way. It will serve as our model for the moment. Now that you know that, and now that you're willing to nurture it and allow it to grow on its own, what do you do?

IMAGINE THIS

In the *Poetics*, Aristotle advises the poet that he should "place the scene, as far as possible, before his eyes . . . seeing everything with the utmost vividness, as if he were a spectator of the action . . ." Note that he asks the writer to be not a writer but a spectator. Two and a half millennia later, it's still good advice. In order to discover more about the impulse, you will first re-create the experience that gave rise to it.

Write out a description of that scene for yourself, what I call an image. You don't need to create every last detail of the scene in an image, but try to find those aspects you find provocative, the things that seem to make it come alive for you. Use all sensory material, not just the visuals. Recall the sounds of the park, the smells, the touch, even taste if it's relevant. Recall the pose of your two "characters": the way they moved, the way they related to each other physically.

Re-create the physical experience of the scene. Not what it means, not the psychology of it, not the story, not how it fits into the mold of dramatic structure. Just the experience.*

Make it specific. Where exactly in the park did the scene occur? An open space? A shady bower? A busy area, or iso-

---

*At the same time, use common sense. Be sure to provide for yourself the basics: two human beings who are capable of talking to each other, even if they aren't the two people in the original experience.

lated? It's autumn. Were the leaves bright? Or is it too early for that? Or too late—are the trees bare with leaves on the ground? What about the sky? Was it cloudy? Bright? Where was the sun as you were walking?

Were there other people around? What did they look like? How close were they?

How cool was it? What was the quality of the air? Dry? Was it windy? Still? Recall what the park smelled like. Was it a heavy smell of rotting vegetation? Or lighter, crisper than that?

What did the man look like? How old? Heavyset or thin? What was he wearing? Hat? Scarf? Was his coat open or closed?

What did the woman look like? How old? What was she wearing? And so on . . .

When you're finished, without thinking about what will happen in the exercise, begin writing. What is he saying to her? What does she say in return? And so forth. Follow your instincts, your impulse, one line at a time.

Don't question the process of writing as you work. Don't critique yourself as you go. Don't apply any rules to what you're doing. Don't control it and guide it with intellectual choices in one direction or another. Don't rewrite or cross anything out, except perhaps for a few words here and there as you go. Even then, do it sparingly.

Let the writing come out as naturally as you possibly can. Listen to the characters. Let them guide you. E. L. Doctorow compares the process of writing a story to crossing a dark forest at night with a flashlight that shines only a few feet ahead. One cannot see the ultimate goal. But one can see enough to take the next step, and by this method reach the other side.

Let the characters take themselves where they want to go, regardless of whether you happen to find it interesting or dramatic, and whether or not it makes sense. Being interesting, or dramatic, or making sense are critical judgments and as such they will eventually be essential in writing your play—but not right now. There's time for them later, and when that time comes you know you have the tools to do something about them.

For now, allow the scene to be interesting or dull, dramatic or not, sensible or irrational. Let the scene be whatever it is, and let the characters behave however they must. Imagine yourself not as a writer but as a transcriber or a stenographer. The job of stenographer is not to be interesting, after all, but to listen very carefully and to get down the words as accurately as possible. Your job is not to be creative but to listen. In this case, you're listening to yourself. Your conscious mind is listening to your subconscious mind. The conscious mind (the writer) must give in to, must give itself over to, the subconscious long enough for the subconscious to express itself.

If the process is working well, you'll feel as though the scene is writing itself. That the characters are speaking and behaving on their own. That you're being pulled along through the scene, rather than forcing something to happen.

Your conscious mind won't like any of this. It's very smart, and it knows it. But your conscious mind, while very impressive, doesn't know everything. It only thinks it does. One thing it doesn't know about is the impulse. And frankly, it doesn't think it's very important.

The conscious mind will always try to take over the writing of your play, and will do so if you let it. It thinks that it always knows best at making the choices we talked about in the previous chapters. But it's wrong, it doesn't always know best. Sometimes, yes. But not always. Right now, it doesn't. You have to put your conscious mind on hold long enough for the subconscious to do the work that only it can do. You have to make sure that you use your conscious mind only when *you* want, not when *it* wants.

The conscious mind will try to wiggle its way into the process by giving suggestions. It will always have better ideas. It will try to be more interesting. But we're not interested in "more interesting" right now. We're interested in truth. And only your subconscious knows the truth. So you have to let it speak, and you must listen to it unalloyed, undiluted, unimproved by the conscious mind. In discussing the impulse exercises after they're written, students often reveal that they've taken a few minutes to think about the scene. Or that they started one way, but threw it out and started over another way. Or that they found themselves getting bored with the scene at some point, but then they thought of an exciting thing that could happen, and away they went.

Though it may sound odd, try not to let this happen. These developments are the antithesis of what you're trying to do. But also realize that this process won't happen perfectly the first time you do it. There will always be times, now and in the future, when you will let down your guard and allow the conscious mind to step in. That can't be helped. We're all human. Do the best you can, and at the very least know when you've allowed the conscious mind to interfere. Don't fool yourself into thinking that a conscious choice was really a spontaneous, subconscious, impulsive one. After all, the next best thing to a perfect, unadulterated impulsive experience is the knowledge of when and where your conscious mind intervened. As you write more of these impulse exercises you'll begin to know more about the difference between what your subconscious and your conscious have to say. That's an important understanding, which will probably only come with time. The more you know and trust your subconscious, the more it will serve you, and in turn the more you will begin to trust it.

The exercise in this chapter is designed to get you started on the process of the impulse exercise. It provides you with an image from which to write a sample exercise. (There are a number of other images in Appendix C.) This image of mine has an advantage over an image you may come up with on your own, but also a disadvantage.

The advantage is that my image is unfamiliar to you, and therefore you haven't had any opportunity to plan anything about the scene you'll write from it. If you write it properly and keep yourself from looking at the image ahead of time, you're guaranteed not to plan, or have any preconceived conscious notions of how you think the scene "ought to go."

The disadvantage is that my image may not mean a great deal to your subconscious. Interestingly, most of them do for the majority of people, which indicates that the subconscious mind is open to many different suggestions. But still, this image (or the additional ones in Appendix D) may not cause any sparks to fly, or at least not very many. That's not your fault, or mine. It's just the way it is. Not all images work for all people.

In general, I recommend practicing on my images at least a few times before going on to write impulse exercises that are based on your own experiences and images. By using my images, you're in a slightly more controlled environment, so you're more likely to come up with good results. But ultimately use your own judgment, and if my images don't seem to work for you, go ahead and create your own.

For a very few people, the images don't seem to work at all. In this case, you'll want to find another way to get in touch with your impulse. I recommend that you find a painting or photograph on which to base an impulse exercise. Also, music, preferably a song with words, has worked for some people.

The essential part of this process is that you get connected to your subconscious, to that part of your mind that is uncritical, emotional, dreamlike. However you do that is up to you. These images and impulse exercises help many people. You may be one of them.

❧

EXERCISE 6: WRITING FROM AN IMAGE

Below is an image designed to give you an impulse. Don't read it until you have at least an hour (better yet, two or three) in which to write your scene. You may use it all, or not. It's better to have enough time than to have to stop writing when things are going well.

You might also want to take a few minutes to relax and clear your mind before you begin. If you meditate, now would be a good time to do that for a few minutes. Or you might listen to some soothing music (no lyrics, please). The main object is to relax and to place yourself in a neutral frame of mind.

When you are ready to write, read the image. You may read it a second time if you need to cement some of the image in your mind. Don't read it again if you can sense that it's just your intellect stalling for time so it can take over the work.

Begin writing immediately—within seconds. Not minutes, seconds. Write until you feel you've exhausted the possibilities. This doesn't mean that you've reached an event for the scene (or for that matter an action or a conflict). It simply means that you have run out of an impulse for these people to say and do things.

At a later date, go ahead and write more exercises based on the images in Appendix D. Or create your own images and write from them. This is an exercise you can do over and over again. Although you may find you don't need to do it after a time, it's also possible that you'll find you enjoy doing it enough that you'll want to do it for its own sake.

A checklist before you look at the image

1. Read the image once, or if necessary, a second time. But no more. Do not try to memorize it.
2. Do not take notes.
3. You are not required to fit any of the details of the image into the scene. The image is only a springboard for your imagination. The details may very well change or evolve as you write. Allow them to do so. Go wherever your imagination takes you. Allow your subconscious to alter or omit details.
4. As soon as you have read the image, begin writing. Do not think about it. Do not plan. All you need to begin is the first line, and that should happen within seconds. From there, follow the voices of your characters.
5. Try writing for at least twenty minutes. If you're really stuck and/or confused, try another image from Appendix D.

6. Do not judge as you write. Do not critique yourself. Do not try to make sense of the scene or predict where it may go. Do not make a conscious effort to apply any of the tools from Part One. If you find that you're using them, and that you're aware of that, fine. But don't force yourself to use them or be conscious of them.

7. Do not rewrite. You may alter a few words here and there if you absolutely must do so in order to make sense of something. But nothing more than that.

8. Think of yourself as a transcriber of the scene. The scene is playing out before you. You are merely writing down what the characters say to each other. You should be a passive participant in the process.

9. Do not try to write an ending to the scene unless one seems to occur naturally. Write until you feel you've exhausted the impulse.

10. Try to keep the scene between the two characters. This should happen by itself if you really listen to what they are saying. If another character absolutely must intrude, allow them to.

The Image

A bedroom in a large country home. Summer. Daytime. The bed is unmade, badly rumpled. A woman lies diagonally across the bed, half dressed in a robe that is not quite fastened, looking as if she had been flung there from a great height. She is staring up at the ceiling, and appears as though she is listening to a melody running through her head. The windows in the room are open and the air is warm, fresh, and dry. The smell of grass and earth comes through lightly on the breeze.

Downstairs, out in the yard, we can hear voices, indistinct snippets of conversation, unintelligible. It is the only sound except, perhaps, for bits of the tune that are running through the mind of the woman on the bed.

There is a bathroom adjoining the bedroom. The door is open. There is someone in it, taking a shower. The water is running, steadily raining down. After a moment the water shuts off. We hear a towel being pulled from the rack. Into the doorway steps the person from the shower, still dripping, drying off.

What does this person do? What do they say?

PROTECTING THE IMPULSE

A painter often makes any number of rough sketches at the beginning of a project, with each sketch containing an essential part of the final work. But these sketches would never be mistaken for a finished canvas.

An actor rehearses for several weeks before allowing his work to cohere into a performance. We would never think to ask him for a performance on the first day of rehearsal. Rehearsals are for making mistakes; they're as much for finding out what doesn't work as they are about finding out what does.

Likewise, a composer tries many different melodies, chord structures, and tempos before the song comes together in its final version.

Yet writers, for some reason, often feel that they've either found the play in their first draft or they never will. Nothing is further from the truth; we are like any other artist in that regard.

Once in a while, of course, we get lucky. A first draft comes out that's perfect just as it is, or virtually so. Also, once in a while, a Mozart turns up among us. He writes perfectly finished work in first draft. But even this doesn't disprove the rule. I'm willing to bet that Mozart also went through multiple drafts. It's just that he did them all in his head. He didn't have to write them down, or play them, in order to figure out how to make them better. He had the capacity to do all the rewrites mentally. But he still did them.

The fact is, artists have to work at it. We have to go through more than one draft before that true impulse, the ur-play within us, reaches its fullest, truest possible expression in the form of a drama.

So now, let's look at what you've got in the impulse exercise you've just written. It may seem to be an amorphous mess in conventional dramatic terms. It may not make much sense to you. You may have just a fragment without beginning or end.

That's fine for now. You weren't trying to write a scene after all. You were finding the impulse.

You've taken the first step in finding and protecting the impulse, though not the last. You have protected the impulse long enough to let it out in its first manifestation. But protecting the impulse doesn't just mean defending it from the conscious mind that would tamper with it before it's ready. It also means actively nurturing it, allowing it to grow into a fully realized scene or play.

How do you do that? How do you allow this first rough draft to mature into something you will be proud to call your play?

The first thing to realize is that, in most cases, the structure is actually already there in the scene. It's hidden, somewhat latent, almost certainly not fully formed. But I can say with confidence that it's very likely there. You don't have to give your fragment structure so much as you have to discover the structure within it, and then support it.

This is one of the mysterious aspects of playwriting. Most of the time, when you follow your impulse and allow your subconscious to discover what's going on, the fragment you write will actually have the basic tools of structure in it. There will probably be an action, maybe some conflict, perhaps even an event. You didn't have to create them. You didn't think about them. You very possibly weren't aware they were rising up as you wrote the exercise.

Nevertheless, they're there.

I discovered this myself as I began to develop the impulse exercises for my own use. I had written several of them in an effort to unblock myself, and to that extent they had been successful. But then I wanted to do something with them, so I examined them to see if any of them might be the basis for an entire play—even a short one.

For example, one of the images I came up with was based on my grandparent's kitchen. For some reason, I don't know exactly why, this place evoked strong emotional memories in me. There was nothing specific that happened in this kitchen, no incident that I could recall, just the sense that this place was rich fertile soil for the playwright in me.

In the image, the time was the morning of a summer's day. The two people in the image were not my grandparents, but another man and woman I recalled from my hometown. They were people I had barely known, but physically I remembered them very well. I wrote a description of the kitchen in as much detail as I needed in order to get a good feel for the place.

The impulse exercise that I wrote from this image was quite short, only a few pages long, and took me a little less than an hour to write. It consisted mainly of the woman (Emma) coming downstairs and into the kitchen to find her husband (Horace) already reading the paper and having his coffee. It turned out that she had a dream (in keeping with the exercise, I hadn't known this until I began writing) that disturbed her. In the dream, the young pilot of a small two-seater airplane was waiting out in front of the house at the curb. He wanted the woman to go with him in his plane but she refused.

In the kitchen, Emma tells Horace of the dream. He insists that it was not a bad, disturbing dream at all but a perfectly happy one. After this, she asks if he will go with her to pick blueberries. (A bowl of blueberries was part of the original image, though I didn't know they would become important until I began writing. There were many other details in the image that were forgotten in the course of writing.)

Horace refuses to go with her, saying she will be fine on her own. He tries to get her to relax about things in general, then leaves for work.

I liked the exercise. It was sweet and simple, and evocative of a time and place long gone for me. But it also seemed to go nowhere and do nothing. It was a short, formless nugget. Delightful in its potential, but only a sweet promise.

But I began to analyze the exercise as if it were a scene I had planned and structured ahead of time. To my surprise, I found that there was action here. In fact, the action was quite clear. There was also conflict. Not much of an event—not yet anyway. But perhaps that was because there was more of a scene to write.

The action, as I saw it, was that Emma wanted a stronger connection to Horace. She felt distant from him and wanted to be closer. Her dream was a manifestation of that action, and so was the onstage act of telling him about the dream. And so, of course, was her asking him to go blueberry picking with her.

The conflict was that while Horace seemed concerned for her in some ways, he was quite happy with this distance. He thought everything was fine the way it was. Her dream didn't bother him, her telling him of it only made him dismiss it as inconsequential. Her wish that he go berry picking with her met with a flat denial.

When Horace exited, this indicated some sort of event had occurred. I wasn't sure what exactly, but in any case it felt fairly minor. It seemed to resolve nothing one way or the other. This told me that the real event of the play was yet to come, that Emma had more to do before she could resolve this dilemma once and for all.

Knowing this, I pressed ahead, putting Emma in a sequence of new situations that allowed her to pursue her action and finally to experience her event. I won't tell you what I did because that isn't my purpose here. My point is only that, by analyzing the structure which my own subconscious had provided for me, I was able to finish a complete one-act play called *Blue Stars.** I never had to create any structure. I only had to serve the structure that was given to me.

Not all of my impulse exercises will yield results like this, and neither will all of yours. It isn't their main purpose. The intent of these exercises is to give you the experience of writing from the subconscious, to let you know how that feels. And to know the difference between that experience and the experience of writing from a preordained set of strictures that may very well be stifling your creative impulse.

When the exercise can be used as the basis of a complete work, so much the better. That's icing on the cake.

Even when you are able to take the exercises further into a complete play, they will not all develop as *Blue Stars* did for me. In this case, it was a fairly simple step. Aside from a few minor rewrites, all I did was keep going. In other cases, one has to go back and write material that precedes that of the exercise. Or you might have a lot of cutting and rewriting within the exercise itself in order to clarify and strengthen the action and conflict. Sometimes you'll find that you have some form of action, but the conflict is rather weak. Or perhaps you'll need to heighten the stakes. Or you might simply want to give the play more room to breathe, to allow it to get more meat on the bone.

And then there are always those occasions, rare but undeniable, when your exercise simply doesn't seem to have any structure latent within it. This does happen. My sense is that when it does, you're better moving on to a new image and an-

---

*If you are interested in reading the play, it is published by Applause Books in *The Best American Short Plays, 1993–1994.*

other exercise rather than spending a lot of time trying to make this one work.

But remember this: you don't have to impose structure onto your play. It will be there by itself.

Why is this so? There are a couple of ways to explain it. One lies in the idea we'discussed in Chapter One—Carl Jung's observation that we dream in three acts. The three-act structure exists because that's the way our minds like to work.

Another way to think of it is that the rules of dramatic structure were not invented. No one ever sat down and imposed the law from above. The rules of drama, like the laws of nature, were discovered. Newton watched an apple fall from the tree and set out to explain why that should happen. The rules of drama were noted by observant people like Aristotle, who could see that all the plays they liked tended to fall into the same general paradigms with similar rules.

Characters in plays have actions because we in life have them. We want things. I am writing this book because I want to express my ideas on playwriting. To pursue my action, I sit at my desk typing words into my computer. My conflict? Well, fortunately, there's no one trying to stop me from writing. But there are a thousand other obligations in my life that beckon me, pulling me away from this task. The event? The day I hand in the manuscript—or maybe I should say the day it's published!

You also have an action; you want to learn how to write plays. To pursue that, you are reading this book. Your conflict? Maybe someone doesn't want you to do that. More likely it's simply the difficulty of the task before you, and the fact that you too have many other competing obligations. Your event will be a finished play—or perhaps opening night.

The rules of drama are the rules of nature. One does not have to bow to them, suffer under them. One uses them, harnesses them to one's own advantage. We don't bemoan the fact that water flows downhill. We put in a hydroelectric power plant. We don't complain about the way the wind carries objects aloft. We build airplanes.

And so you don't need to agonize over the fact that plays need dramatic structure. Nine times out of ten, it's already there; all you have to do is find it and then use it to your advantage.

You may have to write more of these impulse exercises before you get a sense of how the process of writing from the subconscious works for you. Everyone is different, and everyone needs to discover his own process. Begin now to learn how your own process works. Do plenty of exercises—both from my images (Appendix D) and eventually from those of your own devising.

In time, you may feel the need to do the exercises less and less, the idea being that this process becomes second nature to you. Ideally, you will understand your own process well enough that you will, in effect, apply it whenever you write. In other words, you'll be writing spontaneously, allowing your subconscious to dictate the basic flow of the work while you create your actual plays, and not just when you are responding to an image. If so, it's because you've learned to put this process into the scene instinctively. You will no longer need to take the intermediary step of isolating it and working on it as a process apart. Work toward that goal.

In the meantime, you may want to continue to do the exercises. Some people even like to continue to do them indefinitely, as a sort of gymnasium.

• • •

In life, the experiences that give rise to impulses are often more complicated than my park bench scenario. Sometimes they involve experiences that you have over time, with people whom you may grow to know very well. You may even be involved in the scenario yourself, so that you are a character in your own prospective drama. This complicates the process of isolating the impulse. On the other hand, it gives you more information to go on. You have a richer lode of ore to mine.

The process, though, remains the same. You must discover an experience that prompts you to write and re-create that experience for yourself with specificity. Then—and only then—write.

I can't promise you'll never have writer's block, or other problems, again. But I'm confident that you'll have the means to get out of it when you do.

OVERWRITE

When someone doesn't like a play, they often say it's overwritten or needs cutting. Much of the time (but not always) I disagree with that criticism. Often, I think the play is actually underwritten.

That's not to say that I wished the evening had been even longer than it was. I squirm in my seat before most people. But I genuinely believe that many plays so described won't ever be fixed through cutting. They'll be shorter, true, and therefore less painful. But a successful version of the same play might turn out to be longer than the one that already seems to go on forever. How is this so?

Let's take the example of a comedy I once saw in the previews of an expensive, though brief, off-Broadway run. (For simplicity, I'll only deal with the first act.) The plot concerned a young inventor who receives an enormous grant from a wealthy but mysterious benefactor. The inventor hasn't a clue as to why he has been given the money, and the benefactor won't reveal either himself or the reason for the gift. Two thirds through the act, the inventor finally decides to go ahead on his own volition and proceeds to create an invention. At the end of the act, the benefactor reveals himself, lays claim to the invention, and lets it be known that he intends to use it with evil intent.

The act was an hour long, a perfectly standard length even if it seemed interminable—and not just to me. There was endless shifting in seats, riffling through programs, sighs of exhaustion. In the lobby during intermission, one could hear the predictable reactions: "Funny, but way overwritten." "It might work if he cut it." And so on.

My feeling, on the other hand, was that the play hadn't even been written yet. Lots of other things had been written. Scenes of exposition. Scenes that repeated the same plot development we had already seen. Scenes that were utterly irrelevant to the plot. But precious little of the play—of actions, conflicts, and events that might have moved the plot forward—had ever made it onto the page, much less the stage.

So while all that bald exposition and redundancy and irrelevance certainly should have been cut, that alone would never solve the problem. If one had cut all the problems out of this play, there would have been nothing left but a few fragmented scenes.

What should have happened long ago, when the playwright was first writing the play, was this: he should have overwritten. Sound counterintuitive? Maybe it is. But I believe if the playwright had let it all out, the good with the bad, following his impulse and trusting it to take him on the journey of the play (> Chapter 11), he might at least have had something to work with. It might have been many pages too long. It might have been a colossal mess. It might have needed a lot of hard work, including lots of cutting, to get it into shape. But the raw material—the play—might just have been there.

As it stood, though, cutting was beside the point. It was too late, or perhaps I should say too early, for that: the playwright hadn't even gotten to that stage.*

The lesson is this: don't be afraid to overwrite. There's nothing wrong with it, and there is often everything right about it. This is not a license to simply write aimlessly and endlessly without any sense whatsoever of purpose. Try, within reason, to return to what you may know of your story and plot (> p. 206, Tell Me a Story), however tenuous and contingent that knowledge may be. But at the same time, allow yourself the freedom to be imperfect. It's a first draft. No one ever has to see it except you.

A first draft, written from the impulse, is all about overwriting and allowing the impulse to emerge. Later drafts are for cutting, shaping, and supporting the form that is latent within the first (< p. 141, Protecting the Impulse; > Chapter 12).

---

*You may be wondering how such a travesty got produced. The playwright was wealthy: he underwrote the entire production himself.

GOT ANY GOOD IDEAS?

A graduate student of mine, Kara, approached me at the end of a one-term course in playwriting. She had written a number of impulse exercises as well as the four structure exercises in Part One. She had a solid understanding of dramatic structure and a good grasp of how her own creative process worked. She was excited to begin work on her first play, but she had a problem that she wanted to talk about first.

Over coffee, Kara told me that she had an idea she wanted to write about. "Not an idea for a play, exactly," she explained, "but an idea that I want to somehow make into a play. But I don't know how to do it. We didn't do that kind of thing in the class."

Not all plays begin with an impulse. Sometimes we want to write what I call an idea play. Many writers find that the origin for their work is a thought, a question, or a concept.

They may, for example, wish to write about a moral dilemma (*Antigone* or *Hamlet*), a social problem (*A Doll's House* or *Major Barbara*), or a particular human trait such as jealousy (*Othello*) or ambition (*Macbeth*). Playwrights may pose a question that the play attempts to answer: What is the nature of fate (*Oedipus the King*)? What would happen if a daughter told her mother that she would commit suicide that night (*'night, Mother*)? A play may even begin by its author thinking first of the play's central metaphor (*The American Dream, Riders to the Sea*), or of a general social condition such as poverty (*Awake and Sing!*) or the effects of racism (*A Raisin in the Sun*) or the restructuring of society (*The Cherry Orchard*). The author may want to examine a problem in the body politic (*The Crucible*), or even to illuminate and humanize a scientific theory (*Arcadia*, *Copenhagen*).

Of course I can't claim to know that these particular plays began with these particular ideas or with any idea at all. They might very well have grown out of the subconscious impulse. But they certainly may have begun as ideas, and so they serve as good illustrations of the type of play that does.

Kara wanted to know how to go about writing her play, which she said would deal with sexism in the workplace. She said that she felt comfortable with her technique, but she wasn't sure how to bridge the gap between it and the fact that she had a specific but utterly abstract idea about which she wanted to write.

Some writers might easily imagine how to begin such a play. Possible scenarios would present themselves readily, and the writer could pick and choose among them, write them out, and ultimately order them into some sort of narrative.

But this was something that Kara was having a hard time doing. She couldn't make those connections between abstract idea and living play. If you have the same sort of problem, the concepts in this chapter may be helpful to you. If you feel you don't need them, following them is not essential. But if you're stuck and having a hard time finding a way to explore and illuminate and dramatize your idea, read on.

First, I told Kara to define her idea.

Kara wanted to write a play about the issue of sexism in the workplace. I asked her to make a complete sentence of that idea. I gave her an example: "Sexism in the workplace is bad."

"It's more than that, though," Kara responded. "It's not just that it's bad, it's that it's bad for men as well as for women."

"Good!" I said. "So make a sentence."

She thought for a moment, then said, "Sexism in the workplace destroys the sexist as well as the victim."

That's the idea she wanted to write about. We might also call it her theme.

A theme needs to be a sentence, a complete sentence. Only a complete sentence has a subject and verb. It's the subject and verb that give your theme real meaning: "Sexism . . . destroys." The verb, of course, is an action—in both the grammatical and dramaturgical sense. That's no coincidence. You'll find that in coming up with your simple thematic statement, you'll also find crucial information about the action of the play. "Sexism . . . destroys." Now, there won't necessarily be a direct translation. Kara's play may not be about one person wanting to destroy another. Even if it's not that simple, the thematic statement often gives a general sense of where the play is going in terms of its action.

Your theme is what you want to say in your play. Some writers believe that one must have a clear theme, and some writers even insist that the theme must be known and articulated before the writing ever begins.

I disagree. I don't know for sure, but I'll bet Harold Pinter would also disagree. And David Mamet. And probably Tennessee Williams, Sam Shepard, and any number of other authors who clearly write from a deeply personal, subconscious place.

On the other hand, I imagine that Ibsen wanted to know his theme beforehand. I'll bet Shakespeare did too. Maybe

Arthur Miller and David Hare as well. Their plays usually strike me as coming from a thematic idea.

I might be wrong about any of these individuals, of course, but my point is that in the case of theme, you can either have one or not. You can know it beforehand, or you can discover it as you go along. I'm the last person to say you must do it one particular way.

The reason I asked Kara to develop a simple, thematic statement for her play was that I felt she needed to do it in this instance. Clearly the driving force behind the play was an idea, an abstraction. And since that's precisely what a theme is, it was best for her to know what her theme was as long as it was the driving force causing her to write the play in the first place.

As Kara goes along with her play, she might find that her theme alters slightly, or even a lot. She can always adjust it and bring it into line with what is actually happening in the play.

For the playwright, a theme is only a guide, a way of helping you to stay on track, to keep you from wandering so far afield that your play ends up being about everything, and therefore nothing.

MAKE IT REAL

Next, I told Kara to reify her theme, make it concrete, convert it into the raw material of a play.

In other words, I wanted her to transform the theme into an image that would allow her to actually begin writing. I didn't ask her to think about a plot, or an action, or a conflict, or an event. Not yet. Only an image.

Of course, the tricky part here is that she needed to create not just any interesting image, but one that corresponded to the theme of her play.

So I told her to use common sense. If the play is about sexism, for example, it's only reasonable that of the two characters in her image one will be a man, the other a woman. And because her theme involves the workplace, the setting should probably be that as well. That's not to say the entire play will occur in the workplace and involve only a man and a woman, but it's the reasonable place to start.

I continued, "So you have a man and a woman in, let's say, an office. Make it specific. Do you know about advertising agencies? Then make it an advertising agency.

"Where exactly in the agency does the scene occur? His office? What does his office look like? How big is it? Does it have a window? What kind of furniture does it have? What's hanging on the walls? Is there carpeting? What kind?

"What time of day is it? Late afternoon? What season? Winter? Then the sun is probably down, or maybe it's just setting. Is it after hours in the office? How late exactly? Is there anyone else around or is he alone?

"What's the temperature in the room? Is this an old building with steam heat? Maybe it's overheated, stifling. And if it's steam heat, there's a radiator, and radiators bang when the heat comes on. Is the radiator banging right now?

"What does the office smell like? A new carpet? Does the man wear cologne? What kind? Does he wear too much? Is it overpowering, or just right?

"What does the man look like? How old? Forties? Heavyset or thin? What is he wearing? It's winter, so maybe wool pants. Do they itch a little? Did his feet get warm in his shoes so that he kicked the shoes off? And if that's true, has he loosened his tie? It's dinnertime. Is he hungry? Does he want a drink? Or has he already had a drink from the bottle he keeps in his drawer?

"What does the woman look like? How old? What is she wearing? Is she hungry?"

And so on.

Create an image that is as real for you as an actual experience might have been. Don't worry about every detail. We don't notice or remember everything in life, and you don't have to do so here either. But create the details that come to mind, that seem interesting, that make the scenario real for you.

Then write. And remember to do it now, before your intellect intrudes—which it will, given the opportunity.

For now, all Kara needed to know was this: a woman walks into this man's small, overheated office that smells vaguely of cologne and a new carpet, and is lit by a brilliant setting sun. They begin to speak . . .

In some sense, there may be a hidden experience underneath your desire to write an idea play. In other words, even when you get the urge to write such a play, it may be due to an impulse that is really experiential. The subject of sexism may occur to you as an intellectual problem, but there's a chance that you're interested in it because at some time in your life you have experienced its sting.

If this is the case, it's worth investigating that impulse. You may find that the play is more personal, that it comes from a more literally autobiographical place than you suspected.

On the other hand, even if it's true, I don't believe that an autobiographical play is necessarily better. It's just another option—and while it might be better, writers sometimes find it easier to write the less autobiographical material more truthfully. It allows them distance, and therefore the necessary objectivity.

TOPIC FOR TODAY

Another type of play, really a subcategory of the idea play, is the topical play. In recent years the genre has been largely taken over, often in debased form, by television movies. We've all been subjected, for example, to more than our share of disease-of-the-week TV dramas. But theater is still a valid and vital forum for presenting material of this kind. Plays like *Angels in America*, or *A Fair Country* by Jon Robin Baitz, or almost any work by David Hare could be said to be topical in nature.

Again, as with the idea play, if you are having trouble finding the play that's within you, first try developing images that will help you to enter the material on a subconscious level through the impulse exercises.

The key is to find the level on which you connect to the play beneath your intellect. Not that there's anything wrong with the intellect. But in my experience it tends to be easier to manage, while whatever emotional connection you may have to the material is very likely evanescent and easily lost.

Take the aforementioned *Angels in America*. There are plenty of topics in the play. There's the topicality of the gay subculture, of AIDS, of Roy Cohn, of Mormonism, of Reaganism—not to mention the theology of angels. But beneath that topical surface, which is the one most apparent to the audience, is a highly personal connection that Tony Kushner makes in each scene, in every character.

For example, Kushner has been quoted as saying that when he wrote the relationship between Prior and Louis, and in particular Louis's abandonment of Prior in his moment of desperate need, he drew on his own experience with a dear friend of his—a platonic friend—who had been badly hurt in a car accident. Kushner had abandoned this friend in much the same way that Louis abandons Prior. Kushner was able to make that relationship, that act of abandonment, palpable by going back to something in his own life. (This is related to the method acting technique of "emotional memory" that Uta Hagen describes in her book *Respect for Acting*. The actor reaches into his own memory of a time when he was indeed angry in order to perform anger onstage. He remembers the circumstances, the physical experience, the feelings associated with them, and substitutes those into the scene he's playing.)

Kushner may very well not write from images such as the ones I use. I'm sure he has his own methods. What matters ultimately is not that you use my particular system (though I'd recommend you start there) but that you connect to the part of your mind which will allow you to experience something very much like life.

In any case, it is certainly the personal connection that Kushner was able to make with Prior and Louis's relationship and elsewhere in *Angels in America* which is the most significant factor in making the play so compelling to an audience.

IT'S HISTORY

Another subcategory of the idea play is the historical play. *The Kentucky Cycle*, *Amadeus*, *A Soldier's Play*, and *Cloud Nine* all are plays that continue the long and honorable tradition of historical drama.

I mention historical plays here not because I want to make the point that the writing of them, from a creative process standpoint, is so different from the idea plays or the topical plays. In fact, the process of writing a historical play is very much the same as these. You must still convert the history into something that has meaning to you. Again, I recommend using the image and impulse exercises—though only if you feel you need them.

It's true that in the case of a historical play you should probably do some research to discover the "feel" of the time and place you're writing about. You also may want to get down some of the basic information of the period and people about whom you're writing. But as William Styron, author of *The Confessions of Nat Turner*, has said about the writing of that novel, good historical writing should be fed "short rations" of the facts.

And that's the point I want to make. What follows is an observation I would make about any play, but the historical play, because it is based on reality in a way that other plays may not be, makes a good illustration of a larger truth.

Too many writers become bogged down with trying to follow a literal (in this case historical) truth in their plays. Plays are not about this kind of truth, regardless of what many critics, historians, and literal-minded hacks who don't understand the function of art will say. These self-appointed wardens of the theater will often disparage any nonliteral choices a playwright makes and write them off as bowing to dramatic necessity.

But what else should the playwright be bowing to? Certainly not to the history books or some other sort of literal truth. That's what those books (or biographies, or other works of nonfiction) are there for. It is their purpose to inform, and it's an important one. Information, however, is not the function of art (> Chapter 13).

I happily admit to being a crank on the subject. I regularly fire off letters to the editor defending plays (and sometimes novels or movies) against the attacks of those who would demand of a play the same accuracy they would demand of a work of history or biography.

Plays must, of course, be accurate. They must be truthful. But not historically truthful. Not factually truthful. Plays seek another kind of truth. They seek a psychological truth, an emotional or spiritual truth. You must not let the small-minded carpers—the little people who distrust the alchemy of art—to dictate otherwise.

Alan, a playwright who studies privately with me, had a terrific idea for a play. It was to be based on a little-known historical episode, the first Jewish immigrant of the nineteenth century to be tried for murder. The murder and the ensuing trial had been a famous scandal of the time, rife with anti-Semitism and sensational details.

The actual case was this: Pesach Rubinstein, recent immigrant and pious rabbinical student, stood accused of murdering Sara Alexander, also a Jewish immigrant but a socialist firebrand. Rubinstein was married, his wife and family having remained in Russia. As was the custom, Rubinstein had arrived in the New World first, with the others to follow once he established a foothold. But in the meantime, Rubinstein met Alexander and began a passionate affair with her. Ultimately, his wife and family were set to arrive, and Rubinstein was caught in an untenable position. Alexander was found with her throat cut in a remote, rural area of what is now Brooklyn.

Rubinstein never confessed to the crime and technically was never even convicted, though the evidence against him was overwhelming. (Among other self-incriminating acts, he told the authorities of a "dream" that led them to the body.) He escaped conviction only because he died of tuberculosis in jail while awaiting the outcome of his trial.

These were the raw facts. They made a good story, to be sure. More important, they were just the spark Alan needed to get him going on a play. He was thrilled to have something that gave him, personally, such a charge to write.

And he loved not just the raw story but the surrounding ethos of Jewish culture and of Jewish immigrant culture. (Alan is the descendant of Jewish immigrants.) He relished the idea of delving into the intricacies of Talmudic law, about which he already knew a fair amount, to better understand Rubinstein's point of view. He was also fascinated by the conflict between Old and New World values, between religion and socialism.

But therein lay an enormous hidden problem for him, though he didn't know it at the time. In researching all of this religious and historical information, Alan fed himself not short rations but a veritable feast. And all the while, the play remained stillborn. He insisted, when we discussed it, that with a bit more research on the Talmud, a bit more understanding of the finer points of Rubinstein's theological dilemma, he would be able to work on the problems in the play.

I insisted otherwise. "It's the facts that are dragging you down," I'd say. "Every time you discover a new fact, you feel compelled to work it into the drama. But while those facts may be interesting to you, they're not doing the play any good. The play doesn't need more facts, it needs more of you and your passion to tell the story that's inside you." Ultimately, this is not the story of Pesach Rubinstein and Sara Alexander. It's the story of Alan, who's using their story to tell his own. But Alan's story doesn't require any facts, because the more facts there are, the more they prevent Alan's story from getting out and onto the page.

And it wasn't just theology that was causing Alan trouble. The historical facts were a problem as well. He felt constrained to remain as close to the history as he possibly could. If the real Rubinstein had never uttered a word from his jail cell, Alan's Pesach must never utter a word either. If the real Rubinstein had killed Alexander by cutting her throat, then Alan's Pesach must do the same. If the real Alexander worked as a laundress, so must Alan's Sara.

It was driving Alan nuts, and worse, it was keeping him from writing an interesting play. Still, he felt bound never to stray from a historical truth if at all possible.

My point of view was: forget about the historical facts. People don't go to plays to get history. You don't go see Shakespeare's *Henry V* for the history. If you do, you're a fool. Shakespeare never meant any of his history plays as history lessons. It's quite plain that he meant them as studies in human nature. In that regard they are deeply, profoundly truthful. As history, they're preposterous.

I appealed to Alan on a practical level. I pointed out that he was fortunate to be writing of an obscure moment in history. Only an infinitesimal part of the population had ever heard of this case, of that we could be sure. The likelihood that any of them would ever see this play was even tinier. If he was afraid of hearing back from the legions of carping literalists who would be on him in a second if he changed a single gesture of a single character, he could surely relax. Had he been writing about the Lindbergh kidnaping or the Kennedy assassination, it might be another matter. But that was hardly the case here.

Practical reasoning didn't fly with Alan, though, and frankly it was a mistake on my part to try this approach. It doesn't get to the heart of the matter, which is the principle that the playwright's obligation is to his play, not to the facts.

Alan literally spent years going further and further into the details of theology and history. For long periods of time I wouldn't hear from him. When I did, he would ask me to read a draft that was always interesting as a lesson in history and Talmud, but the play remained a faint shadow of its potential. Alan knew it, on some level, but the desire—the compulsion—to hew to the facts remained too strong to break.

Ultimately, though, he had had enough. I'm not sure how or why, but Alan at last satisfied his need for the theological information and finally wriggled out of the tyrannical grip of the historical facts. Now he gave himself over to discovering the play that had been waiting all these years to come out. When he did, the work was remarkable. The characters leapt to life, and the scenes took on a compelling urgency. The play became a moving, wrenching tale of a man torn between his passions and what he saw as his duty to his culture, family, and tradition.

You may be tempted to make the argument that, though he finally dispensed with all that research, it was nevertheless essential for him to have done it. Only with that information tucked away in the back of his brain, you might say, was he able to bring forth the play. But I disagree. The theology was never used in the play, except for a basic understanding of Jewish traditions, which Alan has had in his head since he was a boy. The historical record was discarded or remolded according to the demands of the drama; the further Alan allowed himself to wander from the raw history, the better the play got.

There was still work to be done, of course. The play wasn't perfect right away. But it was a strong draft and, perhaps more important, Alan now accepted that by using these same means, he could do the rewrites quickly and effectively.

As I write this, the play has closed after a successful run in New York and commercial producers are haggling over the right to produce it in a major off-Broadway run.

DON'T TAKE THIS LITERALLY

Another playwright who studies with me privately, Meghan, has a variation on this problem. She is a successful playwright with several professional productions under her belt. She doesn't write historical dramas, or plays that I would categorize as idea plays of any kind. Yet she suffers from being overly concerned with the literal, and in that sense she provides a good way to discuss this issue from another, more subtle angle.

For example, Meghan was once working on a play in which there was some awkwardness in one scene that we both felt needed work. The scene involves three characters. We'll call them Anna, Betsy, and Chuck.

The first part of the scene concerned Anna and Betsy agreeing to enter into a contract together. They did this knowing that Chuck wouldn't like it when he found out. After they made the agreement, Chuck entered. Betsy remained for a moment, then, uncomfortable over the "secret negotiation," she left. Now it was up to Anna to explain to Chuck that she had entered into the contract with Betsy.

The problem was that we in the audience had to hear this same information twice—once when Anna made the agreement with Betsy, then again when Anna told Chuck that she had done so. The second time we heard the same information, it was a lot less interesting.

I suggested that Meghan make the choice that during the time Chuck and Betsy are both in the scene together, Chuck sees her discomfort, puts two and two together, and realizes what Anna and Betsy had been up to before he entered. That way, we leapfrog over the information and go right to the action, which is Chuck's desire to get Anna to break the contract.

Meghan liked the idea of jumping over the information, but she balked at the notion that Chuck could simply make this realization in one brief, silent moment. "Would the audience accept this?" she asked. "Don't I have to show him making the connection, tell the audience how it's happening? How do I convince myself that he could simply get it?"

First, I said she could convince herself of it because in life people sometimes do just such things.

Second (and this was the better reason), I said that in a play, things can simply happen. You don't have to explain them. Plays are not life. They are based on life; they are like life in many ways; and they derive their essential structure from life. But if they operated precisely the same as life, why would we need them? Plays are compressed, highly selective in what they present to the audience. That is their nature. Attempts to explain their distillation serve only to bog down the action and leave the audience bored with too much information.

Ironically, Meghan loves compression when she sees it in other plays, which she invariably describes as smart and fast and elegant. Yet she is terrified to do it herself. Why? Because when she gives it a moment's thought, it doesn't make literal sense. It's not entirely reliable. It's not concretely explicable. She feels that if it happens at all, she has to explain it—even though if it were explained in another person's play, she'd get bored immediately.

The point is that the audience will not give it a moment's thought. They're going to see that Chuck got what happened, and they're going to be far more intrigued about what he's going to do next than concerned over how he has just managed to make the realization. That's always what the audience is most concerned with: not with what has just happened, but with what will happen next.

This is just one example of being too literal. It can take many other forms. Some playwrights feel obligated to provide all the exposition at the top of the play (> Chapter 13), or to allow a precisely naturalistic length of time for offstage events (a trip to the deli takes seven minutes, therefore the character must be gone exactly that long), or to require characters to always answer a question put to them.

I had this last problem when I first started writing. A smart playwright friend pointed out that if my characters would only stop answering questions and instead simply pursue their actions, my plays would move much more quickly and be far more interesting. I protested that the audience wouldn't get things if the characters didn't answer the question.

My friend responded that if the characters answer the questions, the audience will get the answer. But if they pursue their actions, the audience will get the play. And which, he asked me, is more important?

Your job as a playwright, as an artist, is to be true to yourself, to your own inner voice that demands to be heard.

Or, if you prefer a more practical dictum in the case of an idea play, be true to your own thematic statement, such as "Sexism in the workplace is as destructive to the sexist as to the victim." That's the truth that Kara wanted to discover, and it was to that truth that she owed her only allegiance.

Ultimately, what's important is not where your play originates (in an impulse or an idea) but what you do with it. Make sure that whatever intellectual qualities the play possesses are rooted also in experiential, subconscious, imagistic, spontaneous, impulsive qualities.

There is no right reason or wrong reason to write a play. You can make an idea play work just as well as a purely impulsive one, so long as there is a real desire, a genuine impulse in you that drives you to write. But remember that finding and protecting that impulse remains the most difficult and delicate of all the tasks. If you protect it and nurture it and allow it to run the show (and I mean that literally), it will serve you well.

TEN: CHARACTER

WHENEVER I start to talk about a play with someone who's asked for feedback, I start with the question, "Who's the play about?"

I start there because I think that, in some organic sense, that's the starting point of any play. People. Characters. In the gestalt of playwriting, this is one of the parts that truly touches every other.

Back in high school, your English teachers probably talked about something they called "character development" in the stories, novels, and plays you read. They suggested, no doubt, that it had to do with knowing how the character in the story acted and what she said, so that you, the reader, got an idea in your head of who she was. This wasn't simply a description of how the characters looked but how they behaved. Character development was intended, by the writer, to make you feel as though you knew this person—not as you would in real life, but actually more profoundly than that.

Your teachers were essentially right. What they may not have said is that character development is not pursued by the writer as a separate venture, as in: "Today I'm working on character development. I'm saving plot development for tomorrow." Your teachers didn't have to. They were teaching you to be readers, not playwrights.

I don't believe the act of writing a play should, in the actual doing of it, be broken down into its component parts. And nowhere is this more true than in character development. You'll soon see in this section, and in much of the material to follow, that the ideas we discuss will be referring to, overlapping with, and ricocheting off of other ideas in other parts of the book. All these parts are connected, tied up together in one inseparable whole. But we're going to pry things apart just long enough to get a good look at them.

CREATING CHARACTER

"I'm totally confused!" a student of mine, Tanisha, said in the middle of class. "Whenever I think about this character I'm writing, I just get more and more confused about who she is. I feel like I know her in a lot of ways, but then I remember there is no such person, and I just get very freaked out, like I'm going crazy."

I knew just how this student felt. The idea of what a character is, and how to create one, can sometimes seem elusive indeed.

In his book *True and False*, David Mamet proposes that there is no such thing as a character in a play, only words on a page. An actor speaks these words, and so the audience forms a sense of an actual person. The character, though, is an illusion.

I agree with this. It acknowledges, to my mind, an obvious truth, one which is often forgotten because it is so well disguised by the skillful writers who camouflage it with their craft.

Much of what we love about theater is an illusion. We tend to accept this readily in the other theatrical disciplines. For instance, when I saw the set of *A Moon for the Misbegotten* on Broadway, it was quite plain to everyone in the audience that, while the set represented the exterior of the home of Phil Hogan and his daughter, it clearly wasn't anyone's actual home. Certain nonnaturalistic touches toward the back of the set—a painted backdrop, the realistic boulders tethered to what was obviously canvas—made this apparent on one level.

As adult theatergoers, none of us would have ever expected to walk into the "Hogan house," no matter how real it looked, and find a real house inside. Or walk offstage and find the infamous ice pond with old man Hogan's pigs wallowing in it. As a child we might have believed in such things, but as adults we knew that the set was only meant to portray a place, not to be the place itself.

Creating a character is the same as creating that set. What we call a character is merely words on a page, just as Phil Hogan's house is merely some boards painted on one side, and nothing but a skeleton within. Your words will be spoken by an actor who also is not that character.

This might seem limiting to you, but let me suggest that it's actually liberating. All you have are the words, it's true.

But you have every word at your disposal, and it is solely up to you how to use them. To my mind, that's freedom.

However, with freedom comes responsibility—and effort. Like working from the impulse, creating a character is more complex and multifaceted than the structural tools discussed in Part One. This is, in part anyway, because the tools are about structure, which is an abstraction. It's an idea you can get into your head and repeat to yourself. You can learn it. But characters are representations of people, and people are more complicated than ideas. They're unpredictable. You can't "learn" a person, even if you can get to know them a bit.

This is why I often remind my students (and myself) that you never really learn to write plays. You only learn to write the play you're writing at the moment. With each new play, you start the process all over again.

That may seem like hard news, but to me, it's why I feel I'll never get tired of writing plays.

Aristotle believed that it was possible to have a tragedy without character, but not without plot. (To his credit, he only said it was possible, not desirable.) The observation might have seemed bloodless to the Greek playwrights he was writing about, had they been alive to hear it, for they were certainly very concerned with character. Some of the most vivid, unforgettable characters in dramatic literature come from their plays—Medea, Oedipus, Clytemnestra, Antigone—all of them as lifelike today as they were 2,500 years ago. With due respect to Aristotle, they are what we tend to remember of these and most other great plays. Characters—like Falstaff, Iago, Nora, Blanche DuBois, Willy Loman—haunt us long after the play is over, their gestures and words lingering ghostlike before our eyes. If we can make the characters in our plays half as vivid as these, we'll be doing very well.

What makes these characters so vivid? So terrifying? So funny? So unforgettable? How can one go about creating character?

If you're not sure, or if you're having problems doing so, here is a process that works for me.

FOUR STEPS TO CHARACTER

Tanisha's dilemma, which we began to talk about at length, was that she knew a lot about her character—or at least she believed she did. She knew just what the action was, and the conflict, and the event—everything about how the scene transpired. And when she described it to me, it sounded like a good, workable plan.

But she also felt dead in the water, unable to create the slightest sense of life, particularly from the main character. As she put it, "I feel like I have a character out there somewhere, I just don't know who she really is."

At this point, some writing teachers might suggest that Tanisha write a character biography, a free-form exploration of this character's past to discover that elusive "who." I don't have a problem with these biographies, and I know that many writers rely on them and get good results. But in my opinion they're a lot of work, and although they can produce all manner of information, they may not yield the kind you need to create your character. Go ahead and write biographies if you like to. But, in addition, consider the ideas I'm about to offer which, like so many other ideas in the book, are derived from

Aristotle. If you're like me, you may ultimately discover you don't need to write a character bio at all.

Aristotle redeems his somewhat high-handed (if philosophically defensible) remark about characters not being essential when he offers a very smart idea on the subject of how character is created. He suggests that underneath and previous to the actions of any character lie "ill-defined feelings and emotions" (his word is "pathos").

In other words, emotions lead to action. If I want to strike you on the face, it's because first I was angry. If I want to kiss you, first I was attracted to you. Before I want to run away from you, I am afraid.

Emotions cause action to happen. And as we already know from Part One, action leads to speech or behavior.

If I want to strike you, I might go ahead and give you either a whack on the cheek (behavior) or a good chewing out (speech). If I want to kiss you, I might either plant one on you (behavior) or whisper sweet words of love (speech). If I want to run away, either my legs will seem to have a mind of their own (behavior) or I might babble nervously to try to calm you down (speech).

Action leads to speech/behavior. And speech/behavior has a lot to do with what we perceive as character. Aristotle's theory bears out pretty well.

I would add only one thing: that there is something which precedes even the emotions. That something is the unique collection of general qualities or traits that we all, as humans, possess. If I am hot-tempered and pugnacious, I will tend to be quick to anger; if I'm lovelorn, I may find myself easily attracted; if I'm a worrier, I may scare easily.

There's no direct or absolute connection between these general qualities and the emotions a person feels at any given time. God knows we can't precisely predict a person's emotions at any given moment, no matter how much we know about their traits. But we do have clues, over time, as to how they will tend to react.

I believe it's a combination of these four factors (general qualities, emotions, action, and speech/behavior) that together, and in that sequence, give us a sense that something called a character exists.

The following chart lays out this sequence so we can see it in its simplest form:

GENERAL QUALITIES
EMOTIONS
ACTION
+ SPEECH / BEHAVIOR

= CHARACTER

Let's put aside Tanisha's play for a moment and use *Oedipus the King* to illustrate that paradigm. The play is not just a model of structure but of character development as well.

First step. Think of how *Oedipus* begins. In the first moment of the play, the people of Thebes have come to Oedipus, imploring him to help in removing the curse of the plague that is destroying the city. Oedipus is a good, noble, responsible king. Those qualities are the type of person he is, but they're not what we mean by his character in the dramatic sense of the word. They're too general for that. We'd describe him this way regardless of the particular circumstances in which we've found him. They're what we might say of him whether he was twenty-five or seventy-five, was healthy or sick, was actually king or not. They are, in other words, general truths about him. But drama is rarely about general truths. It's about the specifics, right now. So these qualities will only help us to begin defining Oedipus's dramatic character.

Second step. Because he's a good, noble, responsible king, Oedipus does in fact feel bad for his people. He sympathizes with them. Sympathy and feeling bad are, obviously, emotions.

Third step. The emotion of feeling bad leads Oedipus to want to help, which is precisely what he says he's going to do by the time that first scene is over. Specifically, he's going to get to the bottom of this plague. He intends to root out whatever is causing it and deal with it by whatever means necessary. It is a way to describe his action.

Wanting to help leads Oedipus to the fourth and final step. It results in specific speech and behavior designed to satisfy his need to help. He in fact has already sent Creon to the oracle to get Apollo's advice on what to do, even before the play began. (That's not, by the way, an exception to the rule we're discussing here. He sent Creon to the oracle because he already felt bad and wanted to help even before the citizens came to him with their plea.) (> p. 272, In Medias Res.)

In each subsequent scene, Oedipus continues to pursue this same action. While his specific speech and behavior change over the course of the play depending on whom he's interacting with—Creon, or Jocasta, or Tiresias, or others—it's always a result of his action, which is always a result of his feelings, which are always a consequence of his general traits.

The sum of all this leads us to understand Oedipus as a character. We don't have a full, complete sense of his character until he leaves the stage for the final time at the end of the play. We watch as the character is assembled throughout the play. We see him evolve, deepen, even come into apparent contradiction with himself. Oedipus is, after all, a selfless altruist who can also be selfish and blind to the truth.

When the play begins and even after it is over, we have a sense that Oedipus is alive. I speak of him, even now as I write this, as though he were real, though of course he is not.

If we were to make a specific diagram for Oedipus, it would look like this:

NOBILITY, SYMPATHY,

WANTING TO STOP THE

PLAGUE,

SENDING CREON TO THE

ORACLE,

INTERVIEWING TIRESIAS,

SUMMONING THE

SHEPHERD,

REJECTING JOCASTA'S PLEAS,

+ ETC.
_____

= OUR SENSE

OF OEDIPUS'S

CHARACTER

MAKING IT YOUR OWN

After explaining this to Tanisha and the rest of the class, from whom I had heard a groan of familiarity when she articulated her problem, I suggested we go back to our old friends from Part One, the long suffering and very thirsty Joe and Mike.

"Let's suppose," I began, "that Joe again wants a glass of water. Just as with Tanisha and her scene, you've decided ahead of time that this is his action.

"But once you sit down to write, you don't know 'who Joe is.' You don't have a sense of how he behaves, what he says, what he does to get the glass, or any other aspect of his speech or behavior that you think of as being Joe's character. You know his action, but you still can't write the scene. In a word, you're blocked. This could be because you've skipped over the earlier hidden aspects of his character—namely his general traits and emotions.

"You could try using an image and an impulse exercise to discover what your subconscious has to say on the subject. I'd recommend it, in fact. But let's assume you've already tried that and it didn't work. Or for some reason you just don't want to. (And let's also assume you've determined this really is the play you need to write, not just the one you want to write.)

"What do you do? It's obvious, isn't it." And there was a certain amount of nodding around the table. "You need to understand more of Joe's general qualities, and how he feels about that glass of water, and then let the action and his speech and behavior evolve from there."

So, as I suggested to Tanisha and the class, go back a step. "Take Joe's action away from him," I said. "He no longer wants the glass of water, not for right now.

"Instead, let's think about who Joe is, bottom line. Is he based on someone you know? That's not essential, of course, but if you're stuck, consider making that choice. That's why writers base their characters on actual people. Not because they intend to render a biographical portrait (< pp. 160–61), but because it gives them the raw material with which to begin creating their own character.

"Let's say, for instance, that Joe is based on a friend of yours, Andy. Andy is a nice enough guy in many ways, but he's pretty high-strung. He's got a lot of energy, he's rather loud, loves to party. He's very friendly and outgoing, but his friendships also tend to be superficial. In fact, he can seem downright remote if you try to get too close.

"So we could say some of Andy's general qualities are that he's energetic, outgoing, but hard to get close to.

"Now that Joe is based on Andy, ask yourself, how does Joe feel about that glass of water? More important, how does he feel about Mike and the fact that he's competing with Mike for the water? What are some logical deductions we might make about Joe and his feelings on that?

"First, we could say that Joe's feelings are outwardly friendly to Mike. And not just outwardly—Joe really believes he has nothing but warm feelings for Mike. That's the sort of self-image he has: great guy, friend to all, wants to be Mike's buddy. Let's say he's feeling friendly.

"But, on the other hand, Joe also has this intimacy problem. He tends to be friendly to virtually anyone on the surface, but he's afraid of getting close. So it's fair to say, since he's forced into a somewhat intimate setting with Mike, that he's also feeling afraid.

"Friendly but afraid. Sounds reasonably interesting,

doesn't it? Multidimensional. Someone we might all be curious to know more about.

"Now let's move on from there. If Joe is feeling friendly but afraid, then what does that make him want to do in the scene?

"For the moment, let's assume that you can still use the glass of water as the object of his action. Presumably he's going to go about getting it in some friendly, warm way. Kidding around perhaps, or being self-deprecating, but always wanting the water, always wanting all of it, and always wanting it badly. Remember that high stakes do not necessarily mean high emotions (< Chapter 5).

"And let's suppose that this works to some extent. Mike is willing to compromise. He'll let Joe take the water for himself—so long as Joe agrees to come on a monthlong trip to the Australian outback where the two of them will be alone together the entire time. That would certainly test Joe's friendliness, wouldn't it. It might set off those fear of intimacy alarms in his head besides.

"And people who are afraid start to act differently. Joe might very well feel trapped in a corner. He might get belligerent. He might start demanding the water with no strings attached. The scene could escalate quickly into an angry fight. The seeming contradiction of a friendly guy turning angry so quickly could make perfect sense, because underneath you would know that all along Joe has been not merely friendly but also afraid."

I stopped there. The scene could go many other ways as well. This was only an example. But you can see on your own how thinking about Joe's general traits can lead you to some conclusions about his specific emotions in this scene. Then, when you connect them to the action, they can take on a complete and complex life in the form of speech and behavior.

Perhaps the most important thing for you to remember is that while your character may be as mysterious and elusive as we are in life, she is not utterly amorphous or impossible to conceive. Dramatic character is composed of four ingredients (general qualities, emotions, action, speech/behavior) that are simultaneously discrete and inextricably bound together—just as they are in life.

SYMPATHY

Shakespeare's Richard III is one of the most unpleasant characters in literature. Unless you also happen to be a ruthless murderer and plunderer, you probably do not find yourself in "harmony or agreement of feeling" (the dictionary definition of sympathy) with him.

I'm willing to bet that Shakespeare shared your feelings about Richard III. Yet most of us find ourselves engaged by him, just as Shakespeare must have. We may not have the urge to become his best friend, but neither would we avoid spending three hours in the theater with him, complaining that he's an unsympathetic character. We become something like co-conspirators with Richard. We may want him to fail, yet we're mesmerized by his ruthlessness, creativity, and, above all, his self-justifications. He is sympathetic in the dramatic sense, even though we would despise him if we met him in real life.

What's the difference between dramatic sympathy and real-life sympathy? To look for the answer, let's divide dramatic sympathy into two categories: the sympathy that the playwright must feel for her characters, and the sympathy the audience must feel for them. Usually when we talk about a sympathetic character, we're referring to the latter. But I want to begin by talking about the former, because it's my feeling that one leads to the other.

Let's say, for example, that you are writing a play about a certain very nasty man. You're worried that you will not have sympathy for the character. But you don't want to make your nasty character nicer, because that would defeat the whole point of writing about him. What do you do in order to make him sympathetic?

The first thing is to make sure you respect him. Whether you have simply dreamed up an unsavory type in your own imagination or based him on a real person, it's important that the character be a worthy adversary. Make him human.

Let's assume you're creating a character out of whole cloth. Step back from what your own personal view of him might be if you actually knew him. Focus instead on how he feels about himself. No one, even the most cruel of us, thinks of himself as wicked. We may acknowledge that we have done wicked things, but we always have a justification—or at least we did at the time.

Consider the great monsters of the real world. Even Hitler did not wake up in the morning and think to himself, "I'll be tremendously evil today for no good reason." He would have been able to give you perfectly good justifications for his unspeakable acts—from his point of view. And in dramatic terms, his point of view is all we care about.*

---

*If you want to write about another point of view, write another character. When the two characters meet: conflict.

"People always have their reasons," the character Octave says in Jean Renoir's film *La Règle du Jeu* (*The Rules of the Game*). That is what's terrible about those things that are truly evil—not that they are so fantastic or unfathomable, but that they are so perfectly reasonable to the one who is evil.

In life, people do indeed always have their reasons. If the characters in your play don't, the audience becomes confused. It is at this point that they may say, "That character was unsympathetic." But what they really mean is "I didn't understand why he did such a terrible thing."

For dramatic sympathy, we don't have to agree with a character, only comprehend him.

The answer ultimately lies in your ability to give the characters words and gestures that reveal those reasons. So give voice to your characters, all of them, including the ones you find distasteful. In fact, especially them. And find the things in them that you, personally and honestly and passionately, believe that your characters believe are good reasons for their behavior. You don't have to make them nicer. You do not have to create a harmony or agreement of feeling. But you do have to make their behavior comprehensible enough that we understand why they as characters do what they do.

Dramatic sympathy and real-life sympathy are two distinct phenomena. The difference between them is important to the playwright because if it is not made, you can spend much time and energy twisting and bending a very naughty character into a rather nice character. This wouldn't be such a terrible thing except that this new, nicer character may have nothing to do with the play you want to write, and by making such changes you may destroy the integrity of your work. This is not an argument to make all your characters rotten, no-good finks. Certainly make them as pleasant as your creative process dictates. Just don't make them nice if it contradicts your impulse.

We live in an age when some people do in fact seem to want characters onstage to be sympathetic in the real-life sense. What these people really want, I think, is for the characters to be likeable, which is quite another thing.

It is not the dramatist's job to make the world, on the stage or off, a more pleasant place. The dramatist's duty is to reveal the truth as he sees it. That truth is often harsh and unpleasant. It is an unfortunate hallmark of our age that some would have it otherwise.

One can only imagine how these people might have reacted to the great plays that are now considered classics. They might have asked that Richard III settle for a cozy dukedom just outside York; that Medea merely give her children an undeserved spanking; that Hedda Gabler return Eilert's manuscript when she sees how upset he is; and that Stanley steal a fleeting kiss from Blanche and then, ashamed of himself, mumble an apology. Revisions like these would certainly make the characters more likeable, but at what a terrible cost! And not simply at the cost of the plays' dramatic power but of the essential truths that they tell about the world.

Still, it's a fact that there are people who would prefer such travesties in today's plays. And many of them are producers of plays, not just audiences. So as a practical matter you may have to deal with this problem at some point. Naturally, the choice will be up to you. But if you do bend to their will, at least know that it's a choice you're making. Another one is always possible.

PASSIVE CENTRAL CHARACTERS

We tend to identify with our own central character more closely than with the others. I don't claim to know exactly why this is true, but I believe it may be because we often see ourselves as passive in our day-to-day life. Our instincts tell us that the world happens to us, rather than that we act upon the world. We often say, "Guess what happened to me today," when in fact we mean, "Guess what I did today."

This identification is only natural, and in many ways it can be a good thing. We come to feel we are on the side of our main character. We sympathize with her and see the world from her point of view. But this identification also has its dangers, because in seeing ourselves in the central character we may make her passive instead of active.

A passive central character is not necessarily a bad thing. King Lear is often described as one—accurately so in my view. (What *does* that man want?) But often, because we don't know what she wants, a passive central character is a frustrating cipher: unknowable, tiresome, and unclear—the last things you want her to be. Shakespeare avoided this in his creation of Lear, managing to make him compelling and vivid despite his passivity. But if this is a problem in your play, it's important to know more about it.*

The first step in dealing with the passive central character can be the most difficult. Before anything, you want to see if your central character is indeed passive.

---

*In keeping with the gestalt concept, you could probably think about the problem, if it is one, by going back to the basic concepts of action (< Chapter 2). But sometimes this doesn't really help to solve the problem; it might be easier to think of the problem in terms of character.

There are two ways in which she may be. First, the character may be active in your mind, but not on the page. (And, as the saying goes, "If it ain't on the page, it ain't on the stage.") You think of her as being active because you know all the thoughts in her head, all her passions, all her secret longings, and so on.

The trouble may be that, while her secret longings technically make her active (an action is always internal, as we saw in Chapter Two), they may not make her active in a way that we can see. We only know about a character by what she does and says. Action is expressed through word and gesture. Your private knowledge that the character has an action is not good enough.

You have to take a good, hard, objective look at your play to determine whether the words and gestures of your central character actually express her action. Are other people going to be able to see and hear her in such a way that they will understand that action? In other words, it isn't enough that you understand it, though that much is certainly essential. You're going to have to let the audience in on the secret.

Of course, this doesn't mean to add bald exposition (> Chapter 13). It doesn't mean that at some specific moment in your play, your central character must stand and state in plain, unvarnished language the core of her action. (Though doing so isn't always a bad idea. Think of Blanche saying she wants magic. It's loud and clear for anyone who listens.)

Find a way of letting your particular character express her particular action in her particular language throughout the play, in every scene, in every gesture (> p. 194, Language). In a good play she will do it many times, in many different ways—some of them overt, some subtle—continuously throughout the work. Everything she does will, in some way, be an outgrowth of, a result of, an expression of her action.

The other possibility is that your main character really is passive, without any action at all, even an unexpressed one. This is a little easier to recognize. You can do it, knowing what you know of action. Just remember that action is within; it's not external behavior.

You can also test whether your character has an action by asking others what they think. As always, choose people you trust. Even so, don't ask questions that are either general or leading. Be direct, but don't make suggestions. Ask them, very simply, if they know which is your main character and what she wants.

If their answer is a character other than the one you intend, you probably have a problem. Even if they name the correct character, but they cannot identify what she wants, or identify something completely different than what you intended, again you can be fairly certain there's a problem. This isn't a sure test—and as always you must rely on your own judgment. But you can use people to help form that judgment.

Let's presume that you have identified your central character as passive. What to do? First, make certain that you have a clear idea of what her action is, even if, for the moment, it remains inside your own head and that of your character.

Now examine one of your scenes objectively, as though someone else had written the play. Ask yourself at literally each of your central character's lines whether the line is spoken because it is an expression of her action. If so, fine. If not, you have a problem. If it's in the gray area, consider making it less gray.

It's just that simple and just that hard. It's close work and it demands that you be objective and removed. It demands that you be your own best critic. It is an analytic task, reserved for the intellect. That's because in this instance we're talking about a scene that's already written and needs work.

What about a scene that is not yet written? Is there a way of grappling with the problem of the passive central character before you begin writing and as you are doing so? Yes, but it's difficult in the way that Zen meditation is difficult, in the way that writing an impulse exercise is difficult.

In my experience, a central character becomes passive because, ironically, you have paid so much attention to her. I'm not saying, of course, to lessen your actual interest in your central character. Naturally, you must be fascinated with her, concerned about her problem, eager to explore her situation.

But such concern can also be a trap. Too much control on your part can lead to passivity in your central character.

Why? Think for a moment about your secondary characters and the fact that (let's presume) you're having no trouble with them at all. Your secondary and minor characters are full of life. They have strong actions, they pursue them with vigor, they're vivid and lifelike. They almost seem to write themselves.

Why do they seem to do that? We could explain it the same way we explain writing the impulse exercise. And that makes a lot of sense. But there's another way to look at it.

We've already compared plays to children. If that's a good analogy, then the characters in our plays are even more like one's own offspring. It follows that one should treat them accordingly—as children one loves and cares about.

A healthy way of raising a child, we would all agree, is to combine freedom and discipline in measured amounts. We all know what happens if the child is allowed too much freedom: he becomes unmanageable, wild, and very disagreeable.

But too much discipline is also to be avoided. One wouldn't want a child to do precisely as one wishes at every moment, even if such a thing were possible. One is raising a child, after all, not a robot. Part of the joy of watching a child grow is seeing what he will do on his own.

Characters—central and secondary alike—must be allowed to write themselves. You as the writer set their boundaries— whether by conscious decision or through the discovery process of writing from the impulse. In either case, you create a general set of rules for them within the play. For example, you may determine their age, their sex, their general traits, possibly even their emotions and actions. You know basically how they will respond to the various situations into which you may put them. But after that, you set them free to behave as they will. If you control too much, they may very quickly become passive.

You know, for example, that Joe will not offer to take Mike skiing in order to get the glass of water. Why? Because *your* Joe is ninety-six years old and wheelchair bound. In order to know that he doesn't ski, you didn't have to create a biography for Joe that included the phrase "does not ski." It's something you intuitively know about him based on your general concept of him as a character. You've discovered that particular detail only in the act of writing.

You might also consciously set the boundaries of the various scenes. You create the situation, determining the time and the place, the physical surroundings, and so on. You may also determine what has just happened to the character before she entered this scene, what sort of emotional or physical condition she may be in. So there are certain boundaries over which—in your mind—it would not be logical for your character to cross, either because of who she is or the situation in which she finds herself.

But even if you set all these boundaries ahead of time, and consciously, there is still part of the process that almost certainly needs to happen on its own. Like a child growing up, let the character express her own feelings, her own thoughts, her own quirks of behavior and speech, and, most of all, her own needs. If you don't, you run the risk of making her passive.

As illustration of that—and at the risk of contradicting myself—let me suggest that it's just possible that your ninety-six-year-old, wheelchair-bound Joe does get it into his head to offer to take Mike skiing. It might be crazy. It might be illogical. He might not ever be able to follow through on it, no matter how hard he tries. But since when aren't people crazy and illogical and unable to do what they insist they can do? If that's what your Joe wants to do, let him. Let him be active the way he wants to be active. Your play will almost certainly be the better for it.

One of the basic elements of Zen meditation is not to focus on the subject of your meditation directly, but to concentrate instead on the proverbial lotus blossom. In doing so, the real issue about which you are meditating ultimately becomes clear.

You might think of writing your central character in the same way. Don't focus on her quite so hard. Don't put her under pressure to behave as you want her to. Leave her alone a bit, as you leave your secondary or minor characters alone.

And just as your secondary characters come to life because your intellect is not hounding and harassing them every time they open their mouths, so will your central character.

One of the most difficult lessons some playwrights have to learn is that audiences are not interested in what the playwright has to say. They are interested in what the characters have to say. That's why you want the characters to write themselves. They will do so—but only if you let them.

You set the boundaries. But within them, let your characters play. They don't call it a play for nothing, after all.

THE CENTRAL CHARACTER

So much talk of a central character suggests that all plays have one. They don't, of course. Many good playwrights write about a group of characters, each of whom are more or less equal in focus. Chekhov comes to mind first, along with other wonderful writers like Lanford Wilson, Kaufman and Hart, and Shakespeare.

Others write plays in which there are two (maybe even three) characters who might be considered central, depending on your criteria. Who is to say that Romeo is the central character of *Romeo and Juliet*? By some measures, Juliet is. Is Blanche really the central character of *Streetcar*? I could make a convincing case for Stanley.

But the fact is, many times a play with only one central character is, structurally speaking, easier to write. (I emphasize *structurally*; it may be difficult in other ways.) This is a simple matter of mathematics. If I write a play with one central character, I am concerned with one central action. The actions of all other characters are secondary to it, and I can adjust these actions to bring them into conflict pretty much as I choose, since they are by definition secondary to my purpose.

But if I write a play with two central characters, I must contend with two central actions, both of which I consider to be of more or less equal importance. Therefore it's not so easy to make adjustments. I must make sure both remain truthful to the impulse (and perhaps also to the intellectual purpose) of my play, yet still come into conflict with each other. A third central character complicates the level of difficulty to another power, as does a fourth, fifth, and so on.

It's similar to the problem of writing a fugue. A song with a single melody may be relatively simple. Any person with a rudimentary knowledge of music can do it. Add a second melody line, however, and a far deeper understanding of musical structure is required. Add a third, fourth, or fifth, and only composers like Bach, who have a powerful command of musical technique, can bring off the feat in such a way that we can actually enjoy the results.

This doesn't mean that a play with a central character is superior to one without—or vice versa. It's just easier to write. And that's the point. If you're having trouble with what you feel is the size or scope of your play, consider identifying a character as the central one for your personal use. Think of this character as having the primary action to which everyone else in the play relates.

The audience may never be aware of this and doesn't need to be. Their perception of the play may be that all the characters are given more or less equal weight: they may all have the same stage time, all be equally interesting, all go on a significant journey.

Kaufman and Hart's *The Man Who Came to Dinner* is a good example of this. The play has a huge cast, but Sheridan Whiteside is clearly the central character, and not merely because he is the "man" of the title, or because he has the wittiest barbs to toss, or even because he has more stage time than anyone else. Instead, the plot is structured around his need, which is to keep his secretary from running off with the local newspaperman. The vast percentage of that play concerns characters responding to, being manipulated by, fighting back at, or supporting that action. That's why he's the central character.

If you begin by assigning the basic structure of the play to one central character and then build all the other characters around him, making adjustments in them as necessary, this can give you a way of sorting out everyone's actions so that you can keep the entire picture in focus. It provides you with a simple structure (action, conflict, event) around which you can build a large play that may be complicated in other ways.

And like any other aspect of good structure, the whole thing can stay your little secret.

LANGUAGE

"I write good dialogue," a student will sometimes say to me when interviewing for my private class. "It's the other parts of playwriting that are hard."

We all know what this means: that he writes words that sound good together, words that flow easily, words that are, perhaps, poetic.

I can't pretend that I don't know that. I do. But at the

same time, saying that dialogue is easy but plays are hard always strikes me as a little funny. It's like saying you're good at everything about swimming except staying afloat. After all, what else is there to playwriting except writing dialogue? Well, stage directions maybe—and numbering the pages. Not much else.

Dialogue, however, is the one, solitary means by which you have to express everything you have to say: theme, character, story, plot. Everything. Yet I don't have a single chapter in this book devoted to it. Just this one section tucked into a chapter on character. And even so, I call the section not "Dialogue" but "Language."

There is a reason.

Before I get to it, allow me an observation that might seem like going off on a tangent but in fact leads to my point. The observation is simply this: we all know that dialogue can be poetic. I don't just mean literally as Shakespeare or Racine are poetic. Writers like Tennessee Williams, August Wilson, Eugene O'Neill, Lorraine Hansberry, David Mamet, and Jon Robin Baitz all have a rhythm and a sound which is, to me, as poetic as any verse.

If you, too, want your dialogue to have a certain sound or rhythm, that's fine with me. But these qualities do not result so much from your desire that they be so as from a consequence of who you are, how you write, what you write about, and so on. It's what a lot of people call the "writer's voice." That's a good phrase; so is "finding your voice." But note the phrasing: you don't create a voice, you discover it. And you discover it by getting down to work and writing as honestly as you can.

And that is what this section is about. My advice to people who have problems with dialogue is that you concern yourself less with the sound of your dialogue, or with trying to separate the dialogue from the rest of the play, and instead think of the ways that language actually operates in a play.

There is not much to say, in my opinion, about how dramatic language works except for the following, which is crucial: the words you choose, and the order in which they are delivered, will determine what people think of your play.

You may very well not be consciously aware of your word choice as you write (> p. 227, Make Your Choice), but you are making choices nevertheless. The degree to which you or your subconscious makes them cohesively and clearly, while still admitting the complexity of the human psyche, will be the same degree to which they are perceived by the audience as lifelike.

This is so obvious that we often forget how powerful language really is. But like other powerful tools at your disposal, you can break them down and make them work for you.

Let's suppose that you've written the scene about Joe and the glass of water, and that you've done so strictly from impulse, without any planning.

And let's suppose that in this rough, impulse draft, Joe has displayed, in general, certain emotional states. He seems, overall, to be belligerent, though early in the scene he seems neither belligerent nor sweet, merely neutral without any particularly defining emotional color.

Here is an instance in which you can bring your intellect to bear in order to improve the scene. First, confirm for yourself, by reading through the scene, that Joe's belligerence is his dominant emotion in the scene. If you find this to be true, then it will be safe to say that the belligerence has probably given rise to the need for the glass of water. Emotions lead to action.

After you've determined that belligerence is Joe's primary emotion in this scene, read it through to discover which precise lines, even which individual words, express this state and which don't. Don't make any changes yet. For the moment, just mark the scene, indicating any lines that fail to express what you want them to.

Let's say that you marked many of the lines at the beginning of the scene. This, then, is the point in the scene when he was saying things neutrally, without any defining emotion. Do you simply cut these lines?

No. There are other possibilities you're going to want to consider before making cuts.

First possibility. We'll assume for the moment that you've followed your impulse. Maybe it has told you that Joe isn't angry yet. Maybe he doesn't get angry until Mike says a particular thing to him that sparks his anger. Look for that moment. If you find it partway into the scene, then it only makes sense that Joe's anger begins at that moment. In this case, maybe your scene is fine the way it is.

Second possibility. Though the above may be true, the scene simply isn't interesting to you until Joe gets angry. In this case, you may indeed want to make at least a few cuts in order to get to Mike's inciting line sooner.

Third possibility. Our first assumption was wrong and you didn't find the strongest dramatic impulse in the first place. Looking over the scene, you now realize that Joe really ought to enter the scene angry and you've simply failed to write him this way, in which case the remedy is obvious: you need to rewrite that early portion of the scene to express Joe's anger. Cut yes, but only so that you can replace those lines that better reflect the character's emotion and action.

Fourth possibility. Joe is angry in the early part of the scene, but he's deliberately disguising that fact. Be careful of this. It's easy to use this explanation as an excuse not to work on the scene. Even if it's true, it may still be possible to rewrite the scene, discovering subtle, subtextual indications of Joe's anger.

Fifth possibility. Joe may be angry but unaware of it. Again, be careful of using this as an excuse. If it's a valid interpretation of what you've written, consider strengthening it through subtle moments that heighten the sense that there is anger about which even Joe isn't aware.

In the end, remember that a play is all dialogue, so thinking about dialogue as this separate entity won't do you a lot of good. It's language, really. It's words. And those words convey meaning. The particular words you choose, whether you do so instinctively or consciously, will have an impact. You want that impact to be as strong, clear, complex, and forceful as possible. Out of that clarity, that lifelike complexity, that truthfulness, your voice will begin to emerge. And your voice is really that of your characters. Let them speak what they will and how they will, regardless of what your opinion happens to be. Only then will your dialogue ring true.

PHYSICAL BEHAVIOR

Physical behavior, as we've seen, is not the same as action. Nevertheless, it is the only method, after language, that you have at your disposal to communicate action. While we normally think of physical behavior as the province of actors, you can dictate some of the behavior of the characters even if it is not to the same degree that you dictate their language.

There are two ways you can use to dictate behavior: explicit and suggested.

You may, for example, write into the stage directions that Joe walks over to Mike and punches him in the face. Or that Joe congratulates Mike enthusiastically. This, obviously, is the explicit method and doesn't need much explanation.

Though it might seem like the simplest, most direct way to get what you want, it can also create problems. First, it may become a crutch that you use to express information that you're otherwise at a loss to convey. If the behavior is appropriate, maybe that's no problem. But it may turn out not to be, and when a director and actors get hold of the script, they may find it difficult to carry it out.

Second, whether the stage directions are appropriate is a matter of opinion. Let's say your actors are having a hard time delivering the line according to your stage directions. It might be that your directions are perfectly appropriate, and your director and actors simply haven't found the internal logic behind them. That's happened to me. I've sat in rehearsal for a long afternoon watching actors and a director struggle with a scene. Finally, at my wit's end, I've pointed out a stage direction that has been there on the page of the script all along but whose existence everyone had quite assiduously denied. After I pointed it out, suddenly the scene made perfect sense, and we could get on with rehearsal.

But as much as I patted myself on the back after that episode, and a fair number like it, there have been many times when I had to admit that I had asked my actors to deliver a gesture that made no sense once the scene was on its feet. After watching them struggle to do it my way, I finally had to confess that they needed to find their own. Nobody likes to admit they've been wrong, but when you are, better to say so in the interest of the play. If you rely too heavily on stage directions, don't be surprised if you're saying so often.

That's where the suggested method comes in. Though it seems like a weaker, less effective means of getting the physical behavior you want, in reality it's a good deal more powerful.

In the suggested method, you incorporate the physical action into the dialogue itself. Shakespeare is a good model for this. Think of Macbeth: "Is this is a dagger which I see before me/The handle toward my hand? Come, let me clutch thee!" There are no stage directions telling the actor what to do, but what choice does any decent actor have but to try to clutch that dagger? He'll look ridiculous if he doesn't do something that at least approximates grabbing it.

This feature of Shakespeare is often attributed to his use of verse, but really it has nothing to do with that. You can do the same thing, though your plays may not have a line of verse in them. For instance, a character of yours might be punching someone in the arm. You could write that behavior into the stage directions or you could have your character say something like, "How do you like that, huh? You like that? How's the arm now, big boy? How about now? You tell me when you had enough." This will make it hard for an actor to be doing anything but taking jabs at his fellow actor.

Of course, there are no guarantees that this method of suggestion will work. The resourcefulness of bad actors can be boundless. But the act of making the character speak words that correspond to his behavior will accomplish two things:

first, it tends to make the playwright more honest with himself about what is truthful and what is not; and second, only the very densest of actors will be able to ignore completely your suggestion in the dialogue.

IDIOSYNCRACIES

A student once brought in a scene that featured an older man who, according to the stage directions, walked with a limp. He also had a tic in his eye (again according to the directions), and a stammer, and he unconsciously shook his head violently when he got angry.

When the scene was over, I (and the other students) expressed interest in the scene, though the older man seemed enigmatic to us. The playwright was taken aback by this. "But I worked so hard on his character!" he complained. "I really thought he was so clear, with all his attributes."

Some playwrights begin constructing a character by assembling a list of various behavioral quirks. When they have arranged the quirks in the proper order and given them a proper balance, they believe they have created a character. They couldn't be further from the truth.

The small idiosyncracies that a character may have—a lisp, a limp, a tic, a peculiar way of phrasing words—do not actually constitute a character in and of themselves.

Think, for example, of yourself, or someone you know in real life. Let's suppose you have a limp or a stammer or a particularly high-pitched voice. Do you want people to view your character—the essence of who you are—in terms of these particular attributes? Of course not. We rebel against such superficial labels for just that reason: they're superficial. "That's not who I really am," you say to the world. And you're quite right.

You are made of stuff that is at once stronger and less tangible. You are your emotions, your thoughts, your desires. You're not your quirky behavior. You're not your stammer, over which you have no control. You are your dramatic behavior, which results from your needs and desires. Judge a person according to what they do, we tell each other, and rightly so. And by that we mean what they do by intention, not coincidence.

So when you create a character for your play, allow her to be composed of the same strong stuff.

This is not to say that your characters may not have quirks. Give them all the quirks you like. Indeed, the quirks you associate with certain actual people may be part of the impulse behind the play (< Chapter 9). These may help you create a sense of reality for the writing of the play and of the characters. Or they may be a final layer that is added on after building a character on the foundation of his action. Any of these possibilities may be fine. Just don't mistake them for the real stuff of character.

***

EXERCISE 7

1. Creating Character: Take a character from a play you've already written and write a description of his general traits and characteristics. This should not be long—a sentence or two at most. Then read your play again to see if the emo-

tions, actions, and behavior of this character correspond to these traits. You can also do this analysis to a play you admire. Or do both.

2. Sympathy: Create a character who wants to commit what you consider an evil deed. In order to commit this deed, he needs help. In the scene you will write, he will try to persuade the other character to help him commit this act. Make the first character as sympathetic as possible.

3. Passive Central Character: Read the first scene from *A Streetcar Named Desire* to see how Blanche's action is expressed in every line.

4. Language: Write a series of letters between two characters in which each is trying to attain an action of your own devising. Remember, these people never meet. They can only write to each other.

5. Physical Behavior: Write a scene in which one of the characters is engaged in an ongoing physical behavior (jumping rope, playing the piano) that is a result of an action. In writing the scene, discover how this behavior presents a conflict to the other character.

ELEVEN: THE JOURNEY OF THE PLAY

A PLAY is a journey you take alone first, then with your collaborators, and ultimately with an audience. By the time this final passenger steps on board, your journey is in some sense over, while theirs is just beginning.

The journey you take as an artist is the subject of much of this book. It's the how-to part. If you complete your journey successfully, the audience stands a better chance of successfully completing theirs. Some effort will be required on their part (any art worthy of the name demands something of the viewer), but your hard work will guide the members of the audience, encourage them, intrigue them, motivate them to keep going. They will invest the time and energy and money it requires to take the journey because they will want to find out what happens at the end of it.

What do we mean by this journey? Where are we going in a play, and how do we get there? We could talk about the journey as a function of the basic playwriting tools. A character begins *here*, in a state of need and longing, unfulfilled, and he ends *there*, where he is at last satisfied, no longer empty, but full. No longer without, but with. Or, as in a tragedy, he has died, or gone mad, or destroyed himself in the attempt. He is not fulfilled in the conventional sense of the word, but his journey is certainly, clearly, over.

A journey, then, implies a change. The end of the journey is not the same as the beginning. One is in a different place. In a literal journey, it's a different physical place; in a play, also, the journey may be physical, but one hopes it's metaphorical as well. Lear journeys over a fair portion of his kingdom in the course of that play, ending his life near the cliffs of Dover; but he also travels from blind arrogance to the profound humility of self-knowledge.

As an audience, it is the change we seek. The journey isn't taken for its own sake. It's not a circular path, leading far out into an unknown region merely to see the sights, only to return to the same spot from where we started. (The modern existentialist plays like *Waiting for Godot* or *No Exit* challenge this notion, though they don't necessarily refute it.) We in the audience go on the journey not just for its intrinsic interest (though that's certainly part of it) but because, at the end, we arrive at some new place.

We have dreams because we need to work something out. Dreams, as we saw in Chapter One, use the same basic tools that plays use. In our dreams, we struggle to do something, and that doing has some result, some consequence, some event.

Just as in a dream, the main event of a play is its single most powerful moment of change. This change can assume different forms, occur in various ways. Being art, it's always open to interpretation. Different people will describe the nature of the change (and therefore of the event) in their own way.

For instance, I would propose that, for Lear, his event is the moment when his entire being is focused on the question of whether Cordelia's breath is misting up the tiny shard of mirror that he holds to her lips. If the mirror has a mist on it, she lives. If not, she is dead. Lear, at that moment, has finally managed to concern himself with something utterly outside his own ego. Moments later, he himself dies.

Literary critics often focus on the question of whether Lear dies knowing that Cordelia is dead or believing that she is alive. It's a perfectly good question for literary analysis. But dramatically speaking, what matters is simply that he has learned to care one way or the other. That, I believe, is what gives the play its final bit of structure, the sense of a journey completed.

Aside from these tools, about which you've already heard a lot, there are some other ways of thinking of your play's journey. In keeping with the gestalt approach, these ideas will relate to the tools, which you can apply to what you're about to discover.

TELL ME A STORY

The terms story and plot are often used interchangeably. For the average person, this overlapping doesn't matter much. Even in this book, I've used them somewhat loosely to mean more or less the same thing. But sometimes it's useful to make a distinction.

Story is a broad, loose term. E. M. Forster, in his book *Aspects of the Novel*, defines a story as "a narrative of events in their time-sequence." He gives an example: "The King died and then the Queen died." It's a neat little illustration, but Forster was speaking of novels, which themselves tend to be rather broad and loose. We playwrights may want a little more definition.

Here are some defining characteristics of a story.

A story may have a beginning far in the past (Hollywood has dubbed this part the backstory, but that's just jargon—it's story, pure and simple) and may not reach an end for a very long time afterward. The beginning and end points of a story may be arbitrary. Two people may choose to tell the same story, yet begin and end their versions at different moments.

A story may be familiar to many people, all of whom tell it with their own variations. A story may even take on the shape and import of a myth or legend shared by an entire culture, or by many different cultures. Different cultures, like different people, will have their own versions.

Let's take, for example, the story of Oedipus. The Oedipus story was a Greek legend. It was familiar to everyone in the Greek culture just as Santa Claus or Cinderella is familiar to us. No one knows where or when the myth originated, much less who might have been the first to tell it. There is undoubtedly an ur-myth of Oedipus, now long lost.

The story of Oedipus had many different parts and was rather long. In fact, the Oedipus myth was itself part of a much larger story concerning the history of the city of Thebes, its founding, and the many curses it suffered. As different people told this story over many hundreds of years, they began and ended it at different moments. Each storyteller had his own particular way of relating the events that occurred within it.

If they had wanted, some of these storytellers could have determined the beginning and end of the Oedipus story by saying that it starts at Oedipus's birth and ends with his death. But this too would have been arbitrary. Why not start with Oedipus's parents' birth, for instance? Why not end with his children's death?

So, as you can see, when Sophocles decided to write a play based on this story in the fifth century B.C., he had a lot of material he could choose from. He had already written at least one play based on the Oedipus story: *Antigone*, which occurs after Oedipus's death and concerns the death of his daughter. Much later in his life, he would write a third play, based on Oedipus's death, called *Oedipus at Colonus*. But on this occasion, Sophocles selected the moment in Oedipus's life when he confronts the truth that he has unwittingly killed his father and married his mother. He called it *Oedipus the King*.

In the course of *Oedipus the King*, we discover a certain amount of information about Oedipus's story previous to this play. We learn about his birth, his being left on the mountain to die as an infant, his rescue and upbringing by the King of Corinth, his flight from that city and his killing of a group of men on the highway, his solving of the Sphinx's riddle, his arrival in Thebes, and his subsequent crowning as king and marriage to the widowed queen. We also hear other things that happen in the story, events that are concurrent with the play but which occur offstage. These include, for instance, Jocasta's suicide by hanging and Oedipus's self-blinding. And we know at the end of the play that the broken, blinded Oedipus has been exiled from the city he loves.

None of these things happens onstage. Yet they are all part of the story of the play. What's more, Sophocles did not change any of these parts of Oedipus's story in order to fashion his play. These same essential events occur in the same time sequence. What, then, did he change?

THE PLOT THICKENS

Plot is a much narrower idea than story. In the same book, Forster also gives an illustration of plot which differs from that of story only by two words. But those words make an enormous difference: "The King died, and then the Queen died *of grief* [emphasis added]." The time sequence remains the same, but now our attention is drawn more to the fact that there is an effect brought about by a cause.

Aristotle bemoans the fashion of his day, which was to write what he termed episodic tragedies. In good plays, he believed, each episode (what we would call a scene) has the effect of causing the next one. The sequence of events should appear unalterable, creating the impression that their order is inevitable. By calling a play episodic he meant that there is none of this cause-and-effect relationship between the scenes. Instead, they are strung together in what appears an almost random order.

Today, we hear a lot about plays (and movies) being plot-driven or character-driven. In a general sense, we know what this means. Plot-driven work has a sequence of occurrences that stands out in relief more than the characters who make them happen. Character-driven means that the occurrences are not as noticeable as the rich and interesting characters.

Those definitions may be fine for critics. But I think they're dangerous for playwrights because, underneath, they don't describe how a play actually works. Characters, in fact, drive every play that ever was. As we know from Part One, a character needs something, he struggles to get it, and finally some kind of event occurs; the order in which these events occur we call the plot. In this sense, characters are the plot. It's an instance in which the gestalt concept comes in very handy, and the temptation to break that single idea into two can only lead to confusion. Many plays these days are episodic in the way that Aristotle meant it: lacking cause and effect. Further, they are episodic in, we could say, both a macro and a micro sense.

In the macro sense, there are plays in which the scenes have a clear time sequence (seasons change, people get older, develop diseases, etc.) but no cause-and-effect relationship. They're stories, yes, but not plots. Structurally, they're really more like vaudevilles, or blackout sketches dressed up to look like plays.

I once saw a play like this. At the time, it was enjoying some success. It had gotten positive reviews, had a good run off Broadway, and many people were talking about it. But I thought it was overpraised, and worse, praised for the wrong reasons. It certainly had some very funny lines and some startling images in the text, and it benefited from an excellent production that brought out these good qualities. But I didn't feel it was a play.

So I bought a copy and read it to satisfy my curiosity as

to what struck me as missing. I began with the unconscious assumption that the play had a plot. After all, things happened in it; time marched forward. In one scene it was morning, in the next it was evening, and so on. But I soon came to realize that what looked like a plot was really just a string of events. I could literally take two scenes of this play, read them in reverse order, and they made equally good sense.

There may have been other things I didn't like about the piece, had I taken the trouble to examine it more closely. But this struck me as the core of the matter. It was a play that assumed it had a plot, but in reality it had nothing of the kind. That might be fine, but I didn't sense I had experienced a drama because it was not true to the convention that it proposed for itself.

Most people didn't agree with me on this, though some playwright friends did—emphatically so. But at least I had satisfied my own sense of wanting to know why I felt the way I did. (The object, after all, is not to be right. There is no "right." The object is to understand one's own opinions.)

In the end, though, I felt my opinion vindicated by this playwright's next play, which also received a superb production but had the same essential problem: no plot, just a string of amusing/startling incidents. By now, though, people seemed to have caught on to the trick. It received poor reviews, poor word of mouth, and limped along to an early closing. I thought it was very much the same as the first play—just as good, but with the same problems. Perhaps it was a trick that could be pulled only once.

An episodic play in the macro sense, then, contains scenes that neither result from those preceding them nor cause the ones that follow. The incidents or behavior of the characters in Scene One do not significantly influence the occurrences or the behavior of the characters in Scene Two. The event at the end of Scene Three, for example, does not influence the way the characters behave in Scene Four. Except for the change of season and the fact that the characters are a year older, one could easily rearrange the order of scenes and they would continue to make as much psychological sense. For a play to be dramatic, characters must change not just once at the end of a play, but many times, in many subtle ways, throughout its course.

There are certain plays that do not follow a linear chronology but which do have plots—often very good ones. Harold Pinter's *Betrayal*, which reverses the order of time, is one. *Six Degrees of Separation* jumps back and forth in time, as does *Death of a Salesman*, and *Sight Unseen* by Donald Margulies. *Sight Unseen* seems particularly elegant to me. It has significant cause-and-effect relationships between the scenes. While the reordering seems random at first look, it is, in fact, very skillfully done. It allows us to perceive the cause and effect in a new, illuminating light. It's a good example of a playwright coming up with his own convention (in this case, a temporal one) and making it work through consistency and close attention to detail.

In general, though, I think plotlessness is a serious problem in writing plays, one which is common in beginning playwrights. It wouldn't be so bad, except that it seems very clear that many playwrights who are writing plotless drama intend to be writing otherwise. They end up with a plotless play by mistake.

This doesn't mean you have to come up with a play that's heavily plotted (another phrase for plot-driven). In this definition we're using here, even Chekhov uses plots. Not as Ibsen does, certainly. But as we've seen, plot is a question of cause and effect, not necessarily a complicated sequence of mistaken identities and narrow escapes and abrupt changes of fortune.

As a means of studying the problem, it's useful to examine plays in which cause and effect are used well. The great plays of literature are a good place to start: *Oedipus the King*, *Hamlet*, *Hedda Gabler*, *A Streetcar Named Desire*, *Death of a Salesman*. Or choose excellent modern plays like *The Homecoming*, *Plenty*, or *The Real Thing*. Because of the manner in which these plays are written, the order of scenes seems to be inevitable. They aren't inevitable at all, of course. Those plays might have been written a thousand other ways and still be magnificent. But the impression is one of inevitability, that one scene has caused the next.

I mentioned that we could think of episodic plays in a micro as well as a macro sense. In the micro sense, the lack of cause and effect is within each scene. This happens when characters don't listen to each other, ignoring the pleas, demands, insinuations, etc., of each other. If your play is to have plot in the micro sense, your characters must listen to each other. They don't have to respond logically. People don't always respond logically in life and they don't have to in plays either (< pp. 160–61). But they can acknowledge in some way that the other character has done or said something. You can show us that actions and behavior have a consequence.

I sometimes hear a student tell me, "My play is about how this particular character *doesn't* listen," and that this should excuse them from this particular rule. This is a fallacy. Not listening to someone is, first of all, not an action. It's a state of being. It is passive. Trying not to listen may be an action. And if a particular character is trying not to listen, so be it. But in doing so, he will in fact be listening—or at least hearing. In order to be dramatic, what he hears must have some effect on him. It must influence him in some way, no matter how subtle, causing him to behave differently than he has before.

We can find a good illustration of this in improvisational theater. When two actors are doing an acting improv, one of the basic rules is that if the first actor says, "There's a dinosaur out on the front lawn," the second is not allowed to say, "No, there isn't." The second actor must accept the reality as presented by the first. The second actor may say, "Yes, and it's dead. I just buried it." But she is not allowed to deny the reality of anything that another actor has said.

It's possible to take this rule too literally in writing your play. Obviously there may be times when a character simply doesn't listen. But the spirit of the improvisation rule applies to playwriting. Characters need to listen to each other. They cannot simply block out and ignore the fact that the other character has something to say.

This micro cause-and-effect phenomenon can even, in theory, be brought down to the level of the relationship between one line in a play and the next. If your characters are really listening to one another, each line will have an effect on the next. It will have some influence—whether large or small, obvious or subtle—on the line that follows it.

I wouldn't recommend thinking about this while you're actually writing the play. You could go crazy. But the idea, like the others in this chapter, is at the foundation of the play's journey. It's something to aspire to in your writing, something you want to ultimately make second nature. In life things often happen that don't matter, they don't seem of any consequence. That's the mystery of life. In plays, things should matter; they should always have an effect. That's the function of drama.

In the discussion of story, we saw that a story has no beginning or end. Plot is a small slice of that story. It is that portion which has been deliberately selected by the playwright. This is true whether the story is a well-known tale or one you made up entirely in your head.

Plot is what happens on the stage. Story is what happens both onstage and offstage—before the play begins, after it ends, and everything that happens concurrent to it but which we don't happen to see.

In his *Interpretation of Dreams*, Freud claimed that the power of *Oedipus the King* to move audiences as much today as it did 2,500 years ago "can only be that its effect [lies] . . . in the particular nature of the material." With all due respect to Dr. Freud, that statement betrays a serious ignorance of dramaturgy and a profound disrespect for the skill of Sophocles' art. Others have tried writing their versions of the same segment of the Oedipus story. Seneca, Voltaire, and some twentieth-century writers too. None of them have matched Sophocles' skill in creating a plot that delivers that story in such a forceful way.

In the course of creating the plot of *Oedipus the King*, Sophocles did make some changes to the story. The most notable of these changes forms the basis of the play's action itself. In earlier versions of the myth, Oedipus was happily going on with his life when, through no act of his own, the truth of his parentage happened to be revealed to him. In

Sophocles' version, Oedipus makes his discovery as a result of his own relentless pursuit of the truth concerning the death of King Laius. That's an enormous change that profoundly affects the way we experience the occurrences in the story. It creates a cause-and-effect relationship between Oedipus's action and the result it produces. And what a thrilling result it is! Sophocles, in many ways, taught us all how to write plays.

Today, we no longer base our plays on well-known stories as the Greeks or Shakespeare did. For them, the stories already existed and they needed only to create—to select, to derive—a plot. Our stories tend to be more personal—they're either autobiographical or a manifestation of some mysterious portion of our inner psyche (< Chapter 9). Therefore you probably have a different kind of work to do than those early playwrights. You have to create both the story and the plot.

Begin with whatever works for you. Perhaps you like to start by writing the play itself before you know any of the background. That's fine. But at some point you'll almost certainly want to know more about what has happened before the play begins, as well as some of what is occurring offstage concurrent with the action onstage. You may even be curious about what transpires after the play is over.

Go ahead and fill yourself in on this information. Only remember not to confuse the results with plot. What you will have come up with is story. Don't make the mistake that just because something occurred in the past or is happening offstage during the play you must include it in the plot. What you include in the plot is up to you. You will make the decision by selecting those incidents that you believe have a crucial influence on—or are influenced by—the surrounding scenes.

SUSPENSE

There's nothing like a good thriller. You're on the edge of your seat, anxious over the fate of the characters, chewing your nails over what might be about to happen. Thrillers are known and enjoyed for the great suspense that they create in the audience. When they're good, they're not so much journeys as roller-coaster rides—exciting, mesmerizing, utterly engaging.

But it's good to remember that suspense is not just the province of thrillers. All plays—comedies, dramas, musicals— can make use of it. Suspense is, really, just another way of making us wonder about that basic aspect of storytelling: what happens next.

We're going to look at suspense here for that very reason. It's part of any good story and any good plot, regardless of whether the play is a thriller, or even whether average audience members would consider the play suspenseful.

Suspense is created in two basic ways.

The first may seem counterintuitive. Suspense can in fact be created by providing more information to the audience, not less.

Alfred Hitchcock, who knew a thing or two about suspense, once used something like the following example to illustrate this idea: a man walks into a coffee shop carrying a briefcase, which he sets down beside him as he drinks a quick cup. Then he puts some change on the counter and walks out of the coffee shop, forgetting the briefcase as he goes.

There's not much here to hold our interest.

But add information to this scenario and watch what happens: previous to this scene, we observe the same man placing a time bomb into the briefcase. Now we watch him enter the coffee shop, set down the briefcase, and bolt down the coffee. Leaving the change on the counter, he walks out, leaving the camera to linger on the briefcase.

By adding one bit of information, we've added a lot of suspense.

Many inexperienced writers make the mistake of thinking that by omitting crucial information they are making the play suspenseful. "It's more mysterious this way," is a common explanation. These playwrights don't understand that what to them seems mysterious to an audience appears a confusing muddle. Mystery and suspense, on the other hand, are clear as a bell.

Suspense may also be created another way: by forcing the audience to wonder whether the character will accomplish his goal. This is a manipulation not of information but of action.

In his delicious thriller, *Sleuth*, Anthony Shaffer makes good use of this method in the first act. What exactly is the wily Andrew up to with Milo, whom he has invited out to his country estate? I won't give anything away about the play (that would be a crime), but suffice it to say there aren't many people who have escaped this cunning work without getting caught up in the iron net of "What is Andrew actually doing with Milo?"

Again, the rule can apply not only to thrillers, but to any play. It's just another way of thinking about the power of dramatic action. What does Willy Loman really want from Biff? It's a mystery through much of *Death of a Salesman*. We're in suspense about it until their climactic scene, in which Willy exclaims in wonder, "Biff—he likes me!" In *Six Degrees of Separa-*

tion, what does Ouisa want from Paul? For a long time, we know there's something, but not until the end do we discover her yearning for something and someone "to believe in."

❦

EXERCISE 8

1. Story: Find a play you admire. Write out ten things you know about the story of the play but which do not occur in the plot.

2. Plot: Examine the plot of a play you admire. Try to determine how the characters change—growing or disintegrating—over the course of the plot. Now try to arrange the scenes in another order while still retaining the sense of the play. Or rearrange the sequence of scenes and see how it fails to make any sense. Or read the scenes of *Betrayal* by Harold Pinter or *Sight Unseen* by Donald Margulies in chronological order; then read the play again in the order chosen by the playwright.

PART THREE

DEALING WITH
PROBLEMS

MOSS HART sat down with the great George S. Kaufman and began work on their first collaboration, *Once in a Lifetime*. Hart had already written a draft of the play, and Kaufman had now come on board as co-writer. A producer put them together hoping that Kaufman would give the play the structure it needed to become truly wonderful. He did. But not without some effort.

In their first meeting, Hart watched eagerly as Kaufman's pencil "suddenly darted down onto the paper and moved swiftly along the page, crossing out a line here and there, making a large X through a solid speech, fusing two long sentences into one short one, indicating by an arrow or a question mark the condensation or transference of a section of dialogue so that its point was highlighted and its emphasis sharpened."

Hart was awestruck. He had never known a person could

do such brilliant work on a script so quickly, so surely. He loved Kaufman's rewrites and told him so immediately. "The scene really works now, doesn't it?" Kaufman, already the battle-scarred soldier of the theater, was gentle in his reply: "No, it doesn't work at all. I thought the cuts would show you why it *wouldn't* work."*

Rewriting is hard work; there's no doubt about it. It's probably the single largest problem the play will offer you.

So let's suppose you've written your play. Or if you're in a class, maybe you've written your first complete scene. In either case, we'll assume you've completed something that has a beginning, middle, and end. You've concluded that part of the journey.

Your first assignment? Enjoy it! A lot of people never get this far.

And enjoy it while you can, because there's a good chance the work isn't over. Playwrights often do much of their work in the rewrites. It's true that some rewrite as they go, and some rewrite in their heads before they put finger to keyboard. But these are usually experienced writers who have made their craft second nature. We aren't talking about those people right now. We're talking about the majority of writers, and certainly the majority of new writers, who still have a lot to learn about what writing a play is all about.

You'll recall that the Roman poet Horace quipped that one should leave a poem on the shelf for eight years. Only then could the author know if it was any good. There's some-

---

*From Moss Hart's autobiography *Act One*, published by Random House.

thing to that. One thing is sure: to do a good rewrite, you need perspective. So take a little time. Maybe a week is enough, maybe you need a month or even more. However long it may be, take the time you need. Do other things. Write another play. Read a few plays (> p. 287, Read!). Go see some plays (> p. 290, Production Versus Play). Do whatever you need to do in order to come back to your first draft and look at it as a stranger would—with that same dispassionate eye. After all, that's how an audience will look at it, and you're wise to get there ahead of them.

Then, when you're ready, here are some ways to bring your play into its fully realized form.

DOCTOR, SPARE THAT KNIFE

I'm going to risk repeating myself right now because it's so important that you not forget one, basic idea. It won't even be the last time I admonish you on this subject, so you might as well get used to it!

Your first rule in rewriting must be that if you like the work, if it is what you want it to be, leave it alone. Don't start applying the tools or any other ideas for their own sake. As Duke Ellington said, "If it sounds good, it is good." Or as John Cheever, the short-story writer, used to say in his classes, the most important criterion for measuring a work's worth is: "Is it interesting?"

Take it from them. As you consider your work, the first questions to ask yourself are, "Do I like it? Does it say what I want it to say? Is it what I want it to be?"

If the play holds your interest, if it is compelling to you, if you feel it lives, then you've met the most important criteria. All other questions are secondary. Should you ask others the same questions? Of course (> p. 231, Feedback). But only after first satisfying yourself, and only to help form your own opinion. It's your play: you take responsibility for it.

Some people are not good critics of their own work. They simply find it nearly impossible to see the flaws in it. Or they're so overly self-critical that they don't see its strengths. Either case is a problem. Constructive self-criticism is a necessary skill to develop.

It's not good enough for you to be self-deprecating and say, "I just don't know whether what I do is any good." By saying that, you're abdicating a primary function of the artist. Besides, it's probably not true. I'll bet you do know what you think of your work—if only on a gut level. Chances are you're either being modest because you like it quite a lot, or you're embarrassed to admit you can't stand what you've done. Either way, face up to your feelings. They're one of your greatest assets in writing your play.

Try to be balanced in your assessment of your play. Step back from it. View it as you think others will view it. At the same time, apply your own sensibility to judging it. Use your own standards and your own feelings, even while filtering them through another's eyes.

If you don't like what you see and hear, if it doesn't work, if you are dissatisfied, then use the tools to ask yourself why. Is it because there is no clear action in the scene? Is it because there is no conflict? Or is there action and conflict, but no event? Are the beats unclear? And so forth. If you grow frustrated building your house with your bare hands, pick up the hammer and some nails. That's what they're there for.

Here are some ways to wield them.

MAKE YOUR CHOICE

I once began writing a one-act play called *Levels of Perception*. I wrote a draft of the opening of the play and liked a lot of it. Though it was only a fragment, the characters seemed interesting. The situation concerned two painters, one an aging abstract expressionist and the other a young installation artist. Two very different camps in the art world. That intrigued me. Also, the dialogue had a nice feel to it.

On the other hand, something was not quite happening for me. The indefinable sense of moment, of two characters immediately engaged with one another, was weak. And, most troubling, I was having difficulty pressing forward with the rest of the play.

These are the feelings to pay attention to. It is just such feelings that should be the reason, your only reason, to think about a rewrite. If you rely on others, you will almost surely find it impossible to rewrite well despite your best intentions. Until you internalize the dissatisfaction with your play, you'll simply be taking shots in the dark in trying to solve its problems. Trust your own gut instincts (with, perhaps, the guidance of the opinions of others) to tell you that something is amiss. Then—and only then—try to find out what that something is.

So I began to look at what was wrong with the piece.

Everything seemed right. I thought the action was clear, as was the conflict. While the event was a little weak, this might be right since the play had only just begun. Anything too big would be inappropriate so early in the play.

I gave the fragment to a friend of mine, Ted, and asked him what he thought of it. We talked about it after he'd had a chance to read it over a few times.

He began by asking about all the things in the play that I had considered givens—things that I never remembered choosing to be in the scene, though on some level of consciousness I obviously had selected them. To me, they were basic assumptions. They seemed intrinsic to the scene, unchangeable.

A few examples:

1. The scene took place on a terrace in back of an artist's home in the Hamptons on Long Island.
2. The scene had two characters—Alan, the twenty-something installation artist, and Bert, a man in his sixties, whose identity was something of a secret to both Alan and the audience (and, for that matter, to me). In spite of Alan's attempts to find out more, we only knew Bert's name and that he had some sort of friendship with a third character, Gene, a famous abstract expressionist painter.
3. It took place on a bright summer's day.
4. Alan had just arrived in this place a few minutes before the scene begins.

There were many more givens, but that's a good sample.

I asked Ted what he was getting at. Why was he asking

about all these givens? After all, I wanted to talk about what was wrong with the scene dramatically, not whether it took place on a bright summer's day.

Ted admitted he didn't know exactly what he was getting at. "But," he said, "I've got a hunch that since we can't find any other problems with the scene, the real issue may be with some of these underlying choices."

Choices.

In writing plays, we make them all the time. Literally. Everything is a choice, whether conscious or not.

That's what Ted was saying to me: don't make the assumption that some element of the play must be what it is. Maybe it was an unconscious choice that, upon sober reflection, might be better if it were different.

I went back into the scene and considered all these choices we'd talked about. In doing so, I realized that the choice of Bert had been made for no particular reason. He had simply come to me that way.

Now, a lot of things come to me without my realizing it—and that's fine. Many unconscious choices are right just as they are, as we know from the impulse exercises and as we'll see further in the course of this chapter. (Many conscious choices are also fine as they are.) If you've examined the choice and it feels right (that is, you've decided it's what you want it to be), then leave it alone. But when something feels wrong, unfulfilled, or murky, or uninteresting, make sure the choice has been examined to see whether it's working.

It began to dawn on me, for example, that Bert was a choice that wasn't working.

I realized that, first, there was no reason why he should

be a man in his sixties. For that matter, there was no reason he should be a man. I soon saw that if Bert were a woman, she could be married to Gene.

So that's what I did. I called her Sally and made her Gene's wife. Now she had an immediate relationship to Alan, which was to protect Gene against Alan's exploitative designs on him. (I could also have left Bert as a man in his sixties, and made him Gene's lover. While this would have technically created the same dynamic, I couldn't make it work for me.)

The scene suddenly took off. Alan and Sally's relationship is now clear from the start, meaning not only their feelings about each other but also the action and conflict. Before, Alan's action had been simply to find out who Bert is. Now Alan wants to get Sally's permission to go to Gene with his idea for a co-installation. That's more specific and, to me, much more interesting. Sally isn't about to give this to him, and she (unlike Bert) has the power to say no. And while Alan and Sally still don't know each other at the top of the scene, they know who the other is. They know they matter to each other, and Sally particularly matters to Alan.

I often use this example in workshops. When the two versions are read aloud, most people agree that the scene is better now. But some don't. A few are in between—they think that in some ways it's better, but there were things in the original that they liked better. I respect all those opinions. If I were actively working on this play, I'd listen to them and take them into consideration. But ultimately, I would have to make the choice myself, and I would make the choice that satisfied me and no one else.

And that's what I did. Never feel obligated to please others. Be your own toughest critic, and then satisfy yourself. As an artist, that's all you can do. Anything else will be an endless, not very merry chase to please an audience which, as a group, will never be happy. There will always be someone who doesn't like your play, after all. Not everybody liked Shakespeare in his day, though it didn't seem to bother him much. He did the best he could and left it at that.

By questioning very basic choices—the things you may be thinking of as givens—you can often find a new way of approaching your play that will begin to make it work. But you have to be willing to examine everything. Nothing is sacred, and nothing too trifling to be overlooked.

This should be your first step in rewriting. Let's go on to some more.

FEEDBACK

I've just suggested how important it is that you listen to your own gut about your play and make your own choices. But I also allowed that you should be open to other opinions. That may sound like a contradiction to you, so let me expand.

Ultimately, the play is yours. You must do with it as you will. That is the role of the artist. Very few plays that I have ever heard of, which were worth anything at all, were written by committee. For better or worse, a play is the vision of an individual.*

In an ideal world, we would all be able to step back from

---

*You'll think immediately of my reference to Kaufman and Hart. There are always exceptions to the rule, of course. In such cases, the two partners manage to conceive a single vision, even if they are two people.

our work (in less than eight years, one hopes) and look at it with an objective, critical eye. In that ideal world, our critical eye would have a direct line to the impulse that gave rise to the work in the first place. The critic and the creator in you would work hand in hand, as one.

But we do not, as you've probably noticed, live in an ideal world. So, while you alone must be completely and solely responsible for that creator in you, you can also seek out a little help for the critic within. That's where other people come in.

Show your work, once you're ready, to people you trust to be not only smart but honest. Such people may be your friends, but sometimes good friends find it harder to be honest than people you know less well. You might choose to have a reading of the play and tell your friends to bring their friends. That way you'll have both strangers and friends to give feedback. Theater professionals are good, but "civilians" can be very useful too. After all, they will be your audience, ultimately.

By honest I don't mean that you should encourage people to tear your play down. But they should be willing to speak the truth about the things they didn't like as much as the things they did.

They might need help with doing this, and you should encourage them. Let them know repeatedly that you're interested in what they really think. Show that you're genuinely eager to hear their response. Assure them that you won't take any criticism personally, that you would consider it a genuine favor to know the bottom line.

This is truly important. On numerous occasions I've seen

a playwright walk away from a reading thinking that everyone loved her play. And then behind her back, "to protect her feelings," the real opinions begin to come out. Her feelings are spared, sure. But at the expense of the play.

Don't be that person who gets her feelings spared. Show your friends, and anyone else who will give you helpful feedback, that your interest is not in your own feelings but in the work.

So let's assume that everyone in the room is being honest with you. That's great, but it's not enough. You also need to know what to do with all this honesty.

For instance, you need to know which questions to ask. I can't think of anything worse than those feedback sessions in which the playwright is not allowed to speak. The idea behind this is to prevent him from defending his work. Fair enough. A playwright who is busy defending his work isn't listening to the criticism. So let's be sure that the playwright isn't being defensive. But at the same time, let's give him credit for knowing a thing or two about his own play. Let's presume that he has some questions that need answering. Let's allow him to respond to the feedback so that he can dig deeper into the responses he's hearing.

There are an infinite number of questions you might ask. Each play suggests its own unique issues, so it would be foolish to suggest any specific questions here. But I can give you a guideline for the kind of questions you'll want to propose:

1. What do you think my play is about? (You're asking them about your thematic statement here. By the time the

first draft is finished, you should be able to come up with one. Check to see if their answers correspond to your own.)

2. What parts were you interested in? (Start with getting positive feedback. It will help cushion some of the rough stuff later.)

3. What parts were you not interested in?

4. Can you say why you weren't interested? (Their reasons may be idiosyncratic, such as, "That scene has a plumber in it, and plumbers really bore me onstage." That won't be very useful to you. But if the answer addresses the play's dramaturgy, the reason may be very useful indeed, such as, "I could tell what the character was doing, but I couldn't tell why." In that case, for instance, you might consider whether the action was clear.)

5. Was anything confusing or somehow not clear to you? Was anything unresolved? (Again, you'll need to separate the useful from the idiosyncratic.)

Ask them, and persist in getting a truthful answer to your questions. I find that many times people will literally ignore the playwright's agenda and go right into talking about what they want to talk about. More times than I can count I've asked a question like, "Was it clear at the end of the scene why she walks out on him?" And someone will respond by saying something like, "I was confused by the next scene, when she has died and he has started to see someone new . . . "

Of course, people should feel free to address anything they like. They may have something very useful to say on an aspect of your play that you had never contemplated asking about. But you must insist they also answer your specific needs. The discussion is in the service of you and your play, not of them and their preferences. They're doing you a favor by listening and responding, but it's only a favor if they address your concerns.

Don't feel obligated to answer any comment that begins with "Why did you . . . ?" Who cares why you did anything? The fact is you did it—and you may have no idea why. Your entire play, in theory, may have been written strictly from impulse, without any conscious choices. Harold Pinter is known to write this way, and he is famous for refusing to discuss the "Why did you . . . ?" question. He is often accused of being unnecessarily mysterious and deliberately secretive about the meaning of his work. But I suspect he simply doesn't know why he made certain choices. They were, in a very real sense, made for him; that is, by his subconscious.

You, to one degree or another, may find yourself in the same boat as Pinter. Not a bad boat to be in. If so, ignore the "Why did you . . . ?" question and turn it back on whoever posed it by saying, "How do you feel about the fact that I *did* do it that way? Was it confusing? Interesting? Intriguing but ultimately unsatisfying?"

There are exceptions to this, as always. If you really feel that by explaining your motives you can make things clearer to yourself and your respondents, then certainly feel free. But in general, a feedback session is for people to give you their reaction to the choices you've made, not a chance to demand an explanation for how you arrived at them.

There will be times when all your respondents seem to have a problem with a particular aspect of your play—a character, a scene, an event, etc. You must pay particular attention to this, though not to their specific criticisms. Simply make note that they are all talking about the same aspect.

For instance, I once got a wide variety of feedback on a character. Some said she was too unsympathetic. Some said she was too nice. Some said they were confused. Some said she was too clear—overwritten.

One central thing I took away from all of this was that there was something wrong with the character, even if the chances were slim that it was one of the problems offered by my respondents. In the end, it was up to me to figure out what the real problem was. In this particular case, I finally realized that nothing was wrong with her at all, not in the senses that these people had been suggesting. It was her situation that was unclear; her action was not viable. I gave her something positive to want and that solved everything. In the next draft, I heard no more complaints about her.

But my essential point in using this example is that I listened to the fact that almost everyone seemed to have some criticism to make of her. Just because everyone's criticism was different didn't mean I could have the luxury of claiming she was simply deliciously complex. That would have been fooling myself.

There will also be times when you're not ready to get feedback from people. Too often, writers ask for opinions before they've formed one of their own. I have often gone to a reading of the first draft of a play, or of an unfinished fragment, after which the writer in effect announces: "I have no idea what I have here. Would someone please tell me?"

Sometimes this is the only recourse the playwright has, but I believe this method to be overused. It's a danger of our developmental process, which has encouraged playwrights to take on a passive role in their own work, as though we were idiot savants. "Tell me, someone, what I've done here."

If you really find yourself in that position, fine. We all get utterly confused once in a while. Use the reading, or the playwrights unit (> p. 306, Classes, Playwrights Units, Advanced Degrees), or workshop, and the resulting feedback to tell you what you've wrought. But in general, I favor your sticking with the piece until it begins to make sense to you. Then you can have a reading and ask pointed, intelligent questions. You're a lot more likely to get pointed, intelligent answers.

Instead of offering genuine criticism, which is what we've been discussing until now, people seem to love to give playwrights suggestions about their work. Looking on the bright side, it's part of the participatory spell that theater throws. An audience feels involved, part of the event. And indeed you want them to feel that way. Particularly at a reading, or when you're openly asking for their response. But that doesn't mean they should give suggestions.

It's true that sometimes the suggestions are right on the money. Usually that's when the person has taken the trouble to grasp and understand your impulse. He has gotten inside your head and knows where you're going and what you're trying to do. In such a case, the suggestion may be helpful.

The problem with many suggestions, though, is that they're not based on that kind of inside thinking. Often, a person makes a suggestion simply because that's the play he would write if he were doing it. But he's not. You are. You need to make sure that anytime you're considering taking a suggestion, it's one that's in support of your play, the one you're writing. Otherwise, it's going to take you down a long, dead-end trail into the deep dark woods of confusion. In a worst-case scenario, it will be not just a waste of time, but can seriously threaten your grasp of the whole play itself.

My least favorite criticism begins with the phrase, "I didn't believe it when . . . " It is not the audience's job to sit in judgment of what they believe and what they don't. For one thing, it's arbitrary. It's easy for them to shrug their shoulders and say, "I didn't believe it." Man kills his father and unknowingly marries his mother? I don't believe it. Man spends month after month trying to justify and then commit the murder of his uncle to avenge his father's murder? I don't believe it. A woman walks out of her comfortable marriage just because of a misunderstanding over a letter? I don't believe it. A salesman commits suicide because he's disappointed in himself and his sons? I don't believe it.

See how easy?

And for another thing, it's arrogant. "I don't believe it," therefore "it" has no validity. I don't believe it, therefore I don't have to give "it" a second thought. I'm not going to let the horses even get out of the starting gate before I call off the whole race. With the casual flip of a mental switch, I refuse to acknowledge the worthiness of this work. Done, over, next play please.

"I don't believe it" is the enemy of art. If one is going to have an artistic experience, one better start by deciding that, no matter what, one is going to believe it. We suspend our disbelief, and we do it willingly—because if we don't we've locked ourselves outside the room where the art is happening.

If a person wants to lock himself out, fine. But the problem, then, is not that he doesn't believe, it's that he refuses to participate.

Now, this is not to say that people have to like what they see, or find it interesting. That's another matter altogether. And I think that's what people are trying to say with "I don't believe it." They're really saying: I can't accept it, or it's off-putting, or offensive, or difficult, or just plain dull. Any of these feelings are perfectly valid responses to art. But they are purely subjective.

When I was young, I used to go to the plays with Henry, a smart, experienced man of the theater. Once, on the way out of a show we'd seen, we agreed it wasn't a terribly good play. Partway into the first act was a scene in which a man's mother has died just moments before the beginning of the play. The man's girlfriend, whom he has known only a short time, arrives to comfort him. He comes on to her sexually, wants to make love to her with his mother lying dead in the next room. The woman refuses. It was a relatively short scene and the play went on from there.

Afterward, we were laughing about how awful the piece was, and I brought up this scene. "That was so unbelievable," I said, "when he started to kiss her and he wanted to make love to her right then."

"Why unbelievable?" Henry asked.

"People don't do things like that," I scoffed.

"The play's not about 'people,' " he said. "It's about this particular man. Who's to say this man wouldn't do such a thing? I say he would do it, might do it. In fact, he did do it."

"Then you believed that?" I asked.

"I believe everything I see in plays," he said.

"But you didn't like it, did you?"

"I hated it. It was awful, boring, silly. But I believed every word."

Henry went on to say that it was a fact of clinical psychology that people often found themselves highly aroused after the death of a loved one. But that wasn't his main point, which was that even if this weren't a well-observed phenomenon the playwright is still allowed to write it and expect us to believe it.

"He may not be writing naturalistically for one thing," Henry said. "Maybe the play is symbolic. You wouldn't condemn all the crazy goings-on in *The Ghost Sonata* for not being realistic would you?"

"No, but this wasn't *The Ghost Sonata*!" I complained. "It was obviously meant to be a realistic piece."

"Then the problem isn't that the scene was unbelievable, but that the author was confusing his conventions. He led the audience to expect one thing, then gave them something out of the blue, and then tried to return us to his original set of expectations. It doesn't make that sexual advance any less believable on its own terms. People do such things. In fact, people do much stranger things than that."

That made me think. But still, I pressed on. "What's the difference between saying that I didn't believe it, and saying that it was confusing?"

"Huge difference," Henry said, "especially to a playwright like yourself. You have to do rewrites, don't you?"

"Of course. All the time."

"If you listen to people who tell you they don't believe what's in your play, you'll never finish it. Because there will always be some guy in the second row of the audience ready to stick his hand into the air and say, 'I didn't believe it.' And the minute you make the changes to make him happy, the woman over in the fifth row will raise her hand and say now she doesn't believe it. You could go on like that forever."

"Then what's the answer? They're always going to say that. How do I get around it?"

"By cutting the Gordian knot. Instead of worrying about making your writing believable, worry about making it interesting. The problem with that play we saw tonight was that it was so dull, such a muddle. If a play is interesting enough, most people won't give any thought to whether they believe it or not. The issue won't even enter their heads. They'll be too busy paying attention to the play. There will always be some nitpickers, of course, but you'll never please them anyway, so you might as well write them off right now."

I've never forgotten what Henry told me, and it hasn't failed me yet.

FOCUS GROUP

I once worked with a writer, Travis, who had begun a rewrite of his play. The play is about Daryl, a young man who depends heavily on his father for guidance and counseling and support, yet also, underneath, resents these same things when they are given. In the end of the play, he finally resolves the problem, breaking free of the dependence on his father, while learning to accept his father's love in a healthy way.

The first scene of the play takes place in the waiting room of an admissions office of a prestigious school that Daryl is eager to attend. At the moment, though, he's panicking over actually going into the office. He knows he needs to go inside in order to have any hope of being admitted, yet the fear is overwhelming. He also knows that he's being neurotic. He's conscious of the irrational fear he's experiencing, aware that he needs his father's help to get him through the door.

The basic dramatic structure of this scene seemed quite plain to me. It also seemed effective, particularly since the situation of the entire play was encapsulated here in miniature. Daryl wants his father's help (action), but his father wants him to do it on his own (conflict). Ultimately his father gives him the help he seeks (event). Yet this dynamic is precisely the problem that creates the resentment in Daryl, which is the subject of the play. It was ingenious.

Unfortunately, although we had talked about the scene in the terms I've just described, Travis had not actually written it that way. In his first draft, Daryl sat passively waiting for his father to convince him to go into the office. It defeated the whole point of the play, which was that Daryl first sought out his father's help, then later resented it.

Even more unfortunate, Travis was having a very hard time rewriting the scene this way, though he knew that's what he wanted to do. He tried several times, and each time the scene veered off into some course other than this very simple and effective one. In one version, Daryl wanted to go into the office without his father's help, thereby ignoring the central action; in another, the father offered help right away and thereby neutralized the conflict; in yet another, Daryl talked about his feelings of resentment instead of pursuing the action of this moment. There were still more versions I don't remember. Some of them were actually fine as isolated scenes. But none of them were the play that Travis wanted to write. None of them, he and I agreed, were nearly as effective as the one in his head.

The problem was that Travis wasn't focusing on the play that he had decided to write. He kept allowing other, easier versions to emerge. Versions that didn't address the hard reality that Daryl is a confused, frightened character, full of contradictions.

Is it that Travis identified with Daryl so closely that it made him afraid to write the scene honestly? Was he so close to the material that he instinctively pulled back when it came time to step up to the plate? Very possibly. And there might have been other reasons why it was proving difficult for him. There are always a myriad of difficulties that keep us from doing the kind of work we ought to be doing on our plays. It hardly matters what they are. Or if it does matter, then only to your therapist.

As a playwright your concern is simple. You need to focus on and then commit to the version of the play that you have decided is the one you need to write.

After you've examined the choices you've made and gotten feedback from others, it's time to really think about what exactly you're going to do with this rewrite. You have to ask yourself the basic question: Why am I rewriting this play? Or: What do I hope to accomplish in this rewrite? In a word, you have to focus like a laser beam on what your play is about, and once you are settled on that question, hew to that course of action.

Travis finally, after several weeks of fits and starts, did just that. It was a terrific scene and the beginning of a terrific play.

STICK TO YOUR GUNS

And finally, let's suppose that you've stayed close to the one true path of your play. Stick to it. Don't let well-intentioned but wrongheaded people try to pry you away from it.

In *Levels of Perception*, I wrote a line at the end of the play which began: "I told him, let me save a few. *One*, even. They were gorgeous. Like Matisse . . . " The character of Sally was describing some artwork that her husband, Gene, the aging abstract expressionist, had painted but then destroyed.

The question of the play was: Did he destroy them because he suffered from dementia and had lost his ability to see their beauty, or had he painted them while suffering from dementia then destroyed them in a moment of clarity?

Until this moment in the play, we've only heard his side of the story. He says he destroyed them because they were poor, second-rate work. But now, at the very end of the play, Sally comes forward to another character, and we get a new version: she thought they were beautiful. She hated to see him destroy them, but she loves and respects Gene enough that she allowed him to follow his own wishes.

In its proper context, which I can only suggest here, that line of hers expressed the ambiguity of our relationship to art—that some people love the things that others hate. There is no objective truth, no final referee. There are just our opinions, and the line said exactly that. That line was why I wrote the play, and I got a lot of grief about it. People didn't like it. For one thing, they didn't believe it: "I don't believe she would have let him burn them." I was told I should change the line. "She should say that she actually saved one or two of the paintings." Or, "She should say she thought they were second-rate too." Anything but what she says—which is that she loved them, and she let him burn them.

But that line was the truth for me, and I refused to change it. I've never regretted it. It became, in production, the line most commented on, the line many people said made the play for them. Even if the opposite were true, I would not regret my choice to leave the line as it was.

As always, there is a flip side to this. There will be favorite lines that you probably should, in fact, cut. For instance, my student Travis might decide somewhere in his play to write a line in which Daryl says to his father, "I depend heavily on you for guidance and counseling and support, but underneath, I also resent these things when you give them to me. I have to resolve this problem and break free of my dependence on you, while learning to accept your love in a healthy way."

That's a line that would need to be cut, not because it isn't true, but because, if Travis writes the play well, the play itself will be speaking that sentiment in every scene. The line would be redundant. (And if the play itself, as a whole, doesn't already say it, putting it into the play in such a bald way won't solve anything.)

This is different than Sally's line that the paintings were gorgeous. That line was needed in order to round out a new and final perspective in the play, to give the audience information they had not yet received: this artist's wife had an opinion that was unsettling. It prevented us from getting away from the play too easily, unscathed.

There is, of course, a flip side of that argument. A line that I think we would all agree should stay in the play would be Blanche DuBois's exclamation that she wants not reality but magic. One could argue, certainly, that the entire text of *Streetcar*, every word Blanche utters and every gesture she makes, indicates that this is precisely what she wants. It's not as if we don't know that about her anyway. Yet we'd miss that line terribly if it weren't there. It doesn't provide a missing bit of information, but neither does it stop the play cold when it is uttered. It's one of many things Blanche says, and, like the others, it is spoken in a very specific context and for a concrete purpose. It's part of the fabric of the scene and of the play.

These kinds of lines are just the ones to look for and allow them expression. Together with other lines and other gestures, they are what you use to limn your character.

To summarize, then, in rewriting the judgment must remain yours. Listen to others, get their opinions, then make the decision according to your own dictates. Once you've done it, and you're sure you're right, don't let anybody tell you otherwise.

THE PERFECT STORY

A student, Chad, was having trouble getting past the first draft of any play he wrote. He always started out with high enthusiasm for a project, but by the time he got to the end of the first draft and looked back at what he'd written, he would realize that it had never been very interesting or promising in the first place. He confided to me that he felt the problem was that he simply "hadn't found any good stories yet." He believed that this was why he was unable to rewrite his work.

I disagreed with him. I told him that his ideas for plays were just as good as anyone else's.

"But some people get great ideas for plays," he insisted. I admitted that there were certainly some ideas for plays that were better than others, some that seemed to lend themselves naturally to dramatic structure. "But," I said, "far more important than the idea is what you do with the idea once you get it."

What, for instance, is so inherently interesting about a depressed salesman who can't get along with his sons? Or about a slightly crazy woman who moves in with her sister and brother-in-law in their tiny New Orleans apartment? Yet those ideas were very promising indeed to Arthur Miller and Tennessee Williams. Why? Because the ideas spoke to them, touched a nerve, created an impulse to write a play. And, just as important, they made something of that impulse. They worked hard on *Salesman* and *Streetcar*, shaping them until they had honed them to a knife's edge.

Ideas are a dime a dozen, frankly. It's what you do with them that makes them worth something. Even the so-called good ones. The U.S. Copyright Office backs me up on this. You cannot copyright an idea; they literally have no value. Copyright a play? Yes, they're happy to do that. Just fill out the form. Try to copyright an idea and you'll be laughed out of the office.

❧

EXERCISE 9

1. Making Choices: Go back to one of the scenes you already wrote in Part One. Make a list of five elements of the scene that were a choice. Make a second list of variations on

those choices—other possible ways that you could write the scene, how those different choices might change the scene, and whether you think it would make the scene better.

2. Feedback: If you have a completed play or scene, make a list of the questions you'd like people to answer (< pp. 233–34).

3. Read a great play, a classic. Find the lines that speak to the essence of the character, that reveal specific truths about him or her. Analyze how the line is used in a specific, concrete context that makes it a seamless part of the text.

THIRTEEN: EXPOSITION

IN TOM STOPPARD'S *The Real Inspector Hound*, the character of Mrs. Drudge, the maid, is given to answering the phone with, "Hello, the drawing room of Lady Muldoon's country residence one morning in early spring?" Or, when introducing herself, to say:

> I'm Mrs. Drudge. I don't live in but I pop in on my bicycle when the weather allows to help in the running of the charming though somewhat isolated Muldoon Manor. Judging by the time [*she glances at the clock*] you did well to get here before high water cut us off for all practical purposes from the outside world.

In fact, Mrs. Drudge can hardly open her mouth without force-feeding us lots of information that nobody ever asked for.

Mrs. Drudge generally gets some well-deserved laughs from the audience. Why? Because she's a trenchant parody of all those characters in plays who speak exposition in a way that the audience immediately and instinctively rebels against. We love Mrs. Drudge because she (or rather, Mr. Stoppard) mocks those awful plays in which we really are being force-fed clumsy exposition by an incompetent playwright.

It's generally assumed that audiences don't like exposition. While I know what is meant by this, I actually disagree. I don't think that audiences mind hearing exposition. Indeed, as we'll soon see, they're hungry for it. And, as we'll also see, exposition is coming at them all the time in a play. It exists everywhere, continuously. I'll even argue that every play, even great plays, are nothing but exposition.

I realize that sounds like some serious dramatic heresy. What exactly do I mean?

Let's go back a step. In the theater, exposition is generally used to mean information. Actually their meanings are slightly different. Information is, according to the dictionary, "knowledge concerning a particular fact or circumstance." It has a static connotation.

Exposition, on the other hand, means "the act of presenting to view." An expository essay, for example, is one in which you set forth an idea. It's not merely a list of information, but an argument. A play too is a piece of writing which sets forth, which actively presents.

That's an interesting semantic side note, but let's face it. When we say exposition, we mean information. There's not much point in quibbling over the fine shadings.

But as the actual meanings indicate, information, whatever its nature, is being actively presented all the time in plays.

Plays are nothing but a setting forth, an active presentation of an idea, or feeling, or person. A play is the visible, audible manifestation of the action. It uses action to transmit the information. The action doesn't transmit anything *but* information. So it follows that plays are nothing but information—or exposition—all the time.

Thinking of your play as having a gestalt once again comes in handy. When you think of the exposition as a thing apart, as a bit of information that you'd like the audience to know about, you run the risk of doing just what you want most to avoid: writing a Mrs. Drudge—but a real Mrs. Drudge, not the satiric one of *The Real Inspector Hound*.

Once you've separated the idea of exposition from the rest of the play, you've removed yourself from the reality of what the play is actually doing—transmitting information. You're much better off, I think, acknowledging that the information is everywhere, in every word and gesture, then letting that idea work for you, rather than fighting it only to find it popping back to whack you in your dramaturgical nose.

What we don't want in a play is static information, unmotivated, the kind that Mrs. Drudge delivers. We want information that has been activated, driven out by the force of a character's action. Witness the first lines of any good play. In *Hamlet*, we hear: "Who's there?"

The information is simple; the action that conveys it is simple too. Bernardo doesn't know who the figure in the fog is, and he wants to know. Perfectly obvious. But it could have been done differently. If Bernardo had been Mrs. Drudge, he might have said: "I'm someone who doesn't recognize that person over there in the fog. I'm wondering who he is."

Laughable, sure. But you'd be surprised how often exposition this clumsy (if not this obvious) appears in plays. We don't always know it as such. We just know we're getting a little bored. Your job as playwright is to recognize it. Especially in your own work. And if you find it, activate it by letting the characters express their needs. When they do, we'll pick up on the exposition soon enough.

I once had a student, Dana, who had an exposition problem in her play. One of her characters, Michael, is upset because he has learned that a young child, a friend of his family, is being molested by a teacher. The teacher also happens to be a close friend of Michael's. Dana had decided it was crucial that the audience know that Michael is upset and why. Yet, no matter how she thought of it and no matter what she tried, it always comes out sounding expository.

That's because right from the beginning, Dana had already made her first mistake. Can you guess what it was?

It was "Dana had decided . . . "

No one goes to plays to hear what the playwright has decided, or what the playwright thinks. They go to hear what the characters have decided and what the characters think. By standing outside the experience of the play, by thinking of the problem as information to be understood rather than exposition to be set forth, Dana had made the problem much harder to solve.

Of course, Dana is allowed to think that such-and-such information is important. It's her play, after all, and she's probably going to have opinions about what belongs in it and what doesn't. (Though it should be noted that some writers don't work this way. They accept whatever ends up in their plays.) (< p. 26, The Ur-play.)

But in order to solve her problem, I asked her to try putting aside her opinion for the moment and think how the characters felt about this issue. (Remember feelings lead to action, which leads to speech and behavior.) How does Michael feel about the fact that he's upset?

We talked it over. Michael, in Dana's mind, was a rather reticent type. Shy, painfully withdrawn. That was one of his general traits. So it followed that Michael didn't feel much like letting on that he was upset, not even under the circumstances in which he found himself. That, I suggested, was probably the very reason she was having such trouble with him, in addition to the fact that he would be turning in his close friend. Her desire to have Michael express his feelings ran counter to her conception of who Michael was. At that point, she had two options.

She had a situation in which Michael's need to express his emotions might override his natural reticence. (If she hadn't already had such a situation, she might have been able to create one.) Michael needed to grasp that, by expressing himself, he might save the well-being of this child. In suggesting this approach, I was actually asking Dana to create an internal conflict: Michael needs to keep his feelings in, but also needs to protect the child. In the end, one action would have to win out over the other.

Dana tried this, but she couldn't quite get it to work well enough to make either of us happy. She simply wasn't able to convince herself of this overriding action for Michael.

Fortunately, I could suggest a second solution that proved equally good: she could use another character to do the heavy lifting. After all, what she required was not that Michael actively express his feelings, but that his feelings somehow become known. Therefore JoAnne, Michael's friend, could perceive that something is wrong. It became her action to find out what it is. She wouldn't let Michael alone until the truth came out. The scene worked beautifully.

The opening scene of *A Raisin in the Sun* is a masterpiece of just this method. Walter pesters Ruth over and over, wondering what's the matter with her: "Something the matter with you this morning?"; "What's the matter with you?"; "That's what you mad about, ain't it." And so on. Ruth denies it every time, acting indifferently. But we very soon know something must be up, in spite of—or because of—her denials.

We won't know exactly what it is until later, but that's exactly the point. Lorraine Hansberry has made us hungry for more exposition. She's set forth some of it: the basic fact that Ruth is bothered about something. Now we're wondering about the rest. I, for one, am prepared to stay planted in my seat until I find out what it is.

ESTABLISHMENT CLAUSE

This leads us to the next aspect of exposition, which is directly connected to the idea of suspense. Suspense and exposition probably never went together in your mind, but in mine they do. As we saw in the previous section, suspense is not the withholding of information but the setting forth of it. Not all of it, of course. Just enough to keep the audience wondering what the rest of it is.

One of the most common questions asked by beginning

writers is, "How do I get all the exposition out of the way so that I can get into the play?"

My answer is, "The last thing in the world you want to do is 'get all the exposition out of the way.' You want to hold tight to it, hoard it like a pirate with his treasure. Then dole it out as you do candy to children: just enough to make them happy, but not enough to make them sick."

Consider any good play. Take the case of *Hamlet*, or *A Streetcar Named Desire*, or *Glengarry Glen Ross*. How much do you really know after the first scene of these plays? Precious little, compared to what you will know later. What you learn is important, of course. But the relative amount of information, in proportion to that which you will have at the end of the play, is quite small. That's deliberate on the part of the playwright. It's a way to keep you interested, in suspense not just about what will happen next but also about all other kinds of information in the play.

As a practical matter, there will always be times when small bits of information can (and should) be tucked into the dialogue. It may be a matter of adding a few words, or changing the phrasing. But generally, the need for those changes comes late in the process, even as late as rehearsals. With the play on its feet, it becomes clear which pieces of information simply must be revealed or made more clear (or, for that matter, omitted).

Don't be afraid of this. It happens to the most experienced playwrights. If the general world of the play is consistent and coherent, you have nothing to worry about. Let your director and actors help you in finding these specific moments, and work with them to make the adjustments.

There's also a chance that, try as you might to enter into the needs of the characters and allow them to express what you happen to believe is important, the exposition simply won't come out. At least it won't come out without being obvious or clumsy. When this happens, consider the possibility that the exposition isn't meant to be in the play, no matter how much you think it is. Think of it not being in the play you need to write.

Many is the time I struggle for days, trying to get out some exposition only to finally realize that if I never bring the matter up at all, the audience will never know the difference. The following may sound like a silly example, but it represents a serious reality: I get it into my head that my character has a wart on his left buttock; I decide that it's crucial information about him and decide I have to let the audience know about it. After much travail and wasted effort, it suddenly dawns on me that it may simply be information that helps me form my general conception of this character. That doesn't mean the audience must be privy to it. If I don't let on, they'll be perfectly blissful in their ignorance (< p. 171, Creating Character).

There's a lot to be said for omitting some exposition, and much to be said for leaving it a little ambiguous. In working on *Levels of Perception* with the director and actors, we came across a problem. I had felt it was important that we know that Gene, the aging abstract expressionist, had destroyed his own work the previous year. This way, it would be clear that the ashes from the fire had been used as fertilizer for the tomatoes that he loves to eat in the course of the play. To me, this was an important metaphor. But it was pointed out to me, and rightly so, that it would be so much more raw and painful for Sally (Gene's wife) and for Leonard (the art dealer who has come hoping to buy the paintings) if the fire had occurred only a few days before the play. It would raise their emotional temperature considerably, with the memory so fresh in Sally's mind and with Leonard's realization that he has missed the chance to get the paintings by such a slim margin.

It seemed plain that I could have it either way, depending on how I phrased the exposition that referred to the actual burning of the painting. But it seemed just as plain that I couldn't have it both ways. The paintings were either burned last fall or last week. One or the other.

But then, thanks to the director, Judy Minor, I realized what should have been obvious to me all along. In drama, it doesn't have to be one or the other. I could leave it ambiguous. Drama is sleight of hand, after all—a deliberate manipulation of words and images. I didn't have to specify for the audience the precise moment in time when the paintings were burned. They certainly had no interest in knowing. They wouldn't care less. Why was I struggling to give them information that they weren't curious about in the first place?

As the play stands in its final version, it's possible, if you study it carefully, to determine that the paintings must have been burned just last week. Given all the exposition that emerges in oblique bits over the course of the play, that's the only way that would make sense. So the actors can use that for their emotional temperature. But the audience's impression—suggested but never specifically claimed by any of the characters—is that the tomatoes were fertilized by the ashes from the paintings, which could only have happened if they were burned the previous year.

Sometimes, with exposition you can have it both ways, if you're willing to do less instead of more. If you're lucky (or maybe un-) your play will be the subject of scholars' interest in the future. They can pick these things apart until the cows come home. Let them. That's their job. Your job is to write your play so that it's as interesting as you can make it. You get to make the choices of what goes in and what stays out. So long as it's interesting, you've made the right decision.

I'M TALKING TO YOU

It may seem unfair to put the subject of direct address, monologues, and soliloquies in a chapter on exposition. They aren't necessarily exposition—not the awful kind that Mrs. Drudge parodies, anyway. In fact, good direct address, monologues, and soliloquies can be very much the fabric of a play, as dramatically valid as any other dialogue. But I put them here under exposition because they are so often misused as vehicles for the kind of sludge that Mrs. Drudge skewers.

First, let's define our terms. "Direct address" is perhaps the broadest of the three. It means just what it says, that a character is directly addressing the audience, as opposed to speaking to the other characters while we in the audience eavesdrop through the fourth wall. Direct address can be of any length. Even a single-word aside to the audience is direct address.

"Monologue" is a slightly narrower term, though it too is quite flexible in meaning. A monologue is any extended speech within a play—in fact, "monologue" and "speech" are often used interchangeably—but it isn't necessarily direct address. It might be spoken to other characters. And "extended" is a relative term, obviously. Monologues can be as short as several sentences in length, or as long as the play itself.

We can break monologues down into two smaller groups: there are those I call seamless, in which the character is speaking to another character onstage, and those that are delivered as direct address. Examples of the seamless monologue are Edmond's monologue about the sea that he delivers to Tyrone in *Long Day's Journey into Night*, or Willy's monologue to Howard about his hero, Dave Singleman, in *Death of a Salesman*.

Direct-address monologues are usually, but not always, separate, freestanding scenes contained in a play that is otherwise composed of dialogue, such as Tom's monologues to the audience in *The Glass Menagerie* or the Chorus in *Henry V*. Or, as I mentioned, a monologue can also be the entire play, as in the case of a one-person show, like John Leguizamo's *Spic-O-Rama*, or David Hare's *Via Dolorosa*, or David Mamet's short play *The Sermon*.

Finally, there is "soliloquy," which is perhaps the least understood and, these days, the least used. The dictionary defines soliloquy as "a speech in a drama in which a character, alone or as if alone, discloses innermost thoughts." I won't disagree with that, but it sounds a lot like information to me, while I believe that soliloquies are active exposition.

As long as we're on the subject, let's examine soliloquies first. What's the difference between a soliloquy and a monologue? It's subtle, but important. A monologue is delivered to another person; soliloquy, on the other hand, is delivered to oneself— the character is "alone or as if alone."

Shakespeare is, of course, our model, and it's probably no coincidence that virtually all of his soliloquies are quite active. He used a variety of actions to serve his purpose. One was to give the character a dilemma that needed to be resolved. Hamlet's "To be or not to be . . . " is the quintessence of this particular model. Aside from its much-praised philosophical depth, this soliloquy also has an elegantly simple structure. Hamlet begins, literally, with the question of whether he should live or die. His action is that he wants to live; his conflict is that he simultaneously wishes he were dead. He then proceeds to work out the difficulties that attend to each alternative. Finally, he arrives at the conclusion, contingent though it may be, to remain among the living.

Not all soliloquies have such a contemplative problem to work out. Macbeth, for example, has a more external action when he sees the apparition of a dagger floating before his eyes: "Is this a dagger which I see before me/The handle toward my hand?" His action is to try to discover whether it's real or imagined.

True soliloquies are rare. Many times, even in Shakespeare, a character may seem to be speaking to himself, but in fact is addressing someone, even if it's the audience. Richard III's "Now is the winter of our discontent . . . " is an example of this. He's trying to persuade us, the audience, that he is justified in his murderous ambitions. I call it a direct-address monologue, not a soliloquy. Many say that Lear's scene on the stormy heath is a soliloquy, but I say he's addressing the storm itself. Edmund, in that same play, has what some people call soliloquies, but to my mind he is usually addressing someone: "Thou, Nature, art my goddess . . . "

In any case, though they are not directed toward another

character, soliloquies may have action just as dialogue does. When they don't, we're often left with the somewhat bald purpose proposed by the dictionary, which is to "disclose innermost thoughts," presumably to the audience. Then we're back to the original problem of clumsy exposition, from which a lot of contemporary soliloquies suffer.

I won't say that all soliloquies must have action. That would be just as foolish as saying that all plays must have it. Some soliloquies don't, and some people like them that way. But, as with the rest of your play, if you're having trouble writing a soliloquy consider finding an action for it to help solve your problem.

Next, there is the seamless monologue that appears in the context of a larger scene. In *Long Day's Journey*, when Edmond speaks to his father about his experiences on the open seas, it is dialogue in the sense that it's prompted by Tyrone's lines that precede it and will be followed by more of Tyrone's lines after. But it is a monologue in the sense that it is an extended speech and could be lifted from the play while still making a certain amount of sense. (Actors, for example, use these monologues for auditions.)

The seamless monologue is easy to place in the context of the tools. Edmond is pursuing an action here; it's simply that his pursuit of the action required, in O'Neill's mind, some extended articulation. (O'Neill thought this a lot.) He allowed Edmond the chance to develop his needs in some detail, to magnify his thoughts. But in its underlying structure, this kind of monologue is no different from any other part of the dialogue. If you're working on a seamless monologue like this, and it doesn't seem to be working for you, examine it using the tools (< Part One: Structure) you already know.

Finally there are direct-address monologues. These can be hard to write in the same way as soliloquies: there seems to be no one to whom the character can direct his action. How can the character want something if there is no one to want it of, no one to provide him with a conflict?

Regardless of whether the monologue is relatively short (up to a few manuscript pages) or play-length, you can use the same device to help activate the direct-address monologue. The key is using the audience as though they were a character or a group of characters.

Take, for example, John Leguizamo's *Spic-O-Rama*. In the play, there are several characters, all portrayed, in sequence, by the same actor. First is Miggy, nine years old and full of it. His opening line, alone onstage, is: "What?? What??!! But Mr. Gabrielli, I've had my report ready—you just never axed me!" And the stage directions instruct the actor to deliver these lines to whom? "To his teacher, *at rear of audience* [emphasis added]."

In other words, the audience becomes Mr. Gabrielli. It has unwittingly, with no warning, been thrust into the center of the play itself. And Miggy is talking to them just as he would talk to an actor playing the role of Mr. Gabrielli.

Similarly, take David Mamet's *The Sermon*. A minister delivers a sermon to his congregation. We in the audience soon realize we are that congregation.

In *Henry V* and *The Glass Menagerie*, Chorus and Tom, respectively, speak directly to the audience, though here the audience doesn't play a role per se. They are spoken to as themselves, as what they are—a group of people in a theater. Spaulding Gray's monologues follow this pattern as well. In *Via Dolorosa*, there is even less artifice. David Hare himself delivered this monologue. In it, he played himself, not a character at all. We in the audience were acknowledged as the audience in a theater. This is perhaps the simplest form of direct address: "I am I, you are you. I am speaking to you without device." Was *Via Dolorosa* a play? Perhaps not. Hare all but says so as soon as he walks onstage. But it was clear as a bell just what the conventions were.

The thing that I find so effective about the direct-address monologue is that it creates a dynamic that is possible only in live theater. It's what Michael Bennett, the director of *A Chorus Line* and *Dreamgirls*, called a hot relationship. He meant that there is a direct connection between the characters—not just the actors, but between the characters—and the audience. In *A Chorus Line* we collectively become Zack, the man for whom all the characters are auditioning. In *Dreamgirls*, we become the audience this girl group plays to.

The audience is really there for those characters, whether simply as an audience or as fellow characters. And the audience is forced (perhaps seduced is the better term) into participating viscerally in the experience of the drama. They have stepped into the play and have begun literally to play a role in it. It is certainly no coincidence that these plays—Bennett's two greatest successes—employed just such a dynamic.

Finally, there is one other way to write a direct-address monologue. (I admit, I find it less effective, and I don't recommend it, but this may be a prejudice of mine.) You can simply allow the character to speak without acknowledging the audience, rather like a person speaking aloud their innermost thoughts. To me, such an unmotivated monologue always strikes me as clumsy exposition. It is not a soliloquy, for there is no action, no problem to be solved. The person just happens to be sharing information, which is why I don't like it. It feels slack to me, without the bracing astringent of a convention. I can never get past the idea that people don't in fact talk out loud to themselves for no good reason, at least not for long, and certainly not by reiterating a lot of stories and information they already know very well. They don't even think such things silently to themselves. So unless the character in the play has some very good reason to do all that talking, I get bored. Let me in on the reason, and I'm all ears.

The retort to this would be, I suppose, that this is theater and theater is not like life. (That's an argument I use myself in other circumstances, after all.) But in the case of these unmotivated monologues, there seems nothing dramatic about them. The idea of a person speaking at length without any motivation runs too much counter not just to life but to fundamental human nature as I know it. I can't recommend that you write monologues in this way, but there are a lot of people who think it's just fine. Some very successful one-person shows are such. Just don't look for me in the audience.

⁂

EXERCISE 10

1. Take a sample page from any play you like. Find all the exposition you can on that page and make a list of it. Examine each line and analyze, as I did with the first line of *Hamlet*, the information conveyed by each line.

2. Write a direct-address monologue that uses the audience as a specific person or persons.

YOU NOW have all the basic information that I believe you will need to write and rewrite your play. Even so, you will always run into other problems that I haven't discussed. There are as many problems as there are plays to write and no book could hope to address all of them. What follows is a list I've assembled over my years of writing and teaching of the most common dilemmas in which playwrights find themselves, along with some ideas on how to address them. Generally, it goes from earlier problems to later ones, but the order is not as important as what's in it.

A LITTLE PROSAIC

Suppose you have an impulse for a story. And suppose that you either don't want to write a spontaneous exercise, or that you've already done so and it hasn't given you much of an idea as to what the actual plot of this play might be. You could work on the plot by simply thinking about it, but I recommend writing down your thoughts.

The act of writing out, in simple prose, the various permutations of what may or may not happen in this play can be a wonderfully creative and stimulating experience in itself—better than mere thinking. The act of writing encourages you to tell the story—moving it forward, spinning a yarn for yourself. At the same time, it allows you to digress on a character, or an image, or a thematic point—and to retain what you discover.

Best of all, this process will probably take only a few hours, a day or two at most. You can lay out an entire rough plot of a play in that period of time—so much more efficient than sitting down to write actual scenes which, as you probably know, can be much more difficult. Writing out the story allows you to see its strengths and weaknesses quickly, and can even show you whether you really want to commit the time and energy it will take to write the play.

Be forewarned that the writing of this treatment will not tell you everything about the play. It may let you discover the general outline of the plot, a rough sketch of the characters, perhaps something of the theme if you're lucky, but not much else. What's more, a play that works in treatment form may not work at all once you start to write it and are obliged to reveal the mysterious essence of your impulse. But it does have the advantage of being a quick, loose, and (for me) enjoyable way to make some basic discoveries about the projected play.

MAKE IT AN OCCASION

Arthur Miller, in an interview in the *Dramatists Guild Quarterly*,* talks about what he calls the "occasion" of a play. "In *The Crucible*," he says, "the occasion of the play is the witch hunt in Salem, Massachusetts, but there is also a conflict [my term would be "situation" (< p. 73)] which makes a *play* of that occasion." It's worth talking about what Miller means by occasion, because giving your play one can make all the difference between success and failure.

I once had a student, Paul, who wanted to write a play about a family that was going through a lot of emotional upheaval. (It was a comedy, even though the situations may sound quite serious.) The father was thinking of divorce; the mother had quit her job and was doing nothing but Tai Chi all day; the oldest daughter (thirtyish) had recently realized she was a lesbian but hadn't come out to the family; the son (twenties) was a pothead; the younger daughter (twenties) thought they were all crazy and wanted nothing more than to get away from all of them.

The first fragments of the play were promising, but there was no question that Paul was having a hard time finding a plot to give a focus to all these interesting people and their problems. I suggested that before he worried about plot, he should think first about an occasion. We talked about it, and he came up with the idea that the youngest daughter might be getting married. The occasion, he said, could be her wedding.

First, this solved the problem that the youngest girl's action was, really, just to get out of this situation (> p. 269,

---

*Vol. 24, no. 2.

The "Locked in the Room" Syndrome). Second, it gave a coherence, a specificity, and a focus to all their actions. The characters could now work to make the wedding happen, or perhaps to sabotage it. But they would all have something concrete to do.

An occasion can be a general backdrop, such as the Salem witch-hunt, or it can be quite specific and well delineated, such as the impending execution in *The Front Page*. An occasion might be an archaeology dig (*The Mound Builders*), a trial (*The Winslow Boy, Inherit the Wind*), or an automobile trip (*The Happy Journey to Trenton and Camden*). But it is not merely the setting of a play. That would simply be a place. An occasion gives you an event (not the dramatic kind from Part One), which is happening behind the play, serving as background. It's something that's going on anyway; the play is another layer of something going on in the foreground.

Not all plays have occasions. Even in the ones that do, the audience may be only vaguely aware of it as a cohering device. That's fine—maybe even desirable. The occasion is not there so much for the audience as for you, the playwright. Like the tools of structure, it can be invisible, or at least unobtrusive. But you can use it as a means to help give the play structure.

THE CENTER DOESN'T ALWAYS HOLD

As you write your play, you may have a sense of what its dramatic center is. It's usually a character, the one with the strongest action. It might also be thought of as two characters, a central relationship.

But as you write, particularly if you're having trouble, stay open to the possibility that this center might change, or might not be what you originally assumed it to be.

My student, Robert, had written the first act of a very funny play about two lesbians, former stewardesses, who had kidnaped the CEO of their airline and were holding him for ransom. In the course of the act, the CEO made his appearance onstage, and then later, his wife also arrived. Hilarity ensued. But by the end of the act, Robert had run into problems. He had no idea where to go next. He had assumed the play was about the two ex-stewardesses, as that had been his original impulse and that's where the play had begun. But now he didn't have a clue as to what they would do next.

When we talked, however, he had plenty of clues about what the CEO and his wife would do next. I suggested that maybe his stronger, deeper impulse was really with them, and he should pay attention to that. Maybe it was really their play.

Making that choice would mean some changes, obviously. But not that many. He wouldn't, for instance, have to begin the play with the CEO and his wife. Lots of plays (most even) begin with characters other than the central ones. So while he had some adjustments to make, I encouraged him to press forward with the first draft, using the CEO and his wife as the center, and leave the rewriting until later.

THE "LOCKED IN THE ROOM" SYNDROME

Long ago, in an acting class, I was playing Peter in a scene from Edward Albee's *The Zoo Story*. Things weren't going very well. The performance was slack, without any real energy. The teacher told me to imagine that I was locked in a room with Jerry and that there was no way out of it except to press through with the scene. I suppose he was trying to get me to focus, or maybe to raise the stakes.

In any case, it didn't make me act that part any better. But the image has always stuck with me, and since then I've come to feel that regardless of whether it's a good acting note, it can be an excellent one for playwriting.

Sometimes, when you're writing a scene, you may get the sense that the characters could just as well stroll away and not much would be lost if they did. This is a question of stakes, obviously. You'll want to consider giving the character something both to win and to lose.

But here's another tip: avoid making the choice that one of the characters wants to leave. It's not that there's anything absolutely wrong with it. And you can certainly provide high stakes to an action like wanting to leave. But it will tend to focus the characters' energy, their actions, toward someone or something offstage. After all, that's where the persons or things that they want are located. But you want their focus on the character(s) here in this place. Allowing them to want to leave the room can dissipate that focus and that energy.

When I find myself writing a scene that seems to have low stakes, I will check to see that both characters want to be in this place, that they want something from the other character(s) onstage, and won't be willing to leave until they get it.

THE PASSOVER QUESTION

Jews reading this book will know immediately what this means. For those of you who don't, the Passover question is: "Why is this night different from all other nights?"*

It's a good question to ask of your own play also. (Obviously, one can paraphrase and ask about this day or this moment.) The answer may be so obvious that it doesn't occur to you right away. Or you may not be able to answer it at all, which could mean there's a problem.

Here are some sample answers to the Passover question from a few good plays. *Oedipus the King*: Today is different from all other days because today there is a plague and the citizens have come to Oedipus to beg him to find a way to end it. *Hamlet*: Tonight is different from all other nights because while the ghost of Hamlet's father has already appeared twice before on the battlements, tonight Horatio witnesses it, and he will bear that news to Hamlet. *A Streetcar Named Desire*: Today is different from all other days because today Blanche arrives to live with Stella and Stanley. *Death of a Salesman*: Tonight is different from all other nights because tonight Biff has come home. *Glengarry Glen Ross*: Tonight is different from all other nights because tonight certain salesmen have hatched a desperate plan to steal the leads. *Six Degrees of Separation*: Tonight is different from all other nights because tonight a stranger named Paul arrives at the door and says he knows Ouisa and Flan's children.

And so on. You can see that a play that answers the

---

*Credit to Curt Dempster of Ensemble Studio Theatre for passing this on to me.

Passover question also has what I call the inciting event. That's the moment that triggers the specific plot of this specific play and starts it on its way. It's a bookend to the dramatic event we discussed in Part One, which ends the play.

Do all plays answer a Passover question? Do they all have an inciting event? Most do, but not all. As usual, the existentialist plays of Beckett and others defy this rule. That's part of their point, in fact. To the existentialist, every day is unbearably very much like another. Godot said yesterday he was coming; he said he is coming again today; tomorrow he will once more say he is coming.

But in general, you can give your play a sense of specific moment if you can successfully answer the Passover question. There is more than one way to answer it. Just look at the examples above. The inciting event sometimes happens before the play begins (Biff has returned home); sometimes not until the play has already started (Blanche arrives at Stella and Stanley's door); and sometimes a little of both (the ghost of Hamlet's father has already appeared, but tonight Horatio, Hamlet's best friend, is among those who see it).

In all cases, though, an inciting event won't be worth much unless it's pretty near the beginning of the play. Don't hold back too long. Nobody likes a play that begins at the start of Act Two.

IN MEDIAS RES

Horace, the patient Roman poet who advised leaving one's work on the shelf for eight years, was not so patient when it came to the question of when to start a play. In his essay *Ars*

Poetica, he said a plot should begin not at the beginning of the story but while it was already "in the middle of things," a phrase that translates into Latin as *in medias res* (pronounced "in-ME-dē-əs RĀS").

Imagine a story as being a string that extends in both directions as far as you can see. You'll make a cut here and one there—and you've made your first choice in forming your plot. The plot begins wherever you make the first snip. Horace wants you to make that first snip as far along the string as possible.

Take *Hamlet*, for example. Before Shakespeare, revenge tragedies were already a very popular form in Elizabethan theater. But, as a genre, they presented an inherent problem to the playwright. The treacherous, murderous act that inspired the feelings of vengeance was beside the point of a revenge tragedy, but you always had to show it before you could go ahead and show the revenge that ensued. The result was a lot of ungainly plays that took forever to get to the good part—the act of revenge.

Shakespeare solved this problem neatly, as usual. The treacherous act in *Hamlet* is long since committed at the beginning of the play. The first thing that happens is that the ghost of the murdered man appears to demand vengeance. (Nice spectacular touch with the ghost, by the way.) We leapfrog right over the very issue that made revenge tragedies rather long and complicated and lumpy in structure. Instead, we're free to watch Hamlet in the act of justifying and pursuing his vengeance, which is the meat of any revenge tragedy. *Hamlet* begins, in other words, in medias res.

Beginning well into the story isn't essential. Moreover, *in medias res* is a particularly relative term. Where exactly is the middle of things? Your middle may be my beginning. My beginning may be your end. It all depends on the story you want to tell. I can only say that your best bet is, as always, to go with your gut. When you sense that your character has a strong action right now—and is ready to pursue it right now—you're probably in the middle of things. So begin.

THE 40 PERCENT SOLUTION

In medias res is related to, but not quite the same as, beginning at 40 percent which is also good advice for a playwright. Beginning at 40 percent doesn't refer to where you decide to begin your plot, but to the level of emotional and psychological intensity with which you begin it. You can see easily why the two ideas often go hand in hand. But *in medias res* is a structural tool, while beginning at 40 percent is a sensibility, the emotional temperature of the characters.

In *Streetcar*, Blanche is already a nervous wreck at the top of the play. She's lost Belle Reve, been run out of town, and has come here to a place she describes as her last refuge. (And indeed, it will prove to be just that.) Williams might have chosen to make her carefree and happy-go-lucky when she enters, and then show her decline over the course of the evening. While that would have been equally possible, it would have been much harder to accomplish. Like all good tools, beginning at 40 percent is meant to make the playwright's job easier, not harder.

Some plays, for particular and deliberate reasons, begin at 0 percent. Nothing is happening. Everything is neutral. The temperature is cool. Then, as we watch the play begin, the wheels slowly start to turn until we're humming right along. You can try this if you like. But believe me, it's the tough way to go. I'd wager that even plays you think begin this way, don't. They may be deceptively designed to appear quite still at the start. But if the play is any good, the playwright has some serious energy pent up under the surface calm.

PLEASE DON'T CALL A DOCTOR

While working as literary manager for the Ensemble Studio Theatre in New York, I read thousands of plays. In one of them, the main character endured virtually every curse known to modern man: divorce, betrayal by his friends, bankruptcy, and more. Finally, in the last few pages of the script, just when I thought nothing else could happen to the unlucky fellow, he developed a very sudden case of cirrhosis of the liver. (The only sudden case of cirrhosis on medical record.) Though he had shown no signs of the disease until that moment, he died of it before the final page. That took about three minutes of stage time.

This may be a hilariously extreme example, but my point, I hope, is clear: beware of using medical conditions in your play. Even if you are not so unwise as to introduce a fatal case of cirrhosis in the last few minutes of your play, a disease is no substitute for genuine drama.

It doesn't matter whether the disease is mental or physical, fatal or merely bothersome. Just as a limp or a tic or a stammer does not make a character, neither do illnesses. And they don't make dramatic situations either. A man dying of heart disease is unfortunate and I feel sorry for him, but it doesn't make me any more interested in his dramatic journey.

Mental illness seems particularly attractive to many playwrights. What, after all, could be more theatrical than insanity? Theatrical, yes; dramatic, not really. When we watch a genuinely insane person, we are not really watching that person at all. Their words and behavior are not emerging from the person but from the disease. The real person is hidden under the cloak of the disease, unseen.

Of course, you can make illness work. Plenty of plays have characters with maladies both serious and mild. *Whose Life Is It Anyway?* is quite successful, I think, for the very reason that the play hardly focuses at all on the medical condition of paralysis. Instead, the play concerns itself mainly with the dramatic action: the character wants the right to end his own life.

You could also argue that a play like *Streetcar* has a character, Blanche, who is insane. While I'd never make any arguments for Blanche's rock-solid mental state, she is surely in her right mind throughout the play, at least up until the last scene. Somewhat deluded, yes, and slightly off her rocker at times. But the behavior we're seeing is, painfully, the real Blanche. Not until the final moment is she so far gone that madness has overcome her. And even then, her true nature briefly shines through with the famous character-defining line, "I have always depended on the kindness of strangers."

So, as I've already mentioned, there is nothing inherently wrong with a character who has an illness, if that's an essential part of your plot. But be wary of falling into the trap of believing that their medical condition is what's interesting about them or the work. Maybe it's interesting to some people. For years, after all, the networks did make a killing on their disease-of-the-week television movies. But who remembers those movies now?

DON'T TELL ME HOW YOU FEEL

When I write the first draft of a scene spontaneously, without editing myself, I often discover, as I look back at what I've written, that the dialogue is full of phrases like "I'm angry at you," or "I feel great," or "I don't like that."

If things have gone well, these phrases come along with other phrases like, respectively, "Don't touch me right now," or "Come on, let's dance!" or "Send this steak back to the kitchen, it's too rare."

I like the examples in the second paragraph a lot better than the ones in the first, which I usually end up cutting. Why? Because the first lines are static statements of being: "I'm angry at you." The second line, corresponding to it, is active: "Don't touch me right now." The state of being is implied by the active line. The audience picks up on the principle of subtext. It's unstated, but quite clear.

In going through your play (or scene) after you've written the first draft, you may feel that the dialogue is somehow leaden, general, and inactive—even if the scene clearly has an action built into the structure. If this is a problem, the answer may lie in the details. Look at each line to see whether the character is really expressing his action or whether he's simply revealing his state of being.

If you're lucky, you'll have both statements of being and active expressions. If so, you only have to pick and choose, cutting the one and keeping the other. If you're not so lucky, you may have only statements of being. In that case, you'll want to come up with better lines that actively express what's now merely static information.

I don't do this until the first draft is finished. I think it's important to allow those statements of being full expression. It may be your subconscious way of getting clear what the feelings really are. (I know that's the way it works for me.) Don't try to stop them from being expressed the first time out. Just look to see if you can cut them in the rewrites.

OPPOSITES ARE ATTRACTIVE

It's almost embarrassing to let you in on this next trick I discovered because it's so, well, tricky. But it's worked for me more than once, and it's worth putting into your toolbox in case it might ever work for you.

Suppose that in writing a play I arrive at a scene in which a character (I'll call him Joe for old time's sake) wants to take his friend Mike fishing, but Mike already has tickets to a baseball game, and he's just as determined that he and Joe will go to the game. Clear actions, clear conflict. Yet for some reason—and who knows why—the scene simply doesn't come alive for me. I've tried examining the stakes, the general traits and feelings of the characters, everything else I can think of.

Then I come upon a solution which is as easy as using the Search/Replace feature on my word processing software. I replace Joe's name with Mike, and vice versa. Now the scene works beautifully. For some reason, I just had the two characters in the wrong positions.

It's not quite that simple. I still have work that needs to be done around the edges in order to make sense out of this change. But essentially, now that I've rearranged them, the characters seem right and I like the scene a lot.

There is an alternative version of this. Sometimes I can reverse an element other than the characters. For instance, I might reverse the action. In a first draft, Joe might want to make love to Mike. But if that doesn't work, in the second, I might try letting Joe want to kill Mike instead.

Why do these reversals work? I can't say for sure. My theory is that when that first choice doesn't work, it's because the intellect has covertly intruded on the work that belongs to the subconscious. It made a choice that wasn't really mine. I can undo that work though, ironically, by using my intellect to deliberately reverse (or at least change) the choice I've made.

You can think of this as another instance when the play you need to write must take precedence over the one you merely want to write. As I've said before, let your subconscious do as it wants. You'll often find the work is easier, truer, simply more dramatic. It ought to be. If it's one thing your subconscious knows about, it's truth.

Another way to think of it is this: in writing, there's nothing wrong with taking the easy way out. Not in this sense, anyway. I believe that when writing is extremely difficult, when every inch of manuscript must be won through hard, bloody battle, then often something is wrong. When you take the right way, the play starts to flow out of you. It's as easy as dreaming a dream.

POURING THE CONCRETE

The first writing assignment that my students get is exercise one from Part One (< p. 47, The Action Scene), which concerns the writing of an action. Within that exercise there's a sort of hidden lesson—one that is often overlooked. It's this: keep the action concrete whenever possible.

For example, I had a student, Maria, who was writing a character, June, whose action was to seek the love she had never received from her mother. To want love is a perfectly good intangible need, but the scene was not going very well because June was quickly reduced to baldly stating that need over and over again.

When I suggested Maria find a concrete representation of that love, she allowed June to want a family heirloom ring. This choice led her to another good, concrete choice: June wanted the ring in order to wear it to her graduation from high school. Now the scene had not only a concrete action but an occasion in which to want it. The scene turned out beautifully.

Give your character a solid, actual thing to want. Not that they can't or shouldn't have an intangible need also. But the concrete objective is often the most playable one. It exists in the real world. It can be held, looked at, talked about in specific terms. An intangible objective will always remain, by definition, something of an abstraction about which there will be less to see and hear.

TEMPUS FUGIT

I had a student, Margaret, who was having trouble with her play. The first scene had gone quite well and so did the second, which occurred only a few minutes after the first. But now, the third scene was giving her problems. She told me that she thought the conflict wasn't strong enough. Yet when we talked about it, the conflict actually seemed quite clear and plenty strong. We also discussed the other obvious possibilities that I've offered in Part Two. But none of them seemed to offer a solution. She had done her work thoroughly, yet the scene didn't seem to want to lift off the page.

Then I asked her how much time transpires between the end of Scene Two and the beginning of Scene Three. She said she hadn't given it a lot of thought. "Maybe a day or two," she said. "Maybe less, but maybe as much as a week."

I said that she should think about that very carefully and make a specific choice. It might very well provide the solution to her problem.

"If it's only been a few hours or a day," I said, "the characters have had little time to absorb the events of the first two scenes. If it's been a week, they've had a chance to process, to think about those events."

"What difference does that make?" she asked.

"A lot. Their general traits probably haven't changed in that time, but it's fair to think that their feelings have. And the amount of time you choose will alter the kinds of feelings they have. Let's say it's only been a few hours. Their feelings might still be raw, exposed. They could be a can of kerosene waiting for a match. If it's been a day, maybe they've had time to cool down and think. If it's been a week, maybe their feelings have calcified and turned bitter and resentful. Also, offstage events might have occurred that will influence their feelings.

"I'm not saying that you should follow any of those particulars," I continued. "You'll have to see for yourself how the characters have responded. But first, select a specific period of time, then consider what might have gone on in their lives—and in their heads—during that specific period. If you don't like the results, choose another length of time. But whatever you do, choose one and make it specific."

I left her to do the work. She did—and the scene opened right up for her.

FRESH PAGE

You're in the middle of rewrites. Things are generally going well, and you've got a handle on what you're trying to accomplish with this next draft.

But you're stuck on a particular line. You know you don't like it. It doesn't say what you want it or need it to say. But you're confused over what to do about it.

My recommendation: cut the line entirely and start fresh. It's often easier to do that than to try to fix what you've got.

If you're afraid of losing the line forever, as it's easy to do in the age of computers, create a separate file called "Cuts." Paste all your cut lines into that file in the order in which they appear in the play. This way, you can go into that file and find the line if you really want to look at it.

I always have a "Cuts" file for any play that I write. Sometimes the file is hundreds of pages long. It's full of lines (sometimes whole scenes) that I was terrified to lose, sure that I would need them someday.

I can't recall the last time I looked to find one of those lines.

THE END IS NEAR

Some writers, and I'm one of them, begin to develop a problem as they reach the end of the play. Suddenly, they feel the weight of all dramatic literature on their shoulders. They feel that somehow now they must write something extraordinary, something with a big bang, an event that will virtually blow the audience out of their seats.

It's a terrible burden, and it's just the thing that can stop you dead in your tracks, even if the rest of the play has been going well. My best advice is to forget this idea. It's a false notion. Some plays, certainly, end with a bang. Big, loud, explosive events. Those plays can be exciting. I like them a lot. But I also like *The Glass Menagerie* and *King Lear* and *Six Degrees of Separation*, which end softly, elegantly, like an elegy.

There's nothing about the end of your play that must be, or even should be, any different from the rest of it. The same tools and ideas apply. You don't have to suddenly come up with something more just because you're writing the last scene.

When we say the climax of the rising action, we don't mean a climax as in sex. The climax here is an abstraction. Yes, it's the highest point of the action. But action, as we know, is internal, silent. Its manifestation, even in its climactic moment, might be the sound of a whisper. That whisper, well phrased and well placed, can have the emotional effect in the audience of a thunderclap.

As a colleague of mine once said, "When you're onstage, the violence of a punch in the face is often far less effective than the violence of the phrase, 'I don't love you anymore.' "

PART FOUR

SOME ADVICE

READ!

YOU NEED to read plays.

In my college courses, I can and do assign plays. In my private workshops, I can't—but I wish I could. In some ways, this advice should be at the very front of the book, in capital letters. It's that important. In order to write your plays, you need to know other plays—classical plays, plays from other periods in history certainly, but also contemporary plays, things that are happening right now. My rule of thumb is one play a week.

In other societies, at other times in history, seeing plays and reading them would have been a matter of course. Shakespeare, we know, was steeped in the dramatic literature of his time. He worked at a theater, and it's obvious from his writing that he knew the other works of his day intimately. The same with the Greeks. The same with European playwrights of the nineteenth century and American playwrights of the first half of the twentieth century. They lived in a culture of theater. Theater was all around them.

That's no longer true. It's harder for you. You have to actively seek out plays and read them. On the other hand, you've got advantages those writers never had. Thanks to the public library system and the Internet, virtually any play ever written is available to you—sometimes for free, or at relatively low cost. But they won't come knocking at your door. You're going to have to go out and find them.

When you do, you're giving yourself the most important part of your education as a playwright. And I mean that. What you learn in this book, or from a class, or from your peers, will pale in comparison to what you can learn from reading other good writers.

Once you've learned from them, steal from them. I don't mean appropriate parts of their plays. I said steal: their ideas, the way they solve dramatic problems, the way they open a scene or end it, the way they create character, pursue action, raise the stakes, provide a sense of hope, or any of the other many issues I've discussed in this book. Go ahead, steal those ideas. That's what they're there for. Chances are, those writers stole from someone else. That's the healthy ferment of art.

I once had a student who was afraid that if she read anyone else's plays, their ideas would infect her own. Indeed they might. That's exactly the point. We should have such problems as to be infected by the Shakespeare virus.

You also need to read plays in order to see what you don't like, to see what doesn't work. When you're reading (or seeing) a play that doesn't work for you, don't simply write it off as wasted time. Figure out what's wrong. Think about what you would do differently. Fix the play in your head. Is that arrogant? Maybe. A little constructive arrogance never hurt an artist.

If you don't spend your time doing this, then your effort in exploring other writers really is wasted. Nothing seems more wasteful to me than a student of playwriting who reads or sees a play that he hates, but when he's asked why he hated it, says, "I don't know."

You need to see plays as well (> p. 290, Production Versus Play). That's crucial. But you may find it expensive (> p. 293, Cheap Seats), and, depending on where you live, you may be limited in what you can see. There are videotaped productions you can rent, but that's not the same. In any case, as a learning process, reading plays is in some ways better. It forces you to deal strictly with the text, which is all you're going to have in writing your own play. Reading allows you to study closely the dramaturgy, the tools, and the other devices that the playwright has employed.

I've included a recommended reading list in the appendix (> p. 324, Appendix B). It's highly biased, and I don't pretend it's all-inclusive. Many playwrights who are considered very significant are not on the list. Those that I'm recommending should, for the most part, help you understand the comments in this book. Some may not help you at all, and there are certainly many not on the list who might.

My list is only a beginning but it will allow you to start forming a basic knowledge of mainstream playwriting of the Western world. You should at the very least know a play by every author on that list, if not every play. From there, you can go on to read in depth.

ACT UP

I advise all my students to take an acting class. For college students, this is easy. Classes are usually readily available, and chances are they are taking one anyway.

But it's just as important for every student of playwriting to study acting. I'm not suggesting you need to become an actor. But even taking a single class will give you some idea of what happens to those words of yours when someone has to speak them. You'll begin to see what active language really means onstage, what high stakes can do for a scene, how to find the event at the end of the scene, and so on.

It's also not a bad idea to take a directing class and one in design as well. The more you can learn about the art and craft of your collaborators, the better off you will be. You'll respect their work more, and you'll gain a keener sense of your own place, as a writer, in the scheme of things.

PRODUCTION VERSUS PLAY

My friend Henry, whom I mentioned earlier, taught me some important lessons. I often walked out of the theater with him saying that I liked the play we just saw. He would ask me why and I would reply, "Oh that lead actress is such-and-such. And the costumes were so-and-so. And the sets were this-and-that." On I went until I had talked about every aspect of the production I could think of. I considered myself very smart.

When I was done, Henry patiently pointed out that I had said I liked the play, but none of those observations had anything to do with the play. They were all comments on the production.

A play is a text; a production is that text in a particular setting, with particular actors and scenery and lights and costumes, directed by a particular individual.

This is the first, most obvious, but most essential distinction to remember. You'd be surprised how many people get it wrong. Learning and appreciating the difference not only made going to the theater more enjoyable, it allowed me to gain a better understanding about what playwriting actually is.

One argument for going to the theater as much as possible, even if it's expensive and inconvenient where you live, is that it's really the only way to learn the difference between production and text. A text is what you write; it's words on a page. Production is everything that puts those words in front of an audience: the direction, acting, and design. It seems like an obvious distinction, and in the abstract it is. In practice, it can often be confusing.

You need practice in making the difference clear to yourself. If you can't make the distinction in other people's plays, it's not going to be much easier to tell the difference when it comes time to watch your own play in rehearsal or production. You'll either end up expecting your collaborators to solve every problem you've created with a flawed text, or you'll keep scrambling to do rewrites of a perfectly good play that your actors and director don't have the skill to produce properly as it is.

Either way, you lose.

So go to the theater and start learning. You need to look

and listen carefully, and you'll almost certainly need to have a copy of the text so that you can read it before seeing the production. Then make notes, mental or written, of what you see on the stage. Make notes about actors, or lighting effects, or stage pictures, and so on. Finally, read the text again afterward, seeing which of these elements of the production are indicated specifically in the text, which are suggested by it, and which were clearly an element of this particular production.

For example, you may walk away from a particular production of a play convinced that there is no action. In a sense, you might be right. Playwrights rely on the actors to grasp the characters' needs, to understand them, and to use them in performance. They rely on directors to guide the actors toward active behavior. If the actors only play the static emotion, or empty behavior, it will often seem to the average theatergoer that the play itself has no action. Bad actors and directors can make even the most active plays seem inactive if they make static choices.

Sometimes the differences between production and text are subtle; sometimes they are glaringly obvious. In either case, you will need to make the same discerning judgments when you're watching your own play in rehearsal and in the early performances.

If it sounds like work, it is. As a serious playwright, going to the theater will no longer be strictly for pleasure. Of course, you can always choose occasions when you just want to go and have a good time. But there's work to do also, and you'll be better off for having done it.

CHEAP SEATS

Cheap theater seats are often available, even if they may take some extra effort to get.

In New York, preview performances are typically less expensive than ones after a play has opened. Resident nonprofit houses like Manhattan Theatre Club or Playwrights Horizons, and sometimes even commercial theaters, make student tickets available at a discount. Many nonprofit houses often have subscriptions or membership programs for tickets at reduced rates. You need to call each theater to find out their policy. The Dramatists Guild offers free day-of seats to its members via a hotline. Sometimes, discounts can be found on the Internet (such as at Playbill.com). Theatre Development Fund offers discount tickets at a booth in Times Square, as well as a voucher system to see plays inexpensively. An organization called Audience Extras offers very inexpensive means by which to see plays. You pay an annual fee, and your tickets to available shows cost only $3.50. (All these organizations are in the phone book.) Nonprofit theaters will also sometimes allow you to see a play for free in exchange for serving as an usher that night.

Outside New York, many theaters also have this ushering policy or other discount tickets available. Call them to see if you qualify for any of these special programs.

RAISING YOUR PLAY

I've already likened a playwright's relationship to his play to that of parent to child. While this may seem a cliché, the metaphor is useful because we can extend it beyond the simple act of creation.

A mother has not only given birth to her child, she also loves it. She has a relationship to the child that goes beyond the mere mechanics of insemination, pregnancy, birth, and breast-feeding. She loves her child. She wants to protect him, nurture him, help him. She wants him to succeed. She wants to give the child what he wants and needs. She wants to satisfy her child's longings, whether in the form of literal hunger or that of the spirit.

These are appropriate things for her to want, essential to the raising of a happy, well-adjusted child. We don't discourage a mother's love for her child. We recognize it as a natural thing, an essential part of the process.

But at the same time, as we all know, a mother's role is not merely to give a child what he wants. There is also a need to discipline, to say no, to draw the line. Discipline is not a sign that a mother doesn't love her child. Rather it's a sign she loves him well enough that she's willing to make him temporarily unhappy so that in the long run the child will be a better person for it. She is trying to shape her child with love but also with firmness.

So too a playwright with her play. She has created her play not only in a mechanical sense, but also in the sense that she loved the idea of the play. That love develops and increases after the play has been created, after it's become a living thing. (Aristotle bases most of his ideas about drama on the notion that art is in many ways comparable to organic life.) This love is natural, "normal" if you will. A playwright should love her play. She should want to protect it, nurture it, allow it to be what it must be.

But at the same time, a play needs discipline. If the playwright lets it be exactly as it wants, she will probably (though not absolutely) run into trouble. Maybe now, maybe later, but it will almost surely happen.

So listen to other people. Maybe they see a discipline problem in your play that you don't see because you love it too blindly. Don't love your play less; love it enough so that you can stand back from it and objectively see it for what it really is.

This doesn't mean listen to anybody and everybody. Listen to people whom you've come to trust. You wouldn't go to that loudmouthed, ill-tempered, backstabbing third cousin and ask him how to raise your child. But you might take advice from a trusted friend, particularly if they've raised a child themselves, or if they at least seem to have the sensitivity to raise a child well.

⁂

EXERCISE 11

Go to see a play for which you can also purchase the text. Read the play first, then see it, then read it again. List ten things about the production which influenced your interpretation of the play as you were watching it.

SIXTEEN: PRACTICAL ADVICE

THIS IS a book on the craft and art of playwriting, not on your playwriting career. For that matter, the term "career" might not really apply to you. Even if you take your playwriting very seriously, you may have no intention of ever trying to earn your livelihood by practicing it. Many very successful playwrights don't, after all.

As Robert Anderson quipped long ago, "You can't make a living in the theater, but you can make a killing." Today, the second half of that sentence is also in doubt. Many well-known playwrights earn only a small percentage of their income from their plays. The rest comes from writing for film or television, novels or magazine articles, or from teaching or sources that have nothing at all to do with writing—Shakespeare made most of his money in real estate; Sophocles came from a wealthy family.

So the fact that you're a serious artist, and that you've committed yourself to the art of playwriting, doesn't necessarily mean that you intend to make all, or even very much, of your income from your plays.

There's absolutely nothing wrong with this. I believe that the original meaning of amateur still obtains: "a person who engages in an activity for pleasure rather than for financial benefit." The word itself derives directly from the Latin word for lover—one who practices his occupation for love. At one time the amateur was considered the more serious artist for the very reason that his efforts were unsullied by money.

Even if you are strictly an amateur, this chapter can help you. Because what follows is not so much about making money—though you can use it to do that also—as it is about showing yourself to the world as an accomplished and serious practitioner of your art. It will also tell you ways to become more accomplished.

There are other good resources for these same ideas, but here are basic, sensible things you should know about taking the vocation (or avocation) of playwriting seriously and presenting a serious face to the world.

STANDARD MANUSCRIPT FORMAT

There are several good reasons why you will want to put your manuscript into standard format. Overall, though, there is one best reason: a play printed in standard format is easy to read. It has plenty of what I call white space. That is, it doesn't look cramped and compressed on the page, but open and loose.

As a former literary manager who read roughly two thousand manuscripts a year, I can attest to the importance of this. The last thing I wanted when I opened the third manuscript of the day was to dig my way through a cluttered, unfamiliar format. I rarely gave those manuscripts a fair reading, partly because I simply couldn't bother with the difficulty of reading them. But also because the nonstandard format said one thing more clearly than any other: this playwright is inexperienced. It led me to evaluate his play—unfairly, but inevitably—with that presupposition in mind.

Here's a sample of what standard format looks like:

Page 19

FREDDY

I've got the order right here, ma'am.
(He shows it to her.)

EMMA

But I didn't call anyone.

FREDDY

I see.
(Beat.)
Maybe you could let me use your phone. Would that be all right?

EMMA

Yes, yes. Come in.
(He enters.)
It's right over there.

FREDDY

Thank you ma'am.

    (He goes to the phone.)

Page 20

FREDDY (con't)

Frank, it's Freddy. I'm over at 122 North Maple, a Mrs. Emma Thorn. She um . . . she says she didn't order any car.

    (pause)

That's right.

    (pause)

Yeah, I know Frank. Uh-huh. Hold on.

    (to EMMA)

You mind if I wait here for a few minutes? They've got to check things out down there and call me back.

Note the following components of the format:

1. The left margin is slightly indented. This is partly to give that overall appearance of openness (lots of white space). But it's also so that if you bind it, the left margin won't disappear into the binding.

2. The characters' names are capitalized and centered. This doesn't necessarily mean the exact center of the page, but it should be within an inch or so. Capitalization is the best way of setting off the character name, but there are some others. Underlining is one.

3. All stage directions are in parentheses and are placed on a single tab setting, approximately halfway between the left

margin and the character name. This is one of the things with which some writers have a difficult time. They are constantly putting stage direction all over the place—after the character name, within the dialogue, on the same margin as the dialogue. It's best if you stick to the rule: all stage directions on one tab setting, even those that occur within a character's speech. The reason for this is, simply, ease of reading. It's particularly crucial when giving the play to actors if they are going read the play out loud for you. The last thing you want is that their concentration is distracted by having to figure out what is stage direction and what is dialogue. You can, in addition, set off the directions by putting them in italics, or by underlining them, or by adding an extra blank line between them and the dialogue.

4. Number your pages. Some people like to number the act and scene along with the page. This is fine and very acceptable, but not essential.

5. You will also want to bind the manuscript if you are sending it to anyone except a casual friend or someone who has specifically requested it unbound.

COVER LETTERS

If you don't know the person to whom you're sending your play, it's best to write a proper cover letter. The fact that you have to write one at all means that you are at the disadvantage of not knowing this person. Don't try to make up for that by being cute or overly familiar. Grab his attention if you can. If you can legitimately use a name as a reference, start by mentioning it. Present yourself and your play in the best possible light, but be businesslike about it. Never lie. Just get to the point, giving the reader a few words of description that you hope will entice him to read the play quickly and with interest. Then thank him and close.*

One of the common misapprehensions under which neophyte playwrights labor is that they mustn't peddle a play to more than one producer at a time. Nothing could be further from the truth. Your play is your property, as any widget is the property of the person who manufactured it. You may do with it as you like. Send it to one person, or send it to a hundred at a time. Send it out by the truckload if you want.

If more than one producer becomes interested, let them fight it out. That's their problem. They'll bargain with you, or with your agent (> p. 303, Agents), and whoever offers you the best deal will receive the award of the first production. This is capitalism at work. Those times when more than one producer may want your play will be among the few instances when the free-market system works in your favor. Don't limit yourself by playing nice guy. You can count on it that producers are smart business people, you may as well be one too.

A rejection from a literary manager may not be the end of the story. If you get a word of encouragement (they might ask for more work in the future, for example), you may want to seize the opportunity to write back a second time. You can now ask whether there is another theater that this literary manager feels might be more receptive to your play. If there is

---

*The *Dramatists Sourcebook* (published by Theatre Communications Group) has good advice on these and related subjects. The Dramatists Guild also sends out helpful publications information to its membership.

such a theater (or theaters), ask whether you can use this literary manager's name.

Now in your new cover letter, you can begin by saying that Literary Manager X at Theater X suggested you send the enclosed play. You're using a rejection (albeit an encouraging one) to leapfrog to the next possibility.

Some theaters automatically include lists of other theaters to try. This is gracious and generous of them. There's no reason not to ask the same favor of others.

BEYOND COVER LETTERS

Another way to get your play out there is to get involved with a theater company that produces new work. Easy for me to say, you're probably thinking. Yet it isn't really as difficult as you may imagine. Granted, your involvement might not begin on a very elevated level. You may usher at performances, or stuff envelopes in the subscription department, or cold-read manuscripts for the literary department. (This last idea could be the best. It will serve not only to introduce you to the right people, but it's an education in itself on what works and what doesn't.)

You will almost certainly be paid nothing, or next to nothing, for your work, but payment may come in other forms. No, you may never be produced by this organization. (Though stranger things have happened.) But perhaps you'll be given a reading with good actors. Perhaps the dramaturg will read your script and give you good advice. Perhaps you'll meet a director who works with the company, and perhaps she will offer to work with you on the play. She in turn may take it to another theater where it might be produced. Some directors, and not just famous ones, have a certain amount of pull, and if they are behind a script, producers sometimes pay more attention.

If you live in a small community that has no professional theater, you may be able to take advantage of local amateur groups. In fact, it's more likely that you'll be produced at one of these, though the quality of production might be lower than you'd get in a professional theater. Still, even an amateur production, if it's done by serious people, can teach you a lot about your play. Tennessee Williams began his career with a local semi-amateur group in St. Louis, The Mummers, about whom he spoke fondly for the rest of his life.

Don't be pushy with the people you work for, but at the same time don't be afraid of asking for a reasonable bit of their time. After all, they're probably getting yours for free (or for very little pay), and it's generally understood that a bit of mutual back scratching is appropriate. Feel your way through the experience, grabbing what you can without becoming a nuisance.

At the very least, your experience with the company will teach you something of the profession of theater, the general climate in which theaters operate. And it will also introduce you to theater professionals who can in turn introduce you to others until you find those who respond to your work.

AGENTS

Playwrights are not, as a rule, business people. They shouldn't have to negotiate contracts or haggle over terms. That's the governing principle behind having an agent. His primary function is to negotiate contracts, to protect your short- and long-term interests, and to help guide your career. He may help you get a job writing for money—probably for television or the movies. And, finally, he may also be able to place your play in a theater for production.

Many playwrights think that if only they could land an agent, their plays would suddenly start getting productions. It isn't true. Agents can and do help. But many of the productions you land will result from your own hard work and your own ability to hustle. Like it or not, there doesn't seem to be any way around it.

However, when submitting plays to a producer, a reputable agent will get a play read more quickly, and perhaps with more enthusiastic anticipation than an unknown writer might arouse. But whether that producer responds to the play and wants to produce it depends on the play itself. An agent cannot reasonably be expected to make a difference in that area.

So if you don't have an agent, don't fret about it. When the time comes and you're in need of one to negotiate a contract, it won't take too much effort to engage one. Many agents will perform that function for you once a contract has been offered. They may not sign you to a full, exclusive deal. But you might not want that anyway until you know them better.

On the other hand, if you have the opportunity to get an agent now, you should probably take it. He can't do you any harm, and it will be handy to have him there when a contract needs to be negotiated or some advice needs dispensing.

He may also get your play done. You never know.

MAKING TIME TO WRITE

You're probably a busy person. It's likely that you have a full-time job and plenty of other commitments that make it difficult to sit down and write a play. This is a real problem for most people, there is no denying it. But don't imagine that other playwrights are successful simply because they have nothing else to do but write plays all day.

These days, even commercially successful playwrights have to do other work in order to make a living. It's true that often this other work is writing. But many playwrights would not write for television or the movies or magazines if they didn't need the money. They consider this type of writing their day job. It keeps them very busy and very much distracted from their real passion, which is the theater.

There are even more playwrights who are successful in the sense that their work is regularly produced, but who don't make a living on those productions. Their income is often supplemented with a job outside writing altogether. Many have jobs that may be very much like yours. Still, they find the time to write.

How do they do it?

They make the time. That's simplistic but also true. You have to make the time, and you may have to eliminate something. If you can't find a way to get rid of something—any-thing—else in your life in order to write a play, then you don't want to write a play very badly. If there are other things more important to you, you should accept that. Instead of being a playwright, become an avid theatergoer.

On the other hand, don't fall victim to the old cliché that a true writer gets up at dawn and writes first thing every day.

Some writers—many of them—do follow this rule. But many don't. I remember, when I was a young writer, reading that Tennessee Williams rose early every morning and worked for several hours before doing anything else. I became convinced that if I didn't do the same, I could never be a playwright. Now I have my own schedule, which generally amounts to four or five hours of work a day. But I don't start until mid-morning. And some days I do no work at all. Other days may find me working well into the evening. I like a regular schedule—but not too regular.

You need to find the best working arrangement for yourself. Maybe you write on weekends. Maybe you write at night, after work. Maybe you write on your lunch hour. Maybe you only write when you feel like it. Maybe you write every day while you're working on a play and not at all when you're between plays. Playwrights I know—all of them successful—each follow their own plan.

The important thing is to find out what works for you, and then stick to that. Then if you can't even follow your own schedule, something's wrong.

CLASSES, PLAYWRIGHTS UNITS, ADVANCED DEGREES

Many playwrights say that playwriting can't be taught. As a teacher of playwriting for fifteen years, and as the author of this book, you would think I disagree. I don't. Playwriting cannot be taught.

But it can be learned.

Classes and this book can be resources for you. There

may be many others in your life: other teachers, fellow play-wrights, playwrights you admire and playwrights you don't, plays you admire and plays you don't, actors, directors, pro-ducers, audiences, people on the street. You can learn about playwriting from anyone, at any time. Life is your classroom.

I can't count the number of times that a passing observa-tion made by a "civilian" has taught me something essential about the workings of a play. This is because so much (but not all) of playwriting is simply human nature, observed in its rawest and most vulnerable state. If you know people, you know plays.

So take what you can from life, learn what you will from structure, and leave the rest.

A good class will do the same for you. Yes, there are ba-sics to be learned. The ones in this book are those which I, ob-viously, think are essential. Other teachers will have different approaches, many of them good. But the decision of whether or not to take a class really should be made on the basis of how well you respond to what that teacher has to offer.

Ask if you may audit a class. At the very least, ask for an in-depth interview so you can get to know something of the teacher and his methods, if he has any. If you find that the teacher's ideas help you in your writing, and if his general atti-tude supports you and makes you want to write more, you should take his class. If his ideas make no sense to you, or if his attitude turns you off and discourages you from writing, then no matter how brilliant his reputation may be, look for another class.

I, for instance, am the first to admit that as a teacher, I'm not for everyone. I believe I can help most of the people who take my class or read this book, but certainly not all. The learning experience requires a good fit. If the fit isn't good, that's not necessarily my fault or yours—but we should both pay attention to it.

The same rules hold for joining a playwrights unit. A playwrights unit is a group of playwrights who meet, usually weekly, to listen to each other's work and give feedback. A playwrights unit may be a function of a theater, or of a developmental body like New Dramatists, or it may simply be formed by a group of playwrights who get together independently.

The rules for admission into these groups vary widely. You'll have to inquire into each of them to determine whether you may join. But your decision to join should be based on whether you think you can learn something from that group. (This is aside from your wanting to be part of a group for political reasons that may advance your career. There may be something to that, but I'd be careful if that's your only reason for wanting to join.)

A playwrights unit may be a good resource for you, but not all units are the same. Again, ask if you may audit. If you can, listen to the group's feedback after a particular playwright has had his play read. Does the group seem interested in helping him realize his vision, or do they seem more interested in rewriting his work to suit their own ideas and purposes? Do they seem genuinely supportive, or are they too mean for you? Or are they too nice, avoiding the real problems in the work? If you're not comfortable with the answers to these questions, this unit is probably not for you.

Finally, the question of whether to get an advanced degree (usually an M.F.A. in playwriting) is also based on these same considerations—and one other. Some graduate programs offer what is essentially a functioning theater, with a company of student actors and directors, all of whom are at your disposal. This is a substantial advantage and worth considering. Of course, you'll also want to know something of the faculty and the kinds of courses. But together with a good, professional teaching staff, this feature might persuade you to pay the difference between the cost of the degree and that of the other options. (Most other classes are fewer than $500 per term; playwrights units are generally free.)

The program you are considering should offer you plausible assurance that your work will be produced, and that you will have reasonably good access to your actors and directors for the purposes of readings and staged readings. If they provide you with this, and if you are happy with the other values discussed above, then your only other consideration should be money.

COMPUTERS

We live in the computer age. Not everyone has one, but most playwrights do and for good reason. Playwriting is such rewriting-intensive work, and so often the rewrites involve just a few lines here and a few lines there, that the prospect of retyping an entire script just for those few changes is daunting except for the most ardent typist. The old method of literal cut-and-paste is almost as tedious, not to mention how unattractive it makes the script.

There are many good software programs designed specifically for the playwright. These can be useful, though I've always found it just as easy to custom design my documents using ordinary word processing software.

Still, there may be some good reasons for thinking twice about using your computer, at least to the exclusion of all other tools. The advantage that a computer offers can also present a problem. Although retyping is a nuisance, it does tend to make you look carefully at each word. In this way, the simple task of retyping often becomes the more serious job of rewriting. A computer user doesn't have to go through the tedium of retyping and may miss out on the opportunity to take a good, hard look—from which the work could benefit.

I've found that a productive solution is to print out the play in a hard copy. Then with a red pen in hand, I read through the script as though I were editing it for publication. This makes me look carefully at every line.

INCOME TAXES

Playwrights, like many other artists, may have peculiar tax problems. That can be equally true whether you're struggling or successful. Either way, there's a good chance that your income derives from many different sources, that it jumps and dips each year, and that your write-offs are as multitudinous as they are idiosyncratic.

The solution? In a word, get a tax preparer. The money you spend on her will be worthwhile in peace of mind alone. When I first went to a professional tax preparer, I learned that I was about to pay too much in taxes and I was accidentally about to do it illegally. The worst of both worlds! My preparer was able to get me a much bigger—and legitimate—refund.

You may not be able to find a tax accountant in your area who specializes in the theater, but you can almost certainly find one whose specialty is the arts. Get a recommendation. Then hire her.

READINGS AND WORKSHOPS

After you've written your play, what you want is a production. Sets, costumes, ushers in uniforms, your name in lights.

It could happen.

But before that, you'll probably be offered something much smaller—a reading or perhaps a workshop production. Both of these terms are rather plastic in meaning and describe a variety of activities. How do you know when to say yes to them and when to say no?

Readings fall into two general categories: sit-down and staged. A sit-down reading is just that: the actors remain seated, sometimes at a table and sometimes not. More important, a sit-down reading also often implies the amount of rehearsal time that goes with it. A sit-down reading will generally have no more than two rehearsals, often only one. It can even be cold—meaning no rehearsal time at all. If it's cold, it will almost certainly have no director involved, except maybe for casting purposes. If it's a rehearsed reading, you will want a director attached unless you intend to direct it yourself (> p. 317, Collaboration Issues).

A cold reading may or may not be useful, depending on what you're looking to get out of it. It is most likely to be appropriate only for a very early draft of the play. At that time, you may not need to have the finer points brought out of the script. You may only require a general sense of the play's overall structure. Also, a cold reading is often particularly safe when the audience is limited to friends and associates of yours whom you can count on to be supportive and understand the nature of this particular endeavor. One attraction of a cold reading is that it is easiest to arrange, because no one has to commit any time except that of the reading itself.

Even in later drafts, cold readings can sometimes be helpful, particularly if the play is cast with talented actors who are well suited to their roles. What these actors may lack in finesse for some of your more subtle moments, they could very well make up for in the general sense of energy that comes when they are forced to improvise and act out of their own first impulses.

A one- or two-rehearsal reading might be in order later in your process. By then it may be essential to hear your finer points made more clearly. And by this time, there may be people in the audience who are strangers, or who are trying to make the decision whether to take a further professional interest in your play. Under these circumstances, you certainly want to leave less to chance and more to the (relative) predictability that rehearsal brings with it.

At these rehearsed readings, a table often gets in the way. To encourage intimacy with the audience, you might want to ask the actors to hold the scripts in their hands. Sometimes, I like to take the next step and put the actors at music stands. This allows them to stand and to put down their scripts. Tech-

THE PLAYWRIGHT'S GUIDEBOOK

nically, of course, this is no longer a sit-down reading. It's a hybrid—not yet staged, but allowing the actors more spontaneous movement and gesture than they are able to provide while seated. This can make the reading more exciting for an audience. It also requires more work and more rehearsal for the actors and director. Be sure you have the time to add this feature before committing yourself to it.

The next step is a staged reading. Again, a staged reading is just that: the actors are up on their feet, moving around, gesturing, perhaps even using some props as they would in a production. But it is still a reading; scripts are in hand. This too is a hybrid, though a more familiar one—the bridge between reading and production.

The staged reading does have a legitimate purpose, which is to provide the playwright (or a potential producer*) with the means to determine whether a play works on its feet. When a staged reading is appropriate, it is because this information can only be gleaned from this particular form and no other. A sit-down reading is not sufficient, and the playwright (or producer) does not have confidence that the play is ready for a production. But there is still work to do, and it cannot proceed until the playwright gets a clearer idea of the problem. That clarity, it is believed, can come only from watching the actors moving and gesturing in a simulacrum of an actual production.

The staged reading is often overused, particularly by nonprofit producing organizations that want credit for developing

---

*Throughout this section, producer refers to any individual or group, including a nonprofit theater, that is in the business of producing plays.

PART FOUR: SOME ADVICE

313

plays but don't have the financial means to actually produce them. These theaters sometimes offer what amounts to an entire season of staged readings, with hardly a production anywhere in sight. This isn't entirely the theater's fault, of course. The problem of lack of funding is too large to be addressed here, but it is very real and beyond the power of a single institution to change. Still, regardless of who is at fault, to substitute staged readings for productions is an abuse of the playwright, not to mention the audience.

It is up to you, the playwright, to insist on the type of reading that is appropriate for you and your play at any given time. This includes the possibility that you do not need a reading at all—particularly if you've already had several. The crucial questions are: Can you learn something from the experience? Have you already learned what this particular type of reading will teach you?

There is also the opposite question: Is it too soon for a more advanced reading? For the audience, a staged reading will raise expectations (consciously or not) far more than a cold sit-down reading. They will tend to ask more of your play than may be fair, judge it by standards that are too harsh for the state it is in at the moment. For this reason, it's wise not to choose a reading that is too advanced for where your play is right now.

Once you have answered these questions, there may be one other: Do you want the reading, even if it is the wrong type, for political reasons? In other words, do you suspect the reading will lead to the play's being produced?

For example, let's say that Theater X, a reputable resident theater, offers you a staged reading of the play, but perhaps you've already had a workshop production of the play elsewhere. This means that a staged reading is really one step back. But let's suppose that no one from Theater X saw that workshop. To them, the play is new and untried. They don't know if it really works when it's on its feet.

Let's also suppose that Theater X actually does produce a solid season of plays, but does some staged readings for developmental purposes. And we'll also assume that people in decision-making capacities have indicated a serious interest in doing your play. As long as you're not personally required to do all the work in putting it together, you definitely want to have that staged reading. Theater X may not ever do your play, but they have clearly put it on the track that leads in that direction.

In fact, even if you suspect beforehand that Theater X won't ever produce this particular play, you might very well want to allow that staged reading anyway. It could put you in good stead with that theater for the future. They may end up producing another play of yours, or commissioning a new one. And in the meantime, if nothing else, it's good credit simply to be able to say in your next cover letter that such a reputable theater took even this much interest in your work.

Finally, a workshop production is a catchall phrase for a wide range of productions. It can mean the most bare-bones production with no set, minimal props, one light cue, and nobody on salary. It can also mean a lavish production that costs hundreds of thousands of dollars and in which the participants are paid a good sum of money. And, of course, everything in between.

But workshops do generally have a few features in common. Most do not open to the press. They are put on in the hope that another, larger production of the same play will ultimately follow, whether at that same theater or at another. And—in theory—they give the playwright a chance to work on her play.

This last feature is often, unfortunately, somewhat of a cruel hoax. Because most workshop productions are done inexpensively, they must also be done quickly. There is only enough money to pay the actors and other artists for a short period of time. Rehearsals, therefore, are crammed into the period of a week or two, rather than the four that are standard for a full production (and which are often inadequate even then). A director is lucky if he can stage the play in that period of time. The actors are struggling to learn their lines and do their work. The last thing the cast wants to hear from the playwright is that she has new pages for everyone to learn.

Some workshops do in fact have adequate rehearsal time. Some can even enjoy a long run during which time the playwright may work on the play, using the run itself as a sort of extended rehearsal process.

The decision whether to put the play into a workshop production again falls to the same question of what can be learned from it. The playwright must decide the answer to that question and proceed from there. She will also want to consider the questions of political expediency and weigh the benefits of a play's being done in a less-than-desirable workshop against its not being done at all.

COLLABORATION ISSUES

Theater is a collaborative art. In a sense, you will be collaborating with everyone from the box-office manager to the producer to the lighting designer. But your director is the person with whom you will have the closest partnership. It is this relationship that will probably prove to be either the closest and most rewarding, or the most troublesome.

There is some luck involved in how the collaboration with your director works out. You probably won't know for sure how strong it is until the project is over and the play has opened. (Much hard feeling can be forgiven when a play is a success.) But it's also more than luck. There are some simple and sensible steps you can take to help make the partnership a better one.

Start at the beginning.

Let's assume you have control over who your director is. (And you certainly ought to have at least equal say with your producer. If you don't, you may already have a problem.) You have several prospects, and you've never worked with any of them. Arrange interviews with all of them. For each interview, allow a period of time long enough that you can talk business and also get to know each other a bit. Part of your final decision, after all, should be based on how you feel about this person. She should be someone you are comfortable with, someone you can go to with a problem, complain to, argue with, maybe—as a bonus—even have a little fun with.

In the interview, you'll want to know one big thing: what she thinks your play is about. This is an abstract discussion. You're trying to get her to talk about the theme of the play. While she may answer with the specifics of staging, casting, design, and so on, you must press her to talk about the ideas in the play. The specifics are also of interest, but they should follow from these more basic questions: What sort of questions does the play ask? What are its issues, both topical and metaphorical? What does the play say to the director? Why is she attracted to it? Why does she want to direct it?

Don't try to put her on the spot. It's an interview, not a pop quiz. You can let her know ahead of time that these are the questions you'll be asking. Allow her to answer in any terms she likes, but if you're not satisfied with the thoroughness of her answer, ask her to elaborate. If you're not comfortable with her answers, you'll almost certainly not be comfortable with her direction.

It's true that for a while, it may work out. She may stage things well. She may talk to the actors incisively about their moments. She may have a wonderful sense of movement and design. But if her ideas concerning what the play is about differ from yours, there is very likely a disaster waiting for both of you.

The moment of disaster may arrive early in the rehearsal, or late. If you're lucky, it will be early, when there's still a chance of getting another director. If it comes too late, you may have no choice but to go on. In either case, the disaster will make itself known when one of a thousand small but crucial decisions must be made. The decision may be about design, or acting, or a rewrite, or some other area of production. Your director wants things one way, you want them the other. No one budges. The small decision becomes a large crisis with no apparent way out. There is no way out because your director is basing her decision on her idea of the play, which conflicts profoundly with your idea of the play. And because you never established a common ground with her from the beginning, it's probably too late to do so now. All that's left to do is fight.

And you'll probably go on fighting over many other decisions, large and small. You'll both be unhappy, and both fail to get the production you each wanted.

If, however, you can agree from the beginning on the essential idea at the core of the play, it's much easier to resolve these small arguments. The decision-making process becomes a shared experience in which both you and the director learn more about the play by talking and exchanging ideas. The argument can now be settled by returning to the essential, mutually agreed-upon idea of the play, using it as the unchanging standard. Now you can measure both ideas against the standard and judge whose is better.

There is no guarantee that this will resolve every disagreement happily. There will always be different takes on things; matters of taste and so forth. But many, if not most, of your problems will be settled creatively and to the benefit of the project as a whole. You'll find that there is no one right answer, but many.

It will also help if you remember that you are all there to serve the play. Don't confuse this with serving the playwright. You are ultimately the play's custodian, but you have to be its humble servant just as much as any of your collaborators.

And there will still be arguments, but arguments are good if they're conducted in the right way. Don't avoid them. Just establish some common ground at the beginning of the collaboration so that you know that both of you agree fundamentally on the nature of the project.

After that, all I can say is, break a leg.

PART FIVE

APPENDIXES

THE FOLLOWING are plays that are referred to frequently in this book. I highly recommend you read them, before or while you are reading it, in order to fully appreciate and understand the concepts herein:

Waiting for Godot, by Samuel Beckett
Six Degrees of Separation, by John Guare
Glengarry Glen Ross, by David Mamet
Death of a Salesman, by Arthur Miller
Hamlet, by William Shakespeare
Oedipus the King, by Sophocles
A Streetcar Named Desire, by Tennessee Williams

THIS IS a highly biased list of plays that I think you should read. It is only a beginning, but it will allow you to start forming a knowledge base with which to approach the many great works of dramatic literature in the world.

Aeschylus	*The Oresteia (Agamemnon, The Libation Bearers, The Eumenides)*
Edward Albee	*The Zoo Story; The American Dream; Who's Afraid of Virginia Woolf?; Counting the Ways*
Jean Anouilh	*Antigone*
Robert Anderson	*Tea and Sympathy; I Never Sang for My Father*
Schloyme-Zanvl Ansky	*The Dybbuk*
Aristophanes	*Lysistrata; The Clouds; The Frogs*

Jon Robin Baitz	*A Fair Country*
Philip Barry	*Holiday; The Philadelphia Story; Hotel Universe*
Caron de Beaumarchais	*The Marriage of Figaro*
Samuel Beckett	*Waiting for Godot; Endgame; Happy Days; Krapp's Last Tape*
Robert Bolt	*A Man for All Seasons*
Bertolt Brecht	*Life of Galileo; Mother Courage; The Caucasian Chalk Circle*
Georg Büchner	*Woyzeck*
Anton Chekhov	*Three Sisters; The Cherry Orchard; The Seagull; Uncle Vanya*
Caryl Churchill	*Cloud Nine*
Brian Clark	*Whose Life Is It Anyway?*
Jean Cocteau	*The Infernal Machine; Orpheus*
William Congreve	*The Way of the World*
Pierre Corneille	*The Cid*
Noël Coward	*Blithe Spirit; Hay Fever; Private Lives*
Alexandre Dumas	*Camille*
Friedrich Dürrenmatt	*The Visit*
Christopher Durang	*Beyond Therapy; Laughing Wild; Sister Mary Ignatius Explains It All for You; The Actor's Nightmare*
Euripides	*Medea; Hippolytus; Electra; The Bacchae*
George Farquhar	*The Recruiting Officer*
Feydeau	*A Flea in Her Ear; The Lady from Maxim's*
Horton Foote	*The Trip to Bountiful; The Road to the Graveyard; Blind Date*
John Ford	*'Tis a Pity She's a Whore*

Michael Frayn	*Copenhagen*
Christopher Fry	*The Lady's Not for Burning*
Athol Fugard	*A Lesson from Aloes; The Road to Mecca; Master Harold and the Boys*
Charles Fuller	*A Soldier's Play*
William Gibson	*The Miracle Worker*
Frank D. Gilroy	*The Subject Was Roses*
Jean Giraudoux	*Ondine; The Madwoman of Chaillot; The Apollo of Bellac*
Nikolay Gogol	*The Inspector General*
Oliver Goldsmith	*She Stoops to Conquer*
John Guare	*The House of Blue Leaves; Landscape of the Body; Six Degrees of Separation*
Christopher Hampton	*Total Eclipse*
Lorraine Hansberry	*A Raisin in the Sun*
David Hare	*Plenty; The Secret Rapture; Amy's View; Via Dolorosa*
Moss Hart	*Light Up the Sky*
Lillian Hellman	*The Little Foxes*
Henrik Ibsen	*Hedda Gabler; A Doll's House; Ghosts; The Wild Duck; Rosmersholm*
William Inge	*The Dark at the Top of the Stairs; Picnic; Bus Stop*
Eugene Ionesco	*The Chairs; Rhinoceros*
George Kaufman (with Moss Hart)	*The Man Who Came to Dinner; You Can't Take It with You; Once in a Lifetime*
George Kaufman (with Ring Lardner)	*June Moon*
Heinrich von Kleist	*The Broken Jug; The Prince of Homburg*

Tony Kushner	*A Bright Room Called Day; Angels in America* (*Millennium Approaches* and *Perestroika*)
Jerome Lawrence and Robert E. Lee	*Inherit the Wind*
John Leguizamo	*Spic-O-Rama*
Federico García Lorca	*Blood Wedding*
Craig Lucas	*Reckless; Prelude to a Kiss*
Charles MacArthur (with Ben Hecht)	*The Front Page*
David Mamet	*Glengarry Glen Ross; Speed-the-Plow; The Crytogram; The Shawl; The Sermon*
Donald Margulies	*Sight Unseen*
Christopher Marlowe	*Doctor Faustus; Edward II*
Carson McCullers	*The Member of the Wedding*
Arthur Miller	*Death of a Salesman; The Crucible; All My Sons; Incident at Vichy; The Price; A Memory of Two Mondays*
Jason Miller	*That Championship Season*
Molière	*The Misanthrope; Tartuffe*
Marsha Norman	*Getting Out; 'night, Mother*
Sean O'Casey	*The Plough and the Stars; Juno and the Paycock*
Clifford Odets	*Waiting for Lefty; Awake and Sing!; Rocket to the Moon; The Country Girl*
Eugene O'Neill	*Bound East for Cardiff; The Moon of the Caribbees; The Iceman Cometh; A Moon for the Misbegotten; Long Day's Journey into Night*
Joe Orton	*What the Butler Saw*

John Osborne	*Look Back in Anger; The Entertainer*
Harold Pinter	*The Caretaker; The Birthday Party; The Homecoming; Betrayal; The Room; The Lover*
J. B. Priestley	*Time and the Conways*
Jean Racine	*Phèdre*
Terence Rattigan	*The Winslow Boy; The Deep Blue Sea; The Browning Version; Harlequinade*
Elmer Rice	*Dream Girl; Street Scene*
Edmond Rostand	*Cyrano de Bergerac*
Jean-Paul Sartre	*The Flies; No Exit*
Robert Schenkkan	*The Kentucky Cycle*
Arthur Schnitzler	*La Ronde*
Anthony Shaffer	*Sleuth*
Peter Shaffer	*Amadeus*
William Shakespeare	*The Merchant of Venice; Twelfth Night; Measure for Measure; Richard II; Richard III; Henry IV (Part 1); Henry V; The Tempest; Hamlet; Romeo and Juliet; Othello; King Lear; Macbeth*
George Bernard Shaw	*Candida; Mrs. Warren's Profession; Arms and the Man; Man and Superman; Major Barbara; Pygmalion; Saint Joan*
Sam Shepard	*Buried Child; Curse of the Starving Class; True West*
Richard Sheridan	*The School for Scandal; The Rivals; The Critic*
Sophocles	*Oedipus the King; Antigone; Electra; Philoctetes*

Milan Stitt	*The Runner Stumbles*
Tom Stoppard	*The Real Thing; Travesties; The Real Inspector Hound; Arcadia*
August Strindberg	*The Father; Easter; The Ghost Sonata; Miss Julie*
William Synge	*The Playboy of the Western World; Riders to the Sea*
Ted Tally	*Terra Nova*
Terence	*The Woman of Andros*
Sophie Treadwell	*Machinal*
Ivan Turgenev	*A Month in the Country*
John Webster	*The Duchess of Malfi*
Peter Weiss	*Marat/Sade*
Michael Weller	*Loose Ends; Split*
Oscar Wilde	*The Importance of Being Earnest; An Ideal Husband; Salomé*
Thornton Wilder	*Our Town; The Skin of Our Teeth; The Pullman Car Hiawatha; The Long Christmas Dinner; The Happy Journey to Trenton and Camden*
Tennessee Williams	*The Glass Menagerie; A Streetcar Named Desire; Summer and Smoke; Suddenly Last Summer; Sweet Bird of Youth; The Rose Tattoo; The Long Good-bye; This Property Is Condemned; Twenty-seven Wagons Full of Cotton; Cat on a Hot Tin Roof*
Lanford Wilson	*The Fifth of July; Burn This; Serenading Louie; The Mound Builders; Talley's Folly*

William Wycherley   *The Country Wife*
Paul Zindel   *Effects of Gamma Rays on Man-in-the-Moon Marigolds*

The following are books that may be interesting or useful to you:

Poetics, by Aristotle, Introduction by Francis Fergusson
The Empty Space, by Peter Brook
Aspects of the Novel, by E. M. Forster
Respect for Acting, by Uta Hagen
Three Uses of the Knife and *True and False*, by David Mamet
A Life, by Elia Kazan
Act One, by Moss Hart
Dramatists Sourcebook, by Theatre Communications Group

ON THE following pages you'll find a series of images that you can use if you wish to continue with the impulse exercises. Some of the images are told in the second person, i.e., they refer to "you" in the image. This is simply a way of establishing point of view and does not in any way require that one of the characters in the scene literally be you. In keeping with the instructions on pages 138–40, do not look at the images ahead of time, but wait until the moment you are ready to begin writing.

A meadow on the edge of a wood. A small stream runs through the wood and a small foot bridge goes over the stream. It is early on a summer morning, just after sunrise. Dew is still on the grass. It is very quiet except for the sound of an insect buzzing constantly in the background. The air is cool but the sun is warm. It is cooler in the wood than in the meadow. You are arriving at this place through the meadow and into the wood. You have thrown on some clothes very quickly. You are still sleepy, but you are rushing through the meadow. Standing on the bridge is another person. This person has taken more time to dress, their hair is neatly brushed. They are waiting for you. Who are they? What do you say to them as you approach?

A hotel room in southern Spain on the Mediterranean coast. Late summer. It is night, or late evening. The stars are out but the heat of the day is still felt. A sultry wind is blowing in off the sea. The hotel room has stucco walls, a wood-plank floor. It is lit by a single overhead lamp. There are suitcases open on the bed. An American woman of about thirty is packing them. Her hair is dirty, she has dirt under her fingernails, rivulets of sweat run down her forehead. But the clothes she is packing are clean and expensive, with jewelry and other accessories to match. Also in the room is an American man, older than the woman. He is deeply tanned, with a few days' growth of beard. His clothes are old and worn. He sits in the corner, his hands resting on a cane. Through the open window a scratchy record is playing music on a jukebox in the bar downstairs. As she packs, he gets up and goes to the window and looks out. What does he say?

A large room in a downtown loft space. Night. Wood floors, empty walls, no furniture. It is newly renovated. The sounds of traffic can be heard, but only faintly. The windows are closed, and it is raining and cool outside. It is warm inside. A man dressed only in gym shorts and T-shirt lies on his back on the floor. He's lying on a flat woven-reed mat, his head on a small pillow. He has on a Walkman. He's watching a small black-and-white TV. Next to him is a set of keys and three rolled joints. He taps his foot to the sound on his Walkman that only he can hear. He's lit by the bluish light of the TV. A key unlocks the door, and it opens. Another man steps inside. He carries a leather briefcase and has a wet raincoat over his shoulder. He wears a conservative suit and tie. He steps into the apartment and closes the door. The first man has not heard him come in. What does the man in the suit say?

⚜

Outside a corner bar in a small town. Just after sunset, the glow of the sun can still be seen over the rooftops. The bar is an old brick building from the turn of the century, situated on a triangular corner. There is a sign hanging over the door advertising Miller beer, but it is not yet lit. A dog barks in the background. It is a cool summer evening. A man waits on the stoop outside the bar. Inside, the bar appears to be nearly empty. The man is dressed in a T-shirt and jeans. He holds a beer in one hand. A woman appears around the corner and starts into the bar. The man stops her before she can enter. What does he say?

Inside an automobile. Night. A steady rain. The windshield wipers squeak faintly, back and forth, back and forth. The dashboard lights glow a dim green. The driver's face, damp from the rain, is illuminated by them. The driver's clothes are also a little wet. It is warm and cozy inside, in contrast to the cold, wet conditions outside. The bucket seats are soft. You are in the front seat, next to the driver. Your feet are cold, and your shoes are wet. But you can feel the heater blowing warm against them. Outside, through heavy sheets of rain, you can observe the countryside passing by in the dark—rural farmland with occasional billboards and highway signs. On the radio, a station is playing a country song that keeps fading in and out, with an increasing amount of static and dead air. The driver turns to you as if to say something, but then looks back to the road, and remains silent. What do you say?

❧

The Fourth of July. The kitchen of a suburban home. Outside the bang and pop of fireworks can be heard, followed by the shouts and hollers of what sounds like an excited collection of neighbors—adults and children mixed in equal numbers. Inside, everything is neat and tidy, except that a collection of fireworks—bottle rockets, firecrackers, Roman candles, etc.— is sprawled out across the kitchen counter, next to the sink. The air in the kitchen is cool, air-conditioned. But there is the rich, sweet smell of a blueberry pie cooking in the oven. A young boy, preadolescent, sits at the kitchen table. He is not oblivious to the goings-on outside, but he has no apparent reaction to them either. He seems determined not to look out the windows. Finally he gets up and goes over to the fireworks on the counter and picks up one of the bottle rockets. As he does so, a woman in her thirties or forties comes quickly through the door that leads in from the garage. In her hurry she goes right to the oven to check the pie without seeing the boy. Only when she has checked it and turns around does she see the boy, who is still holding the bottle rocket. What does she say?

You are at a party in a large, rambling apartment. The ceilings are high, and the rooms are large and quite full of people. There is a group at the baby grand piano in the alcove singing "Stardust," a large noisy group standing around the hors d'oeuvre table, and another smaller group sitting around the couch having what sounds like a rather serious discussion about the greenhouse effect. You have had too much to drink. The room is getting very close and much too smoky for you. You take a deep breath and carefully pick your way across the room and push through the swinging door that leads into the kitchen. The kitchen is brightly lit, very white and clean, much quieter, and totally empty of people. A window is open just a crack, and a cool, fresh breeze blows in. There is the rich, welcome smell of hot coffee. You look across the room and see that it is still dripping in the coffeemaker. You sit down at the white enamel table, clean and cold under your hands. It is a relief to sit down. You set your glass down and slide it a little ways away from you. You hear a noise from around the corner that leads into the pantry, and you look up. A teenage boy comes around the corner. He is dressed in baggy jeans but he is attractive and has a very nice body underneath the baggy clothes. He looks surprised to see you, but it seems like a pleasant surprise. He lifts his shirt to scratch his belly. As he passes by you to the coffeemaker, he brushes your arm with his shoulder and says hello. What do you say?

Night, just before dawn. Late May. You are on a dirt road deep in a rural woods. The damp air is thick with the smell of budding groves and fields, but there is also a slight chill to it. The leaves beneath your feet are soaked in dew. You come upon a large house. It belongs to someone you know, it looks familiar to you. You walk across the gravel drive—*crunch, crunch, crunch*—picking your way in the dark around the small pools of water. You hear music, a romantic quartet—Schumann? Chopin? Brahms?—faintly coming from the house in front of you. You go closer, around to the side of the house, to the terrace. The stucco of the house shines a dead white in the moonlight, almost seeming to radiate a ghostly light of its own. Lilac bushes heavy with purple-and-white flowers surround the terrace; a row of tulips, their buds closed against the chill air, lines the walk. You step up onto the stone terrace and walk to the windows. You can see a dim light on inside. You peer through the shutters and see a room, a large formal room, probably once a ballroom or dining hall. A chandelier hangs from the ceiling; it is filled with lit candles—the only source of light in the room. All the furniture has been pushed back against the wall. On a table sits a phonograph player, with a record spinning, pouring forth the fine strains of the quartet. In the middle of the room a young woman stands, dressed as a dancer, poised on the tips of her toes. Her shoes are fastened with black ribbons laced around her ankles. She is just finishing her dance and as her arms fall gracefully down from around her head, her eyes rise up to meet yours. What does she say?

Midday. A large, high-ceilinged room of the Royal Hawaiian Hotel in Honolulu. The long translucent curtains billow in the trade winds. The air is warm in that comforting, breezy Hawaiian way. A man in his mid-thirties, dressed in a pair of shorts and a cotton shirt, sits watching the television, not with the usual apathetic stare, but intently, as if waiting for a bulletin of some sort. The television is droning on with an endless series of ridiculous commercials followed by a soap opera. A woman of about the same age is at the window, facing away from him, looking out through the curtains, presumably out at the ocean. She too seems to be waiting, watching for something. She is dressed in a bathing suit, with a light robe hanging loosely over it. A small child, an infant, plays on the floor between them. The child is barefoot, dressed only in a swimming suit, a lei draped around her neck. The woman taps steadily on the glass of the window—*tap, tap, tap, tap, tap, tap, tap, tap* . . . Finally, what does she say?

A large, empty nineteenth-century theater. The houselights are not on, so the orchestra and balconies disappear into murky blackness, but we can see that the house is decorated in the usual grand manner—red curtains, red carpet, red plush seats. Ornate gold carvings decorate the boxes and the ceiling and the proscenium arch. On the stage, an entirely different scene: a tropical paradise, lit softly by a sky full of stars—an effect created by punching thousands of holes in a cyclorama and then lighting it from behind. The low electric hum of an old-fashioned dimmer can be heard from the lighting platform off-stage. The set includes palm trees and a central sandy playing area. Between the palm trees is slung a hammock. The whole scene looks loosely assembled, as though it had been pulled from the prop room for a rehearsal. The building is quite warm, like the tropics. We can also see into the wings, and there is evidence that a person, or persons, is living in this theater. A little kitchenette with hot plate and refrigerator is set back into one of the wings. A slop sink has laundry soaking in it, and there is more laundry drying from a line slung between two lighting poles. Then, as we look more closely at the stage setting, we see someone in the hammock that is slung between the palm trees—in fact, there are two people in it. One of them wakes up. What does this person say?

Night. Winter. New York City. You are standing in a line out-side of a revival movie house in the Village. The line extends out the lobby of the house, and you are stuck outside—you didn't think there would be this many people. It is cold and you are bundled up against the wind. You've been in line for about twenty minutes now and the cold has gotten down to your skin. You look at your watch; the movie doesn't start for another fifteen minutes, you won't be inside for another ten. You put your hands in your pockets and scrunch up your shoulders. From inside the house, a person appears and comes down the sidewalk in your direction. You make eye contact as they approach. They stop at a pay phone by the curb, put a quarter in, and make a phone call. As they talk to the other party, they turn around and make eye contact with you again. You look back, shivering and miserable, but quite attracted to this person. They continue talking on the phone, looking your way. This goes on for several minutes. Finally the person hangs up and crosses the sidewalk and says hello. What do you say?

Grand Central Terminal, the evening rush hour. You are walking through the main concourse dressed for business, with a raincoat on. The floor of the terminal is streaked with water, tramped in from the outside. The station is dimly lit—outside the sun has gone down and the sky is overcast. You are heading toward the Metro-North gates along the north wall. You go through your gate and down the ramp to the platform. It is quieter here, muted, though there is the constant, penetrating electric hum of the trains waiting to leave the station. You walk to the far end of the platform where the cars are less crowded. You enter one of the last cars. There are a few window seats left, and you take off your raincoat and slide into one of them. As the train pulls out, you look down the aisle. One of the people facing you is looking at you. You recognize the person as someone you know. You hold their stare. Finally, the person gets up and comes down the aisle. The person sits down next to you. What does the person say?

Your bedroom. Early morning. You wake up slowly, drowsily, and for no apparent reason. No alarm goes off, no phone call. You just find yourself waking up, though it is quite early on a Saturday morning. The sun is up and it's a bright, beautiful day. You feel wonderfully warm and comfortable under the covers, completely rested and at peace. You look around the room (take a moment to do this) and see that everything is as it was last night, as it always is. There is a goldfish bowl on the windowsill with a single goldfish swimming contendedly around in it. You hear a noise in the other room, the soft clinking of cups and plates and the gurgle of coffee being made. After a moment, someone appears at the door with a cup of coffee and the morning paper. This person sees you are awake, brings the coffee and paper over, and sets them on the bed. What does the person say to you?

❧

The living room of a beach house very early in the season. The curtains on the windows are still drawn but through them we can see the sky is sunny. The air outside is cool, moist, spring-like. It is utterly quiet and still except that the front door is ajar and the ocean can be heard very softly in the distance. Inside the house, it smells musty and close after being locked up all winter. The furniture is covered with sheets and the kitchen counters are bare. A collection of boxes sits inside the front door, waiting to be taken to their proper places. A person enters the living room from a bedroom, goes to the boxes, looks on the label of one of them, picks it up, and goes into a bedroom with it. As this person returns, another person appears at the door with a bag of groceries. The first person goes to the door to help. What does the person say?

An old lodge deep in the woods. A winter's night. A large, open room, with wood floors, walls, and ceiling. At one end a stone fireplace. The windows are all shut tight, the curtains drawn. It is cold in the room—and also dark: the only light is that which spills over from the porch light, creating deep shadows in the corners. In the dim light, we can see that the wood paneling is old and warped in places, the floor bends crazily here and there. Old water damage from a burst pipe is apparent across part of the the ceiling and down one wall. The room smells faintly of wood smoke; it is not the comforting, cozy wood smoke of a roaring fire, but rather the ashy, bitter smell of a fire long dead—a smell you can almost taste. The room has scattered around it large easy chairs and couches, some small tables, a couple of larger chests of drawers. A black baby grand piano stands near the middle of the room. A double door at one end of the room opens. A few flakes of snow make their way into the room as a person steps into it and slams the door behind them. The person searches for a light switch against the wall and, not finding one, continues across the room to the fireplace. The person kneels to lay a fire. A second person now enters from the same porch door. Again the wind howls and the snow swirls, and the flame is blown out. The second person closes the door after them, goes directly to the middle of the room and pulls the chain on an overhead hanging lamp, which floods the room in light. What does this second person say?

A small, semirural railroad station. It is just before sunset at the end of a humid summer day. Beyond the platform we can see a small river, its dark waters moving slowly and reflecting the last rays of sunlight. The architecture of the station resembles a summer cottage—painted white, with frivolous Victorian trim and a steeply peaked roof. The lamps burn along the edge of the platform in a somber yellowish cast. They are surrounded by halos caused by the moisture in the air. Far, far away we hear the long hollow sound of a train whistle. A man and a woman stand alone at one end of the platform. The woman is dressed in traveling clothes and a suitcase sits next to her. The man is in a coat and tie. They are about the same age. What does the man say to the woman?

The parlor room of a house in the old residential section of a small city. The middle of an afternoon in June. The house is a large old mock-Tudor affair. There is a marble fireplace, crystal chandeliers, faded but elegant curtains, and the room is filled with heavy, dark, Victorian furniture. Though the sun is brilliant outside, it is dark and cool in here. And a little dusty. From the front hall a man and a woman enter. She is in her fifties, dressed in an elaborately brocaded kimono-style dressing gown and shoes with two-inch heels. Her hands flash with jewelry. She is a plump, pretty woman with fair skin, rouged cheeks, china-blue eyes, and silvery blond hair done in a careful, conservative style. He is younger than she, but by no more than ten years. He is wearing a brown suit and a crisp, white shirt with a necktie—office clothes. His hair is black and he is nice looking, but in a reserved way. The woman shows him in and goes to the center of the room where there is a table covered with a white sheet. She hesitates for a moment as though nervous about revealing the table. He waits for her to move. Finally she draws the sheet away from the table and steps back, clutching the sheet to her chest with both hands. What does she say?

The third-floor hallway of a small apartment building. Late in the afternoon in March. Outside the sky is overcast and the air is chilly. The hallway is cool. A window at one end of the hall has been opened and cold air is streaming in. Outside the window on an adjoining roof sits a woman dressed in a sweater and blue jeans. She is not wearing shoes. She has a bottle of wine and is smoking a cigarette. The pitch of the roof is steep, and she is half sitting, half reclining, as if sunning herself—except there is no sun. Another person, carrying an armload of textbooks and notebooks, comes up the stairway and sees the woman out on the roof. This person goes down the hall and puts their head out the window. What does this second person say?

⁂

The living room of an eighteenth-century stone farmhouse. The floors are of wide wooden planking. The roof beams are heavy and close overhead. Outside the window we can see farmland, hemmed in by hedges and rows of cedar trees, all of it covered in snow. The room has a large fireplace in which a fire is burning. It is warm and comfortable in the room. Someone has brought in evergreen boughs and put them along the mantel of the fireplace, and the room is redolent with the sweet, fresh smell of pine. Against one wall are Chinese antique-silk wall hangings. It is still and quiet, inside and out. A person is sitting in a chair near the fireplace, reading a book. Another person enters the room, dressed in warm outdoor clothes that are covered in snow. The first person looks up from the book. What does this first person say?

The room of a small inn in Connecticut. Outside we can see the bare trees of late autumn, a millstream gurgling by. The room is furnished in antiques; it has patterned wallpaper, with prints and watercolors hung on the walls. A key rattles in the door, and after a moment, the door opens. In the hallway we see a woman dressed in a traditional long white bridal gown and a man in a black tuxedo. They both come into the room and close the door behind them. What does the woman say?

A busy coffee shop. An afternoon on a winter weekend. We hear the clatter of dishes and cups being cleared. It is cold outside and the windows have steamed over: inside it is warm, a little too warm, steamy and muggy. Coats and sweaters and scarves are draped over the back of chairs and booths, and hang from hooks on the wall. Puddles of dirty water have formed under the tables—the drippings from shoes. Two people are sitting at a table by a window. One of them studies the menu. The other person does not look at the menu. Finally, the person looking at the menu speaks. What does this person say?

✻

A small, saltbox-style house. Outside the window you can see a small yard—the grass is a little overgrown—lined with high hedges. A sliding glass door leads to a little wooden deck built out from the house where there are a small, white table and chairs, and a barbecue grill. The air is warm and sunny—a cloudless sky. The windows are open and the air can be felt blowing through them. The air smells of freshly turned earth, of wildflowers in bloom. We hear the hoarse, throaty song of a red-winged blackbird repeating itself nearby. This room is a living and eating area adjacent to a small kitchen. In the living room is a brick fireplace, two couches, a coffee table. In the eating area is a round dining table with four chairs. Against one wall is a low bench with a portable stereo. In back is a staircase leading upstairs. A person comes in from the yard, dressed in old jeans and a work shirt; their hands and knees are dirty. Another person comes in from the kitchen carrying plates with sandwiches on them. What does this second person say?

A room in the European wing of the Metropolitan Museum of Art. It is a large, square room with a high ceiling. The light is filtered, diffuse, but quite bright and seems to permeate every bit of space in the room, though you are not conscious of any particular light source. It seems to come from all around. On the walls there are hung paintings by the Dutch masters, portraits of solemn men and women, and sometimes children, dressed in black and staring sternly out into the room. Their eyes are amazingly lifelike and seem to follow you around the room as you move. It is a slow hour for the museum. You hear the clip of the heels of the guard's shoes, and you hear occasional murmurings from nearby rooms, but mainly it is quiet and still. The air is perfectly conditioned, cool, dry. You sit on an upholstered bench in the middle of the room. Your feet hurt, the muscles on the bottom of your feet and up into your calves are sore. The small of your back is sore. It feels good to sit. From the bench, you find yourself fascinated by a particular painting, by the eyes of the subject which are even more mesmerizing than the others. You stare at it. In the room there is one other person who is making their way around the perimeter, studying the paintings closely, slowly, deliberately. They look at a painting, step back from it, look closely again. They move around the room until they reach the painting you have been looking at. They stop, examine it, step back, examine it again, step back again. They do not move on. They remain as though fixated by the work also. They stay there for a long moment. Finally, they turn to you. What do you say?

The deck of a small ferryboat midway on its journey between the mainland and an island. It is out on the open water, though land is in sight. It is late afternoon on a blustery autumn day. Rain splashes down occasionally in tiny drops, or perhaps sometimes it's a light spray blown up by the wind. The taste and smell of salt is in the air. The low growl of the ferry's diesel engine can be heard below, and its vibration drums up through the deck. The wind whips through people's hair and clothes. It is chilly out, brisk, but exhilarating and pleasant in a way. Many people have crowded into the small cabin just behind the bridge, but a few have remained out on deck, excited by the elements. Two people in particular stand up near the bow of the boat, clutching the handrail. Their overcoats flap in the wind. Finally, one of them reaches out and points at a place on the island. What does this person say?

The living room of a small country house. Middle to late afternoon on a day in autumn. A pair of French doors is open and through it we see a compact, neatly laid out garden which, clearly, is well tended in the summer months. Narrow paths of gravel crisscross each other, framing plots of earth in which the dying remnants of flowers and small shrubs shudder in the breeze. The air is warm here in the sun, but there is a coolness detectable just below the surface. It will be cold tonight. The breeze stirs again, and leaves blow in through the open doors, swirling across the bare wooden floor and scattering onto the patterned wool rug. As if oblivious to this little invasion of nature, a person sits reading a book on a couch with plump pillows and overstuffed cushions. There are books all around, stacked on tables, on the floor, on the mantel over the fireplace, leaning against themselves and the legs of chairs. Deeply engrossed in the book, this person slowly turns the page and continues reading as another person appears at the French doors. What does this second person say?

❦

A good-sized living room of a middle-class suburban home. Early morning. The room is filled with the remains of a large celebration of the night before. Crepe-paper streamers hang from the ceiling, the tables are covered with food, half-empty glasses, overflowing ashtrays. The carpet is stained and spotted in places. The musty stench of cigarettes, stale beer, rank mayonnaise, and cheese dip. Morning light can be seen dimly through the curtains. It's very quiet, very still. A figure can be seen sprawled on the sofa, face buried under a throw pillow. Another person comes down the stairs, barefoot, surveying the scene. What does this second person say?

Mid-afternoon on a brisk autumn day. We are inside a rustic country home. It has wood-plank floors, walls of unfinished beams. Another wood beam on the ceiling divides the living room from the dining area. The furniture is antique, eclectic—some old primitives, others Victorian, and so on—a collection. A cast-iron woodstove burns in one corner. Its heat and a slight smokiness pervade the room. Outside the air is crisp and clear, no clouds, no humidity. A slight breeze rustles the trees, and the leaves fall in small flurries. Softly, from no perceptible source, we hear the music of a lute, a light Elizabethan air or dance. The room is brightly lit by the afternoon sun streaming through the dining room window in a bold, golden shaft, hitting the table and reflecting off its brilliant, hand-rubbed surface. At the table is a person, writing on a piece of paper—writing thoughtfully, carefully. Glancing up to the ceiling every few minutes to consider the next phrase. There is a noise from another room—the kitchen. The opening of a cupboard, the rattle of plates. Then silence. Then, still from the kitchen, we hear a voice. What does it say?

APPENDIX D: EXTENDED EXERCISES

HERE ARE two longer exercises that I use in my classes as a means of expanding on both the structural technique and the creative process described in this book. If you are unsure what to write about, you can use these exercises as starting points for your work.

1. Adapt a short story of your choice. Be sure to make it into a play, not just a transcript. Your plot will no doubt end up different than the story's. The characters might also, along with other things. Remember that you must still be faithful to your impulse, not the story itself. Use this as a test of your ability to do just that. Choose a story in the public domain to avoid copyright problems.

2. Write a history play based on a historical event or character. Though you will want to do some research, use this exercise as a way to be faithful to your impulse, not the historical facts.

These definitions may vary from those used by others. My definitions do not presume to be correct—only to be consistent within the framework of my ideas about playwriting.

ACTION: What a character wants; it is itself invisible and inaudible; we learn the nature of the action through the consequent speech and behavior of the characters.

BEAT: The basic building block of a scene and therefore of any play; a beat is the smallest unit of dramatic structure that contains action, conflict, and an event.

BEHAVIOR: A character's gestures and movement; ideally, behavior results from the character's action just as his or her language does.

CONFLICT: Whatever prevents a character from getting what he or she wants; do not confuse conflict with a state of emotion or with an argument.

CONVENTION: The accepted rules by which a drama is constructed; different plays will have different conventions, but each play's conventions should be internally consistent.

DRAMATIC SITUATION: A way to refer to the ideas of action and conflict as one concept.

DEUS EX MACHINA (DA-əs-eks-MÄ-ki-nə): Literally "god from a machine," this now refers to any kind of ending that does not seem organic to the play; a false event, not a consequence of action and conflict; pejorative.

DIRECT ADDRESS: When a character addresses the audience directly, breaking the fourth wall. (See monologue and soliloquy.)

EVENT: The moment when a character either gets what he or she wants, or definitively does not get it; there are normally many smaller events in a play (see beats), but the main event serves to end the play; a genuine dramatic event is the result of action and conflict (see *deus ex machina*); an event may take many different forms, but is always some sort of change.

EXPOSITION: Literally "the act of presenting to view," but generally used in playwriting to mean information and more particularly used pejoratively to mean that information which is not justified by the action; in reality, every word in a play is exposition, whether it is activated or not.

EXTERNAL CONFLICT: Conflict that exists between two or more characters. It can further be divided into direct external conflict (that which occurs directly between two characters who want to possess or control the same object) or indirect external conflict (that which also occurs between two characters, but while action of the first character is directed toward the second, the action of the second is directed elsewhere).

IMPULSE: Whatever makes one want to write a play; it may take many different forms, but is usually some sort of experience, whether first person or not.

IN MEDIAS RES (in-ME-dē-əs-RĀS):   Literally "in the middle of things," it is the point in the story that the Roman poet Horace recommends a playwright begin his or her play; a relative term that must be applied according to one's own instincts.

INTERNAL CONFLICT: Two actions within oneself which give rise to a conflict; sometimes referred to as a character's ambivalence, it is generally easier to think of it in structural terms.

MONOLOGUE: Any extended speech within a play; monologue and speech are often used interchangeably; a monologue may be (but is not necessarily) direct address.

MOTIVATION: The underlying reason for a character's action; often mistakenly used interchangeably with action. (See subtext)

PRAXIS: The ancient Greek word used by Aristotle to refer to dramatic action; also used to mean the main or central action of a play, as opposed to the many smaller, more immediate actions.

SOLILOQUY: A conversation with one's self; often confused with direct address or monologue, a true soliloquy is rare.

STAKES: What a character has to gain or to lose; often confused with high (or low) emotions, it is in fact a function of conflict and/or action.

SUBTEXT: When a character seems to have one action or motivation, but in fact has another; subtext lies under the text, not spoken directly, but nevertheless apparent.

TOOLS: A way to think of all the structural ideas in this book; a more constructive and less restrictive term than rules.

UR-PLAY: The ultimately unknowable play that is buried deep in your own subconscious; your actual play, as written, will bear as close a resemblance to the ur-play as possible.

ACKNOWLEDGMENTS

For their help in seeing this book come together I'd like to thank Susan Cinoman, Mark Farnen, Maureen McDuffee, Keynan Shadd, Robert Shaffron, and Mark Woodcock. For their close, critical reading and feedback I'd particularly like to thank Elaine Berman, Nancy Greening, and Scott Williams.

INDEX

absurdists, 17, 119

acting classes, 290

action, 21, 35–47, 73, 96, 105–6, 111; in beats, 97–100; character and, 174–79, 187–90, 192–93; climactic, 283–84; concrete, 280; conflict and, 66–71; in creative process, 145–47; defined, 361; as dramatic center, 268; event and, 85, 87–88, 91–93; information transmitted through, 251–54; *in medias res*, 274; levels of, 53–54; in monologues, 261; motivation distinguished from, 48–50; occasion and, 267–68; reversing, 279; rewriting and, 228, 230, 234, 236, 242; of scenes, 102–3; in soliloquies, 260–61; stakes as function of, 75; subtext and, 50–51; suspense and, 218; theme and, 154

actors, 291, 292; creative process of, 141; "emotional memory" technique for, 159; physical behavior of, 199–201; for readings, 312, 313; and subtext, 52–53; in workshop productions, 316

acts, 103–6, 112; breaks between, 30–31, 104, 106

advanced degrees, 308–9

Aeschylus, 15, 89, 118, 324; *see also titles of specific plays*

agents, 303–4

AIDS, 158

Albee, Edward, 78, 97, 269, 324

Alexander, Sara, 161–63

alienation, 17

Amadeus (Shaffer), 160

amateur theater groups, 303

ambiguity, 256–57

ambivalence, 67, 69, 70

American Dream, The (Albee), 152

American Theatre, 122

Amy's View (Hare), 53

Andalusian Dog, An (film), 5

Anderson, Robert, 296, 324

Angels in America (Kushner), 158–59

Anouilh, Jean, 119, 324

Ansky, Schloyme-Zanvl, 324

anthropology, 26

Antigone (Sophocles), 43, 71–72, 76, 152, 173, 208